AF781094

# EurographicSeminars

Tutorials and Perspectives in Computer Graphics

Edited by W. T. Hewitt, R. Gnatz, and D. A. Duce

R. L. Grimsdale A. Kaufman (Eds.)

# Advances in Computer Graphics Hardware V

## Rendering, Ray Tracing and Visualization Systems

With 97 Figures, 17 in Color, and 16 Tables

Springer-Verlag
Berlin Heidelberg New York
London Paris Tokyo
Hong Kong Barcelona
Budapest

*EurographicSeminars*

Edited by W. T. Hewitt, R. Gnatz, and D. A. Duce
for EUROGRAPHICS -
The European Association for Computer Graphics
P. O. Box 16, CH-1288 Aire-la-Ville, Switzerland

*Volume Editors*

Richard L. Grimsdale
University of Sussex
School of Engineering & Applied Sciences
Falmer
Brighton BN1 9QT, UK

Arie Kaufman
Computer Science Department
State University of New York
Stony Brook, NY 11794-4400, USA

ISBN 3-540-54291-4 Springer-Verlag Berlin Heidelberg New York
ISBN 0-387-54291-4 Springer-Verlag New York Berlin Heidelberg

This work is subject to copyright. All rights are reserved, whether the whole or part of the material is concerned, specifically the rights of translation, reprinting, reuse of illustrations, recitation, broadcasting, reproduction on microfilms or in other ways, and storage in data banks. Duplication of this publication or parts thereof is only permitted under the provisions of the German Copyright Law of September 9, 1965, in its current version, and a copyright fee must always be paid. Violations fall under the prosecution act of the German Copyright Law.

© 1992 EUROGRAPHICS The European Association for Computer Graphics
Printed in Germany

The use of general descriptive names, trade marks, etc. in this publication, even if the former are not especially identified, is not to be taken as a sign that such names, as understood by the Trade Marks and Merchandise Marks Act, may accordingly be used freely by anyone.

45/3140-543210 - Printed on acid-free paper

# Preface

This volume contains papers representing a comprehensive record of the contributions to the fifth workshop at EG '90 in Lausanne.

The Eurographics hardware workshops have now become an established forum for the exchange of information about the latest developments in this field of growing importance. The first workshop took place during EG '86 in Lisbon. All participants considered this to be a very rewarding event to be repeated at future EG conferences. This view was reinforced at the EG '87 Hardware Workshop in Amsterdam and firmly established the need for such a colloquium in this specialist area within the annual EG conference. The third EG Hardware Workshop took place in Nice in 1988 and the fourth in Hamburg at EG '89.

The first part of the book is devoted to rendering machines. The papers in this part address techniques for accelerating the rendering of images and efficient ways of improving their quality. The second part on ray tracing describes algorithms and architectures for producing photorealistic images, with emphasis on ways of reducing the time for this computationally intensive task. The third part on visualization systems covers a number of topics, including voxel-based systems, radiosity, animation and special rendering techniques.

The contributions show that there is flourishing activity in the development of new algorithmic and architectural ideas and, in particular, in absorbing the impact of VLSI technology. The increasing diversity of applications encourage new solutions, and graphics hardware has become a research area of high activity and importance.

We should like to thank the members of the Programme Committee for the efforts they invested in the planning of the workshop, the Eurographics Association for supporting the event through scholarships, and the Ecole Polytechnic Fédérale Lausanne and Professor Roger D. Hersch for hosting the event so excellently. Thanks also to Michael D. J. McNeill for preparing the book for publication. Last, but not least, our thanks go to all the authors of the volume for the careful preparation of their contributions.

Brighton and Stony Brook
February 1992

Richard Grimsdale
Arie Kaufman

# Fifth Eurographics Conference on Hardware

**Workshop Co-chairpersons**

Professor R. L. Grimsdale, School of Engineering, University of Sussex, Brighton, UK
Professor A. Kaufman, Computer Science Department, State University of New York at Stony Brook, USA

**Local Organisation Chairman**

Professor R. D. Hersch, Ecole Polytechnic Fédérale Lausanne, Switzerland

**Workshop Programme Committee**

Dr. F. Kitson (HP Labs, Palo Alto, CA, USA)
Dr. P. Leray (CCETT, France)
Drs. A. A. M. Kujik (Centre for Mathematics and Computer Science, Amsterdam, NL)
Professor W. Straßer (University of Tübingen, FRG)
Dr. S. Molnar (University of North Carolina, Chapel Hill, NC, USA)
Dr. J. R. Rossignac (IBM Thomas J. Watson Research Center, NY)
Dr. C. Shaw (University of Alberta, Canada)

# Table of Contents

## Part I Rendering Machines



## Part II Ray Tracing



## Part III Visualization Systems

# Part I

# Rendering Machines

# The Triangle Shading Engine

Hans-Josef Ackermann and Christoph Hornung

ABSTRACT This paper describes an algorithm implementing the Gouraud-shading of triangles and its realization in hardware. Different realizations using span shading hardware are discussed. Their drawbacks lead to the concept of a triangle shader, designed as an ASIC. Interfaced to a signal processor for geometry computations, this chip will provide an effective and low-cost 3D-extension to graphics subsystems in the PC environment.

## 1 Introduction

Simultaneously with the growing complexity in VLSI, there has been an explosion of computational power in personal computer systems. Personal or Entry Level Workstations feature system performances, which were reached only by minicomputers and mainframes few years ago. Higher performances and system resources brought up the demand for better user interfaces and, as a picture is worth a thousand words, the new user interfaces were menu systems using simple forms of graphics. New graphics hardware meaning better video adapters were developed, and graphics software standards like GKS and PHIGS were brought from workstations to the PC. The demand for more than low level and faster graphics is ever growing through popular graphics applications like CAD/CAM which run on PC platforms. These applications however, require some hardware acceleration to release the CPU from time intensive visualization tasks.

## 2 Graphics Hardware

Today, all state-of-the-art workstations feature some form of hardware support for graphics. There have been several approaches to achieve major graphics performance in the field of high-end workstations. One of the first to become known was the pixel plane architecture by H. Fuchs which is a massive parallel system [1]. Another approach is the geometry engine now marketed by Silicon Graphics [2] making intensive use of pipelining. Common to all these systems is their complexity, the use of highly integrated custom chips, their restriction to one workstation architecture and their costs.

The rendering pipeline, supported by graphics hardware basically consists of geometric modelling, transformation, clipping, lighting, scan conversion, shading, and in the case of 3D-graphics, z-buffering and hidden surface removal. These tasks can be sub divided into two blocks, geometry calculations and raster calculations. Geometry calculations cover modelling, transformation, clipping and lighting, whereas raster calculations handle scan conversion and hidden surface removal by z-buffering. In order to achieve a balanced system, the units performing the tasks of these two blocks should have a comparable performance. In single processor systems the CPU works on the operating system, the application and the whole geometric and rendering pipeline ne, a burden too heavy even for the fastest general purpose CPUs. In order to improve the performance, accelerators are used. The widest spread form of an accelerator is an arithmetic-coprocessor chip plugged in a prepared socket on the processor board. More powerful and complex accelerators are add-on boards, communicating with the main CPU via its bus-backplane. These add-on accelerators may be classified according to their field of application.

### 2.1 Floating Point Accelerators

This first group uses RISC or Digital Signal Processor systems for the acceleration of floating point intensive tasks. In the case of graphics these tasks are those of the first group mentioned above: transformation, clipping and lighting. With single state-of-the-art processors like the i860 or the TMS 320C30 floating point performances up to 50 MFLOPs can be reached. According to [3] this performance is sufficient for the transformation and the clipping of 100,000 to 300,000 vectors/s.

### 2.2 Graphics Processors

The second group is covered by so called graphics cards. Graphics cards typically consist of processors or controllers with some graphics properties, a frame buffer and the video logic necessary for the connection to a monitor. Processors often applied, are the TMS 34010 and 34020 by TI [4] and the DP 8500 by National Semiconductor [5]. These chips mainly support BitBLT operations and simple 2D-line drawing. 3D-functions are not supported. So these graphics cards do not reach the performance for shading an d hidden line removal necessary to achieve a balanced system together with a floating point accelerator.

### 2.3 Goal for a Hardware Shader

The goal of a hardware shader is to reach an equivalent performance of about 50,000 to 100,000 shaded and z-buffered triangles per second. The shading algorithm to be implemented is the Gouraud Shading [6], which does a linear interpolation of the color between the edges of a triangle. This algorithm is supported by major graphics standards like PHIGS-PLUS. It is well fit for an implementation in hardware. Color and z-values of the vertices have to be computed according to a chosen lighting model.

## 3 Triangle Shading

In comparison to other area primitives, triangles have some major advantages. Triangles are inherently planar. This leads to a constant increment for color (r, g, b) and depth (z) along the scanlines. A fixed shading algorithm for triangle shading can be formulated. This is especially important for a hardware implementation. Arbitrary areas, delimited by polygons can be decomposed into triangles. This shows that triangles are a well-suited rendering primitive.

### 3.1 Conception

The shading of triangles consists of three main steps:

- initialization
- edge interpolation
- span interpolation

### 3.2 Initialization

Initially, a triangle is defined by its three vertices (x, y, z) and the respective color values (r, g, b). This representation has to be converted into another one, better suited for shading. Depending on the requirements to the triangle shading algorithm, different formats may be used. An important requirement has been the implementation of an exact point sampling. Exact point sampling is essential for the support of texture mapping and transparency, planned features of future versions of the triangle shader. Furthermore, during edge interpolation, no pixels are missed or drawn twice. To fulfill this requirement, the following data structure was chosen:

```
typedef struct  short f, i;  tFix;
typedef struct  tFix x, y, z, r, g, b;  tPoint;
typedef struct  tFix dx, dy, dz, dr, dg, db;  tDeltaPoint;
typedef struct
   {
   tPoint          PTop;
   tDeltaPoint     dEdge;
   tDeltaPoint     dSpan;
   tFix            xTop;
   tFix            yMid;
   tFix            yBot;
   tFix            dxMidTop;
   tFix            dxBotMid;
   }
tTriangle;
```

This structure represents a triangle as shown in Figure 1. In our implementation, interpolation always starts from the longest edge of a triangle. Thus, in any case, only one edge-increment *dEdge* of type *tDeltaPoint* has to be calculated. This algorithm requires the ability to interpolate the spans along both, the positive and the negative x-axis.

Figure 1 illustrates the meaning of the components of tTriangle. *dEdge* does not correspond to the exact edge from *PTop* to *PBot.* Instead of the exact edge, the closest edge through *PTop* pointing to the outside of a triangle and having and integer slope dx/dy is chosen. This construction allows the implementation of a Bresenham-like algorithm guaranteeing that only the centers of the pixels are taken into account. All data values are stored using the type *tFix* with an integral and a fractional part, as usual in a DDA-algorithm. Therefore, this concept combines both the accuracy of the Bresenham-algorithm and the speed of the DDA-algorithm.

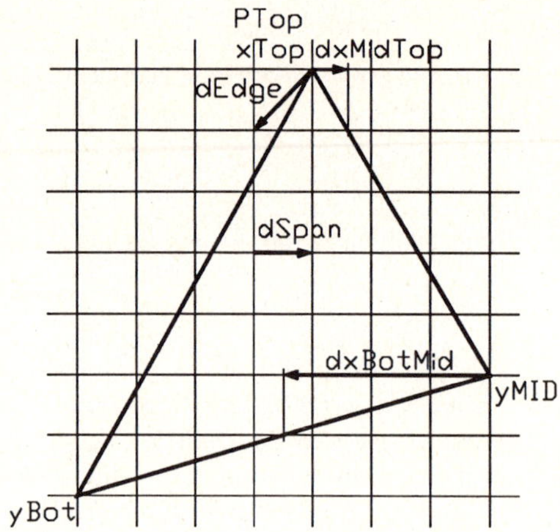


**Fig. 1.**

### 3.3 Edge Interpolation

During edge interpolation, a triangle is scanned along y from top to bottom. This algorithm delivers the boundary of a triangle as well as the initial values of r, g, b and z, which are necessary for the span interpolation.

The initial values for r, g, b and z are calculated by incrementing *PTop* along *dEdge* until *yBot* is reached (Figure 1; $dEdge.dy = 1$ in any case). The final x-value is initialized with *xTop* and first incremented by *dxMidTop* until the line *yMid* is reached, and then incremented by *dxBotMid* until reaching *yBot*.

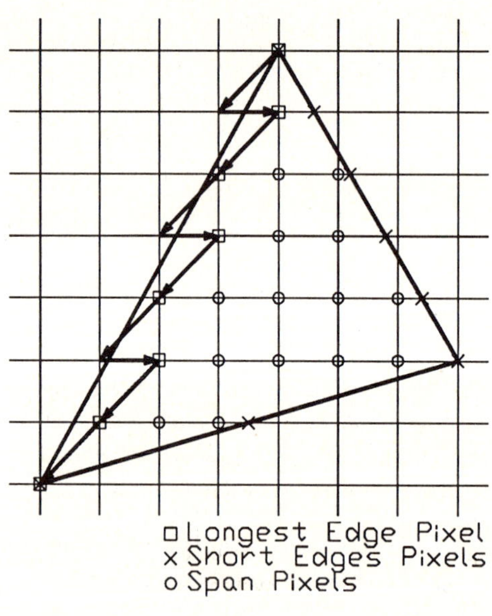


**Fig. 2.**

### 3.4 Span Interpolation

The span interpolation forms the inner loop of the triangle shading. Starting from the longest edge, all pixels are set until the corresponding short edge is reached (Figure 2). This iteration is done using the variable dSpan, including the elements x, y, z, r, g and b. The values of these increments are constant throughout a whole triangle. During span interpolation, the value of *dSpan.dy* is constantly 0, while *dSpan.dx* is 1 or -1 depending on the direction of iteration.

## 4 Realizations of Triangle Shading Using Span Shading Hardware

### 4.1 The Zebra Chip

Starting point for the realization of Gouraud shading in hardware was the Zebra chip [7], an ASIC designed by National Semiconductor to fit into a system controlled by National's raster graphics processor DP 8500. This chip mainly contains a set of four adders for the interpolation of r, g, b and z and a comparator for hidden pixel removal calculation. The minimum cycle time for the interpolation is 100 ns, meaning that pixels could be written to the frame buffer with a maximum rate of 10 Mpixels/s.

As mentioned above, the triangle shading algorithm consists of the subtasks initialization, edge interpolation and span interpolation. Implementing the triangle shading using the Zebra chip, both the initialization as well as the edge interpolation have to be done in software by the host, while only the span interpolation can be boosted by the Zebra chip. Initialization data for each span have to be transferred to the Zebra chip's set-up registers. This leads to a high data stream and communication overhead between the host and the Zebra chip. The maximum performance according to the interpolation rate without communication is 100,000 triangles/s with 100 pixels each. In order to test the true resulting system performance, three different systems using the Zebra chip were designed and analysed.

### 4.2 An Initial Approach

The initial system consisted of a Zebra chip with a $2 \times 256 \times 256 \times 24$ bit frame buffer and a $2 \times 256 \times 256 \times 16$ bit z-buffer, both static RAM, controlled by a hardware state machine for address generation and fed by a T800 transputer [8]. Due to the memory access time of 100 ns and the timing of the z-comparison, an interpolation rate of 4 Mpixels/s was reached.

### 4.3 An Improved System

This system was redesigned using fast page mode DRAMS for a $2 \times 512 \times 512$ frame buffer and a $2 \times 512 \times 512$ z-buffer. The state machine was optimized for the maximum speed which could be achieved using standard page mode DRAMs. The result was an interpolation rate of about 7 Mpixels/s. Like in the first system, initialization and preprocessing is done by a T800 transputer. The z-buffer can be automatically cleared while image data are transferred to the output stage of the system.

### 4.4 A Different Approach

The third approach was an AT-based system [9] built around the whole Advanced Graphics Chip Set of National Semiconductor [10]. In this system the interpolation was controlled by the linedraw cycle of the raster graphics processor (RGP). According to the framebuffer of $2048 \times 2048 \times 8$, the z-buffer was $2048 \times 2048 \times 16$ and the Zebra chip interpolated color indices. Due to the fairly complex timing an interpolation rate of about 2 Mpixels/s was reached. A FIFO for initialization data was used to decouple three possible data sources. Transfer from the FIFO to the Zebra chip's registers was realized by a hardware state machine.

### 4.5 Analysis of the Results Using Span Shading Hardware

The Zebra chip can be parallelly initialized while interpolation is going on. The time required for transferring initialization data for one span depends on different aspects:

- the chosen interface bus width (16- or 32-bits)
- the write cycle time of the initializing device
- the number of color planes (when using index colors, g and b values are not used)
- the type of the transferred span (the transfer of the increment values is required only for the first span of a triangle; see Section 3.4.)

It could be pointed out, that the break even point between initialization and interpolation was in the area of 12 to 29 pixels. There are two consequences:

- the number of spans which can be initialized is restricted to about 400,000/s.
- a higher interpolation rate only pays for spans considerably longer than break even spans.

In advanced quality pictures only a small percentage of lines exceeds this length. Assuming a maximum data block of 44 bytes per span and triangles with 100 pixels and 10 spans, the requested 50,000 triangles/s would require a peek dataflow of 22 Mbyte/s for initialization. In addition, at least the edge interpolation must be done by the transferring device.

This led to the conclusion, that using spans as primitive, our goal of 50,000 to 100,000 shaded triangles/s cannot be reached. Doing the edge interpolation in software and realizing a communication for each span drops down the system performance dramatically. Especially for high quality pictures with small triangles the resulting data rates cannot be handled. The primitive one level above is the triangle. Using triangles as primitive could reduce the datasets for triangles with 100 pixels by one order of magnitude. So the logical consequence was to design a triangle shader.

## 5 The Triangle Shader Chip

### 5.1 Conception

The triangle shader chip was designed to implement both edge and span interpolation described in Sections 3.3 and 3.4. Up to now, the initialization has to be done in software running on the host CPU or the floating point accelerator.

### 5.2 System Overview

A system utilizing the triangle shader chip will consist of three major components. The host processor running the operating system controls the whole graphics subsystem via the standard bus system. The graphics subsystem will be built out of a floating point accelerator and a rendering engine carrying frame buffer, z-buffer, video logic, triangle shader chip and a graphics controller for buffer management. The datapath between floating point accelerator and rendering engine will use one of the accelerator CPU's busses for fast transfer of initialization data. During shading operation, frame buffer and z-buffer are controlled by the triangle shader chip.

### 5.3 Hardware Implementation of the Triangle Shader

The triangle shader chip contains three major functional blocks (Figure 3). A 16-bit-wide data interface provides access to the set-up registers holding initialization data. A 12-bit-wide control interface provides access to the state machine with its associated microcode RAM. Nine memory strobes can be independently programmed within 25 ns periods to fit the necessary frame and z-buffer timing. Furthermore, the control interface provides lines for automatic control of an external FIFO memory containing initialization data. Data are transferred to the set-up registers while the preceding triangle is processed by the interpolators. The interpolator section contains six independent parallelly working interpolation units for x, y, z, r, g and b. The interpolators work on both edges and spans. During span processing, edge data are in internally latched. A mask function protects specified bit planes from interpolation.

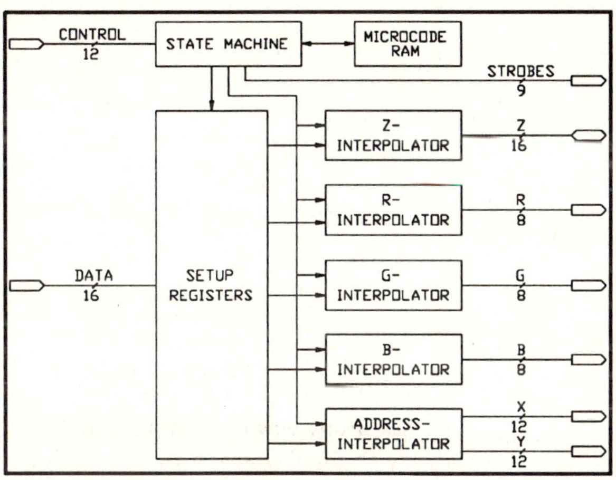


Fig. 3.

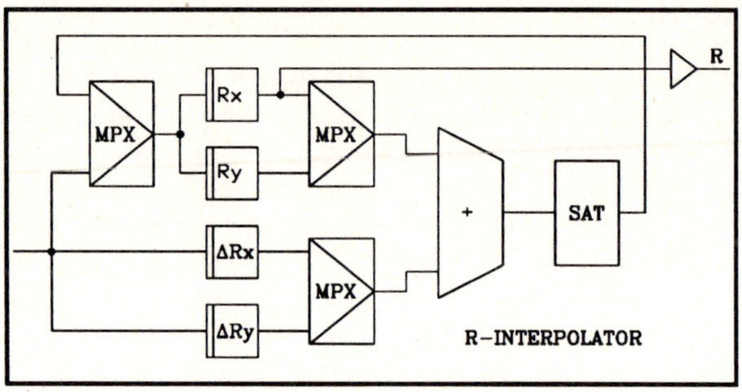


**Fig. 4.**

Figure 4 shows the datapaths of the r-interpolator consisting of registers, multiplexors, adder, saturation logic and output buffer. All values except y are processed in fixed-point representation. The widths of the fractional parts have been chosen to prevent rounding errors while interpolating the longest line possible in a 2048 by 2048 pixels frame buffer. The actual formats are,

| | INT | FRAC |
|---|---|---|
| x: | 12 bit + | 12 bit |
| y: | 12 bit + | 0 bit |
| z: | 20 bit + | 12 bit |
| r,g,b: | 8 bit + | 12 bit |

The triangle shader chip has been designed as an ASIC using a 2 mm standard-cell process. The gate equivalent count is 11,358 (kernel).

### 5.4 Simulated Performance

All simulations have been done assuming a clock frequency of 40 MHz for the internal state machine of the triangle shader chip.

*Initialization Data Transfer*

An advantage of the triangle shading algorithm is, that unlike to the span shading approach, the number of initialization values is constant for any triangle. According to the chosen data structure *tTriangle* and formats, 37 16-bit words per triangle have to be transferred to the registers of the triangle shading chip. The state machine supports the reading of initialization data from an external FIFO memory. Depending on the used micro program, the read cycle time is 50 ns (linear program) or 100 ns (loop). This leads to a fixed initialization time for a triangle of 1.85 ns (3.7 ns). Therefore the number of triangles which can be initialized is 540,000/s (270,000/s). The initialization works in parallel with either edge or span interpolation.

*Edge Interpolation*

Due to the restricted chip complexity, edge and span interpolation have to use the same interpolator circuitry. Therefore, a parallel interpolation of edge and span data is not possible. The cycle time for the calculation of the next longest edge pixel (Figure 2) is 350 ns. If a correction step in y direction is necessary (Figure 2) an additional 100 ns are added. Switching from the first short edge to the second short edge requires 200 ns for loading the new parameters.

*Span Interpolation*

The span interpolation cycle time has been simulated assuming standard fast page mode DRAM timing for z-buffer and frame buffer access. The resulting interpolation cycle time is 150 ns which corresponds to a maximum interpolation rate of 6.7 Mpixels/s.

*Analysis*

In comparison to the span shading approaches, the data flow of initialization data for 50,000 triangles/s could be reduced from 22 Mbytes/s to 3.7 Mbytes/s. The resulting transfer cycle time can be still easily met for 100,000 triangles/s.

The break-even point between initialization data transfer and iteration depends on the ratio between number of spans and pixels per span. In the case of a triangle degenerating to a horizontal line, the break-even point is 9 pixels per triangle. The break-even point decreases to 4 pixels if a triangle degenerates to a vertical line. These values show, that the problems of initialization data transfer have been solved with our design. The maximum shading performance is limited by the span interpolation rate of 6.7 Mpixels/s. Figure 5 shows a performance diagram assuming triangles with 100 pixels and shapes changing linearly from a horizontal to a vertical line. Figure 6 shows a performance diagram assuming rightangled, isosceles triangles.

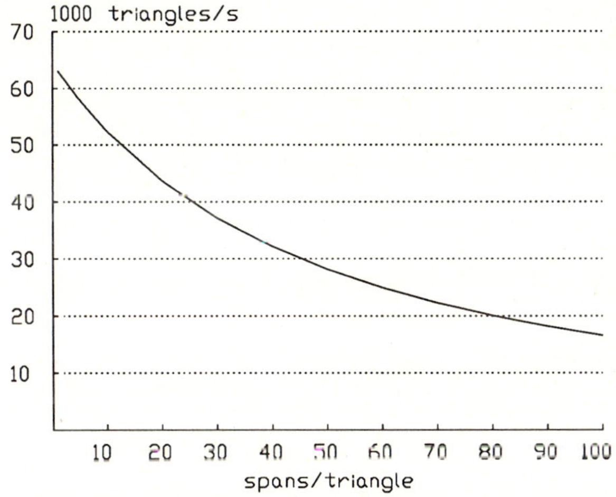


**Fig. 5.**

## 5.5 Status of the Triangle Shader

The algorithm of the triangle shader has been implemented first as a C program. The function of the algorithm has been certified to produce correct results using comprehensive and difficult case test patterns. The transfer from the C program to the VLSI design has been finished including logical and timing simulation of the design. The turn-around time for the chip production will be about six months. During this time, an evaluation system will be designed and built. This system is expected to work using the triangle shader chip in Spring 1991.

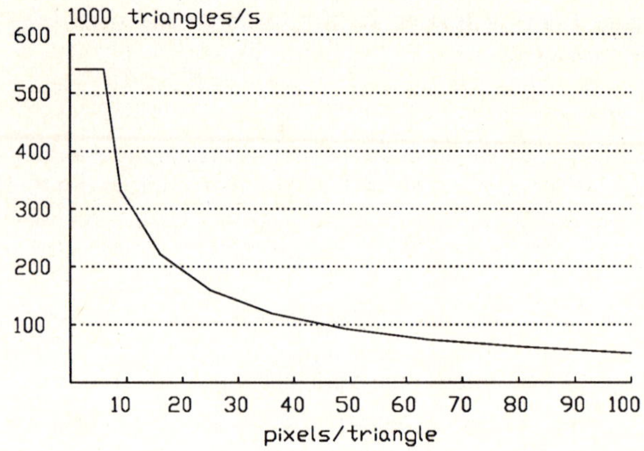


**Fig. 6.**

## 6 Future Work

The triangle shader as described above, is only the first step towards the development of an integrated hardware renderer. Two extensions are planned for the future: higher integration and enhanced, programmable functionality. With a higher scale integration process available, the initialization task will also be integrated on chip. The initialization requires an ALU supporting fast multiplication and division as well as a control sequencer.

Functionality enhancements will include alpha blending and texture mapping. Alpha blending can be implemented by adding an alpha channel to r, g and b. Furthermore, a blending stage consisting of adders and multipliers is required. This functionality can be used for features like anti-aliasing and transparency. Texture Mapping is more complex. A separate address generator and interpolation logic is required. Texture mapping will be combined with alpha blending. Goal will be to design a shading processor, which can be programmed for a flexible use of internal ALU-resources depending on the algorithm to be performed.

It should be noted, that all these extensions are already implemented in software. The conceptional background is clear and the implementation will be done within a short time.

## References

[1] Fuchs, H. and Poulton, J.: Pixel-planes a VLSI-oriented design for a raster graphics engine. *VLSI Design*, 2(3), 1981, pp. 20-28.

[2] Akeley, K. and Jermoluk, T.: High-Performance Polygon Rendering. *Computer Graphics* Volume 22, Number 4, 1988, pp. 239-246.

[3] Wilner, M.: Untersuchung eines Arithmetik-Spezialprozessors auf Eignung zur Realisierung floatingpoint intensiver Grafik-Algorithmen. *Diploma Thesis.* Universität Gesamthochschule-Paderborn Fachgebiet Datentechnik, 1989.

[4] Asal, M., Short, G., Preston T. et al.: The Texas Instrument 34010 Graphics System Processor. *IEEE Computer Graphics and Applications*, Volume 6, Number 10, October 1986, pp. 24-39.

[5] Carinalli, C. and Blair, J.: National's Advanced Graphics Chip Set for High-Performance Graphics. *IEEE Computer Graphics and Applications*, Volume 6, Number 10, October 1986, pp. 24-39.

[6] Gouraud, H.: Continuous Shading of Curved Surfaces. *IEEE Transactions on Computers* C-20, 6, 1971, pp. 623-629.

[7] National Semiconductor Corporation 'Zebra' Gouraud Shading and Z Buffer Engine. *Preliminary Datasheet*, May 1989.

[8] Nicklas, J.: Aufbau, Programmierung und Anschlua eines Graphik-Subsystems Zu Schattierung von 3D-Objekten an das Echtzeit-Bildverarbeitungssystem PEBSY. *Diploma Thesis.* Technische Hochschule Darmstadt, Fachbereich Informatik, Fachgebiet Graphisch-Interaktive Systeme, 1989.

[9] Ackermann, H.-J., Mehl, M., Peischl, M.: Halbjahresbericht des Projektes NT 2815 A 8: *Modulares Graphik-Subsystem für die Echtzeitdarstellung von 3D-Anwendungen*, April 1989.

# The AIDA Display Processor System Architecture

S. R. Evans, R. L. Grimsdale, P. F. Lister and A. D. Nimmo

ABSTRACT This paper describes the Advanced Image Display Architecture, AIDA. The primary aims were to design a graphics display subsystem capable of satisfying the needs of both high performance workstations and vehicle simulator visual systems. AIDA can accept planar triangle primitives which have been transformed, clipped and projected by preceding stages. The system implements many desirable features including modularity, anti-aliasing, translucency, pixel-rate hidden surface removal and Gouraud shading. AIDA has been designed to take advantage of ASIC technology in the implementation of its processing units.

## 1 Introduction

The realization of a flexible Display Processor Architecture, capable of meeting the requirements of radically different applications, requires the use of modular subsystems. Application areas that the VLSI and Computer Graphics Research Group have targeted include high-performance 3D workstations and vehicle simulator visual systems. This paper will introduce AIDA, developed as part of the ALVEY PRISM project, in collaboration with Link-Miles Ltd. and GEC Hirst Research Centre, and initially designed to be used in a graphics systems with the MAGIC I [1] or MAGIC II [4] processors performing the required geometry operations. The algorithms used, the system architecture, its components and configuration details, and an analysis of the expected performance will be discussed. Several similar systems exist [3], but AIDA is considered to be more flexible in terms of configurability. Figure 1 represents the AIDA graphics display subsystems.

AIDA accepts triangle vertex data, face data and gradient information. Subsequent processing steps produce an image with several desirable attributes. These include anti-aliasing, Gouraud shading and translucency. The conceptual display pipeline is used to express the decomposition of primitive objects into spans, then into rendered, depth sorted pixels, without indicating the amount of data produced by each step. This depends primarily, on the characteristics of the database and the effect of preprocessing stages. Section 4 attempts to predict the results obtained from different database types.

## 2 Algorithms

The only primitive currently accepted by AIDA is the planar triangle—the decomposition of a database into triangular elements is assumed to be a relatively trivial task. This primitive was chosen to simplify the span generation process—the planar triangle is always convex, can be described using a small amount of data and can be characterised

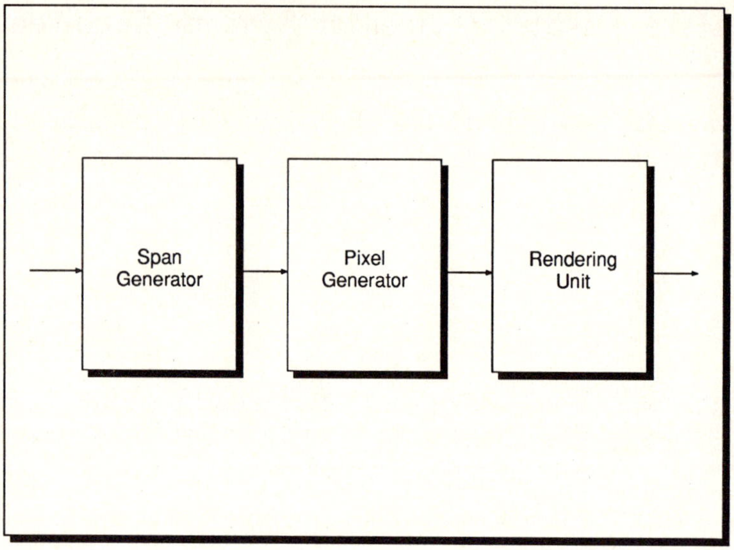


**Fig. 1.** The Conceptual Display Pipeline

simply. However, because the Pixel Generator and Rendering Unit only rely on span and pixel primitives, alternative Span Generators operating on different primitives—line, polygons, parametric surfaces—can be readily employed. Coherency is exploited by using interpolation methods in both the Span Generator and the Pixel Generator.

### 2.1 The Span Generator

The Span Generator is the first processing element of AIDA, generating spans from the display list of triangle data. Triangle primitives are defined for a virtual screen of $4096 \times 4096$ elements, for viewing on a display screen of $1024 \times 1024$ pixels. A span therefore consists of four sub-scan lines and the start and end $x$ coordinates, which, together with bounding information—sub-scan line coverage—provides enough information for anti-aliasing to be implemented in subsequent processing steps. One assumption is made—the triangles to be processed must have the top vertex (smallest $y$ coordinate) passed first, and if two vertices share the smallest $y$ coordinate the one with the smallest $x$ coordinate is to be passed first. The vertices are then passed to the Span Generator in clockwise order. In order to generate spans in a largely autonomous manner, a processing step is employed to ascertain the relative positions of the triangle vertices. This process is known as *triangle typing.* There are four types of triangle vertex orientations that AIDA must distinguish between, although triangle type 0 defines two effectively equivalent orientations. The typing parameters, $s_0$, $s_1$ and $s_2$, are given in Equations 1, 2 and 3.

$$s_0 = y_{v_1} - y_{v_0} \tag{1}$$

$$s_1 = y_{v_2} - y_{v_0} \tag{2}$$

$$s_2 = y_{v_1} - y_{v_2} \tag{3}$$

Type qualifications are allocated using the simple magnitude comparisons,

```
if (s0 == 0)||(s2 == 0)
  type = 0
else if (s0 < s1)
  type = 1
else if (s0 > s1)
  type = 2
```

Together, the typing parameters and the type qualification fully describe a planar triangle for the span generation process. The triangle orientations are shown in Figure 2 and gives the relevant typing parameters. A Bounding Mask is used to describe the span sub-scan line coverage, and is calculated using the current $y$ coordinate and the two closest vertices, information which is type dependent. It is also used to determine the allocation of $x$ coordinate interpolators to sub-scan lines to avoid reverse interpolation when a span does not start on the first sub-scan line.

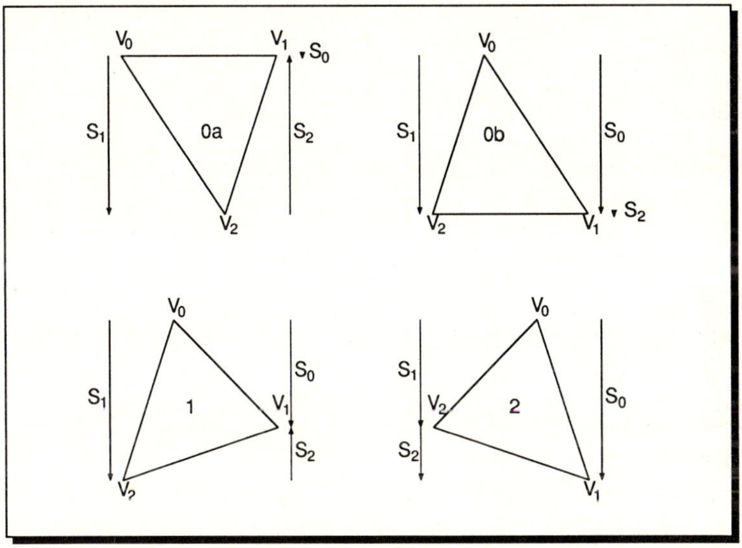


**Fig. 2.** Triangle Types

The development of a suitable algorithm for the Span Generator uses triangle typing and span coverage information, together with counters and comparators, to simplify and aid the production of similar routines for different triangle configurations. An overview of the algorithm is given.

```
per triangle {
    read vertex data, attribute data, write attribute data to face memory
    calculate data s_0, s_1, s_2, type triangle
    y_c = y_{v_0}
    if (type == 0) {
      calculate bound mask (y_c, v_0, v_2), allocate interpolators, write span
      while (y_c != y_{v_2}) {
            y_c++, interpolate
            calculate bound mask (y_c, v_0, v_2), write span
      }
    }
    else if (type == 1) {
      calculate bound mask (y_c, v_0, v_1), allocate interpolators, write span
      while (y_c != y_{v_1}) {
            y_c++, interpolate
            calculate bound mask (y_c, v_0, v_1), write span
      }
      calculate bound mask (y_c, v_1, v_2), allocate interpolators, write span
      while (y_c != y_{v_2}) {
            y_c++, interpolate
            calculate bound mask (y_c, v_1, v_2), write span
      }
    }
    else { /* type == 2 */
      calculate bound mask (y_c, v_0, v_2), allocate interpolators, write span
      while (y_c != y_{v_2}) {
            y_c++, interpolate
            calculate bound mask (y_c, v_0, v_2), write span
      }
      calculate bound mask (y_c, v_2, v_1), allocate interpolators, write span
      while (y_c != y_{v_1}) {
            y_c++, interpolate
            calculate bound mask (y_c, v_2, v_1), write span
      }
    }
}
```

## 2.2 The Pixel Generator

The Pixel Generator follows the Span Generator and has three main functions:

- Interpolation in $x$ for Gouraud shading.
- Generation of the edge mask [2], required to perform antialiasing.
- Depth sorting all the surfaces at each pixel for hidden surface removal.

An outline of the Pixel Generator operations is given,

```
per pixel {
    if (span(s) cover(s) pixel) {
      for (all spans previously read and stored) {
          read span data
          calculate intensity, proximity and edge mask
          depth sort
          keep span if contribution to next pixel
      }
      for (all spans that start at current pixel) {
          read span data
          calculate edge mask
          depth sort
          keep span contribution to next pixel
      }
      while (pixel contributing surfaces exist, until maximum) {
              output pixel contributions
      }
    }
    else {
      output background surface
    }
}
```

The AIDA depth sort algorithm was developed to resolve two problems:

- Surfaces at different distances from the viewing position.
- Coplanar surfaces.

Surfaces with less depth (greater proximity) are placed in front of surfaces with greater depth (less proximity). Coplanar surfaces present an interesting dilemma. Take the example of superimposing one surface on another—typically used for road markings, where texturing techniques may be inappropriate. Each surface will have the same proximity value, making it impossible to predict the visible surface. A label, termed surface i. d. and allocated during the design of a database, comprising a surface identification tag and a priority word tag is used. Identical surface identification tags are given to primitives with the same parent object. The database designer can then choose a priority value for superimposed markings and details depending on the desired effect.

## 2.3 The Rendering Unit

Pixel rendering functionality is provided by the AIDA Rendering Unit. Situated between the Pixel Generator and the frame buffer, it takes depth sorted pixel contributions and outputs rendered RGB pixel data. Desirable features of the design include antialiasing and translucency. An algorithm for the Rendering Unit is given,

```
per pixel {
    set pixel colour zero
    per element {
        read element
    }
    per sub-pixel {
        find depth mask
    }
    do {
        find next unused depth mask
        mark all unused depth masks as used
        find number of depth mask
        calculate initial translucency factor
        for (every surface covering sub-pixel in depth order) {
            accumulate colour
            produce translucency factor
        }
    } while (not all subpixels used)
}
```

The Rendering Unit algorithm takes in a pixel packet, finding which sub-pixels are covered by the same pixel contributions, which will have the same final colour. The colour of each different coloured sub-pixel is calculated then multiplied by the percentage of sub-pixels with that colour. The values for all the different coloured sub-pixels are then added together to give the final pixel colour, Equation 4, where $m$ is number of covering pixel contributions, $n$ is number of differing depth masks, $tf$ is the translucency factor, $tl$ is the translucency level and $w$ is the weighting factor.

$$c_{out} = \frac{\sum_{j=0}^{n} \sum_{i=0}^{m} c_i \times I_i \times (1 - tl_i) \times tf_i}{16} \tag{4}$$

$$tf_{i+1} = tf_i \times tl_i \tag{5}$$

$$tf_0 = w \tag{6}$$

To find which sub-pixels are covered by the same pixel contributions, the bit corresponding to a given sub-pixel in the edge mask is stored. Each sub-pixel has a word, or depth mask, in which the $n^{th}$ bit represents the coverage by the $n^{th}$ pixel contribution in the packet. Comparisons of the depth masks will show which sub-pixels produce the same colour. By resetting the bits in any edge mask covered by an opaque pixel contribution, the number of differing sub-pixels can be reduced, without affecting the final result. This significantly decreases the number of calculations needed to produce the final pixel colour.

# 3 System Description

The AIDA architecture exhibits an hierarchical structure, taking advantage of parallel processing and exploiting coherency. System performance can be optimised to meet a wide variety of applications by varying the number and configuration of processing elements.

## 3.1 The Span Generator

A complete Span Generator is implemented using two instances of the Span Generator ASIC—they are synchronised to track and interpolate the values at the left and right edges of a triangle, Figure 3.

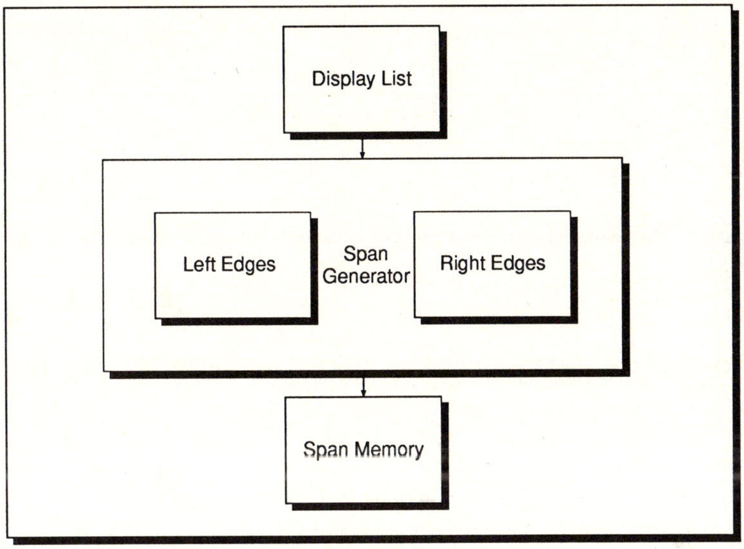


**Fig. 3.** The Span Generator System Architecture

Figure 4 shows the internal ASIC architecture. Interpolation of $x$ values, proximity and intensity occur in parallel. The initial values for $x$ are cascaded from the preceding interpolator, since each $x$ interpolator deals with only a sub-scan line. The interpolated results are buffered in an output memory block, which is sent to the output block when a complete span is present—when the bottom bit of the bounding mask is set, or the bottom of the triangle has been reached. This information is obtained from the span coverage, using the Bounding Mask generator output present at the current scan-line.

## 3.2 The Span Memory

The Span Memory is the first stage of the pixel generation process, sorting all the spans, per frame or region, in XY order. The sort process creates, for each pixel, a null terminated linked list of spans which start at the referenced pixels. This method of span sorting simplifies Pixel Generator access to spans.

## 3.3 The Pixel Generator

Span coherency within the Pixel Generator, Figure 5, implies that only complete scan lines can be allocated per Pixel Generator.

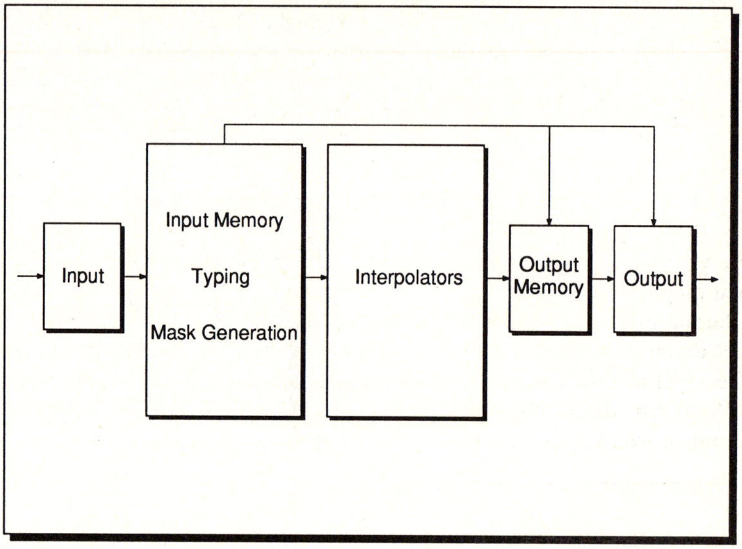


**Fig. 4.** The Span Generator ASIC Architecture

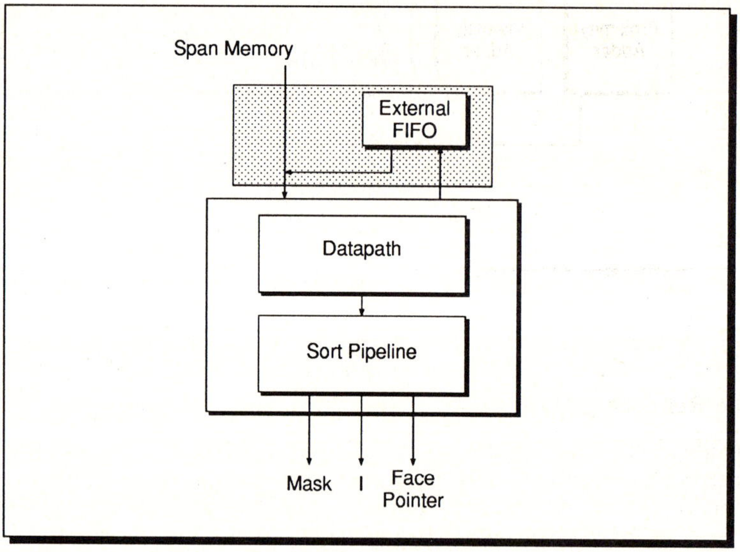


**Fig. 5.** The Pixel Generator ASIC Architecture

The Pixel Generator creates pixel packets, derived from all the spans covering a given pixel, and consists of a depth sorted list of pixel contributions. Two types of span, input through a 128-bit bus, are recognised:

- A *new span*, which starts on the current pixel.
- An *active span*, one which has previously started.

The essential difference between the two types of span is their source. New spans come directly from span memory and are input after all current active spans have been processed. Active spans are stored in an external FIFO instance—on-chip storage of every active span may not be possible because of the RAM size required.

The Datapath, Figure 6 generates the data packet of unsorted pixel contributions used by the Sort Pipeline. For a given pixel, the Sort Pipeline sorts the data in ascending depth order. The pipeline comprises $n$ autonomous modules, where $(n-1)$ is the maximum number of resolved translucent surfaces. Data at the input of each module is either routed to the output or exchanged with the data present in the module.

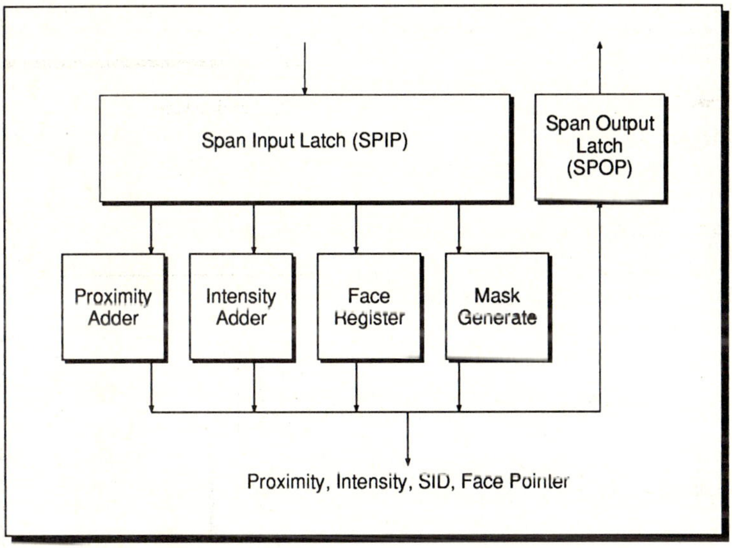


**Fig. 6.** The Pixel Generator Datapath

### 3.4 The Rendering Unit

The Rendering Unit ASIC Architecture, Figure 7, presents a hardware implementation of the Rendering Unit algorithm.

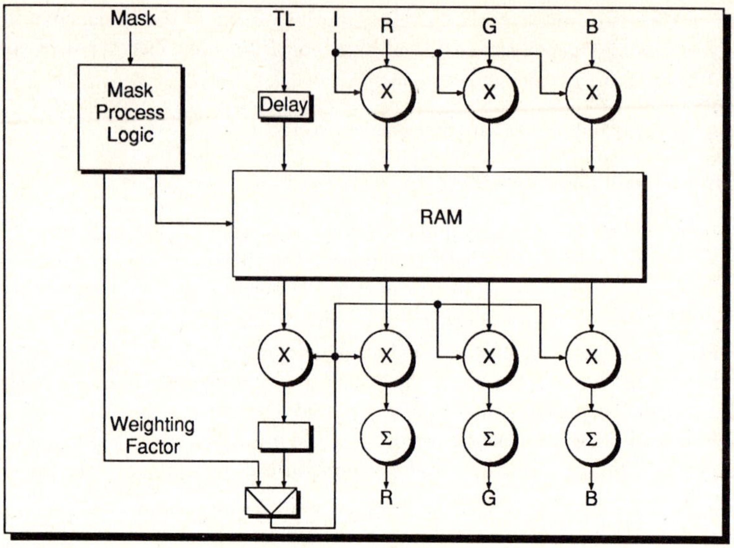


**Fig. 7.** The Rendering Unit ASIC Architecture

# 4 Performance

## 4.1 Introduction

It is widely recognised that accurate performance results for one system often have little real value for comparisons with other systems. More suitable performance indicators are obtained by using a variety of different data, to reflect different applications. The results presented here use several AIDA system configurations, to give an indication of the predicted peak performance.

## 4.2 System Configuration and Triangle Throughput

We have given three example configurations, Figures 8, 9 and 10, together with peak performance rates and memory requirements. These configurations represent typical connection schemes. System Configuration A is used as a reference, Figure 8, with peak throughput and memory requirements given in Tables 1 and 2. System Configurations B and C, Figures 9 and 10, show more complex, higher performance configurations which would typically be used in workstation and vehicle simulator display systems, together with associated throughput and memory requirements.

| Throughput | | |
|---|---|---|
| Δ/sec | | No. of |
| SG | PG | ASICs |
| 1M | **100K** | 4 |

**Table 1.**

| Memory Requirements | | | |
|---|---|---|---|
| | | Sub Regions | |
| Frame rate | Δ/frame | 1 | 64 |
| 1Hz | 100K | 32M (21M) | 19M (328K) |
| 5Hz | 20K | 6.4M (4.2K) | 3.7M (64K) |
| 30Hz | 3.3K | 1M (700K) | 600K (5K) |

**Table 2.**

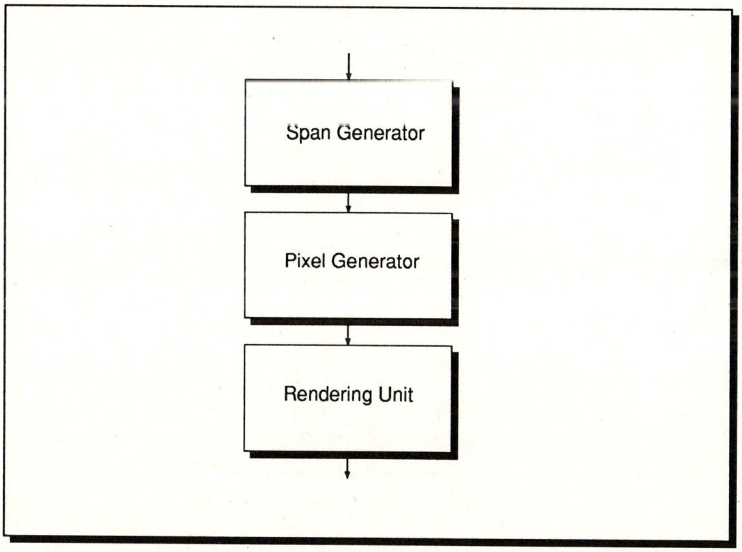


**Fig. 8.** System Configuration A

| Throughput | | |
|---|---|---|
| $\triangle$/sec | | No. of |
| SG | PG | ASICs |
| 1M | **400K** | 10 |

**Table 3.**

| Memory Requirements | | | |
|---|---|---|---|
| | | Sub Regions | |
| Frame rate | $\triangle$/frame | 1 | 64 |
| 1Hz | 400K | 130M (84M) | 74M (1.3M) |
| 5Hz | 80K | 26MB (17M) | 15M (260K) |
| 30Hz | 13.2K | 4.3M (2.8M) | 2.4M (43K) |

**Table 4.**

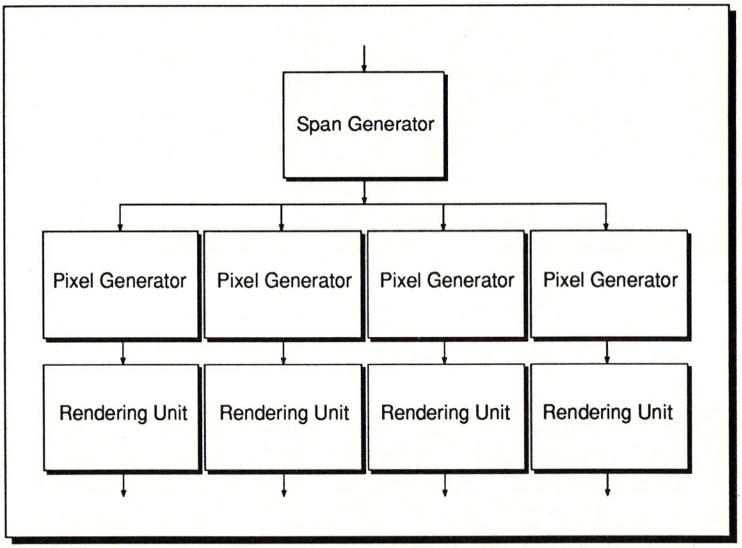


**Fig. 9.** System Configuration B

| Throughput | | |
|---|---|---|
| △/sec | | No. of |
| SG | PG | ASICs |
| **4M** | 6.8M | 72 |

**Table 5.**

| Memory Requirements | | | |
|---|---|---|---|
| | | Sub Regions | |
| Frame rate | △/frame | 1 | 64 |
| 1Hz | 4M | 1.3GB | 741.1MB |
| 5Hz | 800K | 260MB | 148.22MB |
| 30Hz | 133K | 43MB | 24.7MB |

**Table 6.**

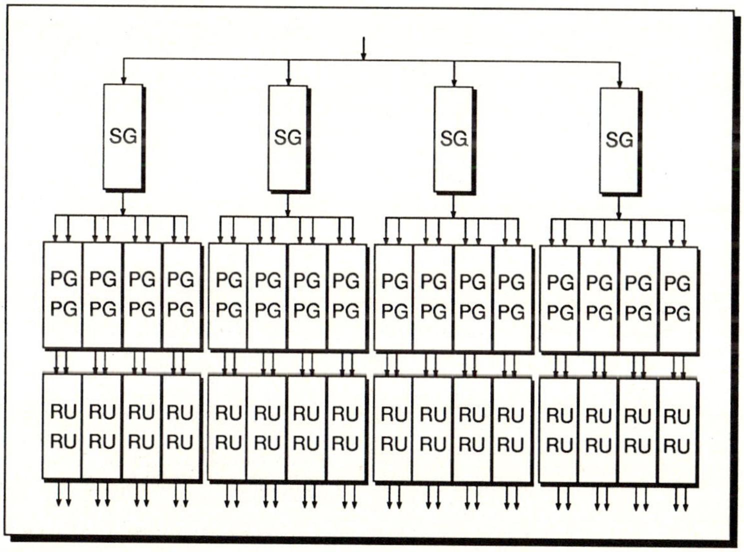


**Fig. 10.** System Configuration C

## 5 Conclusion

We have presented a modular graphics display subsystem, capable of high throughput and different system configurations, for the production of high-quality images. These designs have been developed using techniques presented in [5], and are being implemented in silicon using the GENESIL[1] silicon compiler.


## Acknowledgements

The work presented here has been funded under the UK ALVEY programme, and performed in collaboration with Link-Miles Ltd. and GEC Hirst Research Centre. We would like to thank Alan Cunliffe and Daljit Bimrah of Link-Miles Ltd. for their contributions, and all the members of the VLSI and Computer Graphics Research Group, Graham Dunnet, Marie-Pierre Hébert, Michael D. J. McNeill, Bina Shah and Martin White.


## References


[1] M. Agate, H.R. Finch, A.A. Garel, R.L. Grimsdale, P.F. Lister and A.C. Simmons.: A multiple application graphics integrated circuit—MAGIC. In A.A.G. Requicha, editor, *EUROGRAPHICS'86*, pages 67–77, 1986.

[2] L. Carpenter.: The A-buffer, an antialiased hidden surface method. In H. Christiansen, editor, *Computer Graphics—SIGGRAPH Conference Proceedings*, pages 103–108, 1984.

[3] M. Deering, S. Winner, B. Schediwy, C. Duffy and N. Hunt.: The triangle processor and normal vector shader: A VLSI system for high performance graphics. In *Computer Graphics—SIGGRAPH Conference Proceedings*, pages 21–30, 1988.

[4] H.R. Finch, M. Agate, A.A. Garel, P.F. Lister and R.L. Grimsdale.: A multiple application graphics integrated circuit—MAGIC II. In A.A.M. Kuijk and W. Strasser, editors, *Advances in Computer Graphics Hardware II*, pages 81–92. Springer-Verlag Berlin Heidelberg New York, 1987.

[5] A.D. Nimmo, P.F. Lister and R.L. Grimsdale.: A VLSI strategy for graphics. In A.A.M. Kuijk, editor, *Advances in Computer Graphics Hardware III*. Springer-Verlag Berlin Heidelberg New York, forthcoming.


[1]GENESIL is a trademark of Mentor Graphics Silicon Design Division

# Real Time Phong Shading

Ute Claussen

ABSTRACT Nowadays, hardware support for Gouraud shading is state-of-the-art. Most hardware implementations of the Phong shading algorithm lack flexibility, for example are restricted in the number of light sources. In this paper, we will present a concept of shading processors that has been developed in a rendering system called PROOF. Two types of processors have been designed, one performing the normalization of vectors. The other one is designed for faster and cheaper shading. The capabilities of the processors are demonstrated.

## 1 Introduction

Hardware implementations of real-time shading algorithms are aiming at Phong shading today. Several approaches have been made.

- The 'normal vector shader' developed at Schlumberger [5]. It is restricted to five directional light sources and its performance led to 24784 triangles rendered in less than 50 ms. The resolution of the screen is 1280 × 1024 pixels.
- The 'fast Phong shading' approach [1]. In principle, the computations of the illumination model and of the shading algorithms are combined into one formula. This term then is evaluated as a Taylor series of second order. Hence, rendering can be done with two adds per pixel. Unfortunately, a Taylor series should be developed for every light source. Furthermore, it is restricted to directional light sources.
- The 'faster Phong shading' by Kuijk and Blake [6]. They propose to interpolate angularly along great circles. This is an algorithmic approach that seems to be promising to be built in hardware.
- Another approach has been designed to render bicubic patches [11]. The hardware consists of adaptive forward differencing units and is also restricted to a single directional light source.

Our approach stands in the framework of the PROOF rendering system that has been presented before [3,10]. It is a more expensive but more flexible approach to real-time Phong shading.

First, the concept of the processor will be described. Two instantiations of the processor are developed. Their dataflow and datapaths as well as the algorithms and commands that are implemented will be described. Capabilities, the ways and the cost of its use is described. An outlook to the future and critical discussion will close the paper.

**Table 1.** Naming Conventions of this Paper

| | |
|---|---|
| $I_a$ | ambient intensity |
| $I_d$ | intensity of directional light source |
| $I_p$ | intensity of positional light source |
| $k_a$ | ambient reflection |
| $k_d$ | diffuse reflection |
| $k_s$ | specular reflection |
| $\vec{N}$ | surface normal |
| $\vec{L}$ | light source vector |
| $\vec{H}$ | highlight vector |
| $\vec{E}$ | eyevector |
| $\vec{P}$ | point on a surface |
| $\vec{P}_p$ | position of positional light source |
| $C$ | colour |
| $P$ | number of positional light sources |
| $R$ | number of directional light sources |

## 2 The Processor Concept

The rendering system PROOF consists of three stages. The object processor pipeline is a distributed z-buffer system that solves the hidden surface problem. A second stage, called shading stage, calculates the illumination model, if an interpolation of normal vectors takes place in the object processor pipeline. The last stage, a filter stage, performs an oversampling and filtering of the resulting picture. The object processor pipeline and the filter stage have been described before, e.g. in [9,8].
A standard illumination model for a Phong shading is defined as:

$$C_{amb} = k_a I_a \tag{1}$$

for an ambient light source,

$$C_{dir} = \sum_{l=1}^{R} [k_d I_{d_l} (\vec{N} \cdot \vec{L}_{d_l}) + k_s I_{d_l} (\vec{N} \cdot \vec{H}_{d_l})^m] \tag{2}$$

for all directional light sources, and

$$C_{pos} = \sum_{l=1}^{P} [k_d I_{p_l} (\vec{N} \cdot \frac{\vec{P}_{p_l} - \vec{P}}{|\vec{P}_{p_l} - \vec{P}|}) + k_s I_{p_l} (\vec{N} \cdot \frac{\vec{E} + \vec{P}_{p_l} - \vec{P}}{|\vec{E} + \vec{P}_{p_l} - \vec{P}|})^m] \tag{3}$$

for all positional light sources [12]. The naming conventions of this paper are described in Table 1. Regarding these formulae, it is obvious that a common part of all computations is

$$C = k_x I_y (\vec{X} \cdot \vec{Y})^m. \tag{4}$$

Additionally, these terms have to be summed up.

The basic idea now is to built a processor that computes terms of the form

$$I_{out} = I_{in} + kI(\vec{N} \cdot \vec{A})^x. \tag{5}$$

**Table 2.** Instantiations of $k$, $I$, $\vec{A}$ and $x$ for different types of light source

| | ambient term | | | | diffuse term | | | | specular term | | | |
|---|---|---|---|---|---|---|---|---|---|---|---|---|
| light source | $k$ | $I$ | $\vec{A}$ | $x$ | $k$ | $I$ | $\vec{A}$ | $x$ | $k$ | $I$ | $\vec{A}$ | $x$ |
| ambient | $k_a$ | $I_a$ | d | 0 | — | | | | — | | | |
| directional light source | — | | | | $k_d$ | $I_{d_l}$ | $\vec{L}_{d_l}$ | 1 | $k_s$ | $I_{d_l}$ | $\vec{H}_{d_l}$ | m |
| positional light source | — | | | | $k_d$ | $I_{p_l}$ | $d$ | 1 | $k_s$ | $I_{p_l}$ | $d$ | m |

**Table 3.** Capabilities of the two versions of the shading processor

| version | light source model | illumination model |
|---|---|---|
| without normalization | ambient<br>directional | ambient reflection<br>diffuse reflection<br>specular reflection |
| including normalization | ambient<br>directional<br>positional | ambient reflection<br>diffuse reflection<br>specular reflection |

The instantiations of $k$, $I$, $\vec{A}$ and $x$ for the different terms of Equations 1-3 are shown in Table 2. In addition, the values $\vec{N}$, $\vec{L}$, $\vec{H}$ or $\vec{P}_p$ respectively, and $\vec{P}$ have to be provided.

The provision of $\vec{N}$ and $\vec{P}$ is done by the object processor pipeline. This pipeline acts as a distributed z-buffer system and linearly interpolates the normal vector $\vec{N}$ for triangles. Consequently, vectors provided from this pipeline and passed on to the shading stage are not normalized.

## 3 Datapaths and Algorithms

It has been shown before that the computation of an illumination model without normalization of the interpolated normal can be accepted as a 'cheap' Phong shading [2]. Therefore, two versions of the shading processor are proposed: one that includes normalization in its algorithms as well as in its datapaths, and one that doesn't. An overview of the resulting capabilities of the processor versions is given in Table 3.

### 3.1 Datapaths

A design for the datapath of the simpler processor can be derived from equation (5). Basic functional blocks are dot product computation, vector multiplication, vector addition, and a look-up-table for exponentiation (see Figure 1). The intensities as well as the reflection and the highlight coefficient are represented as integers whereas vectors are represented as 2's-complement fix-point numbers. One of the characteristics of this processor is the high compression rate from input to output data.

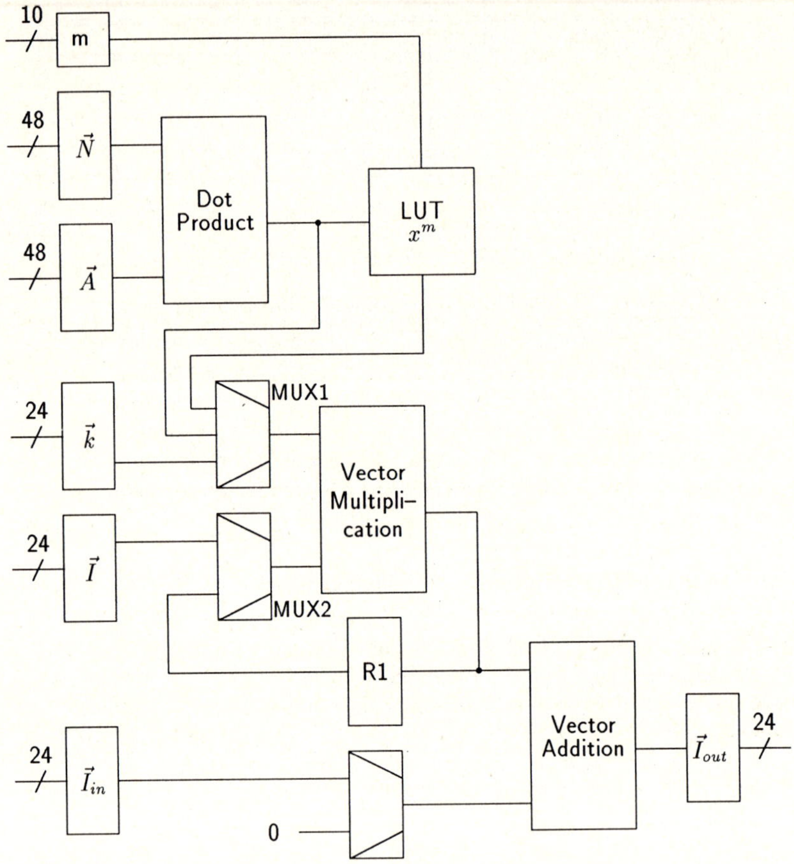


**Fig. 1.** Datapath of the simpler processor. One of the characteristics of the processors is the high compression rate from input to output data

### 3.2 Commands

Though the processor can be implemented in a lot of hardware environments, the following descriptions are restricted to its application in PROOF. It can be shown that a pipeline of shading processors is optimal concerning this implementation [4]. The first processor computes the ambient intensity, hence $I_{in} = 0$ and $I_{out} = C_{amb}$. Afterwards, each couple of processors computes the diffuse and the specular colour component for one light source. Consequently, for a scene with $P$ positional and $R$ directional light sources, $2(P + R) + 1$ shading processors are needed.

The processor can act in two modes, a loading mode and a pixel mode. In the loading mode, light source data is loaded into the registers of the processor where they remain constant during pixel mode. During the pixel mode, object data are passed through the pipeline to compute the colour of the object. Loading can be done with the two commands *define* and *redefine*. Light source data can also be *deleted*.

During pixel mode, *new pixel*, *new scanline*, and *new frame* indicate the respective change. A fourth command indicates a change of object without changing the pixel.

### 3.3 Shadow Polygons

One sort of objects that can be handled by PROOF are shadow polygons [7]. They don't have to be rendered by the shading processor but they influence the rendering of other objects. Furthermore, shadow polygons will be removed from the list of objects that are passed through the shading stage.

An object will not be illuminated by a certain light source, if it is inside the shadow polyhedron that is generated by the light source. Hence, in each shading processor, it has to be determined, if a shadow polygon 'opens' or 'closes' a polyhedron. Therefore, an additional counter has been implemented to do this determination. If the counter equals zero, the respective object will be illuminated. Otherwise, the current intensity will be passed on.

The extended datapath including this counter and the components for the normalization are shown in Figure 2. An additional vector adder and a look-up-table for the computation of $1/\sqrt{x}$ have been included and the dot product unit is split to make intermediate results available.

## 4 Capabilities of the Processors

The complexity of operations lead to the assumption that the clock frequency of the shading processor will be about 20 MHz. The number of cycles that is needed to compute the illumination for a certain configuration is listed in Table 4.

To support real time shading, a huge number of shading processors will be needed. This number depends on the number of pixels on the screen ($M$), the number of light sources ($P$ and $R$), the average number of objects per pixel ($o$), and the cycle time of the shading processors (see Table 5). Here, it is assumed that to preserve the clock rate needed in a real time system, parallel pipelines are used.

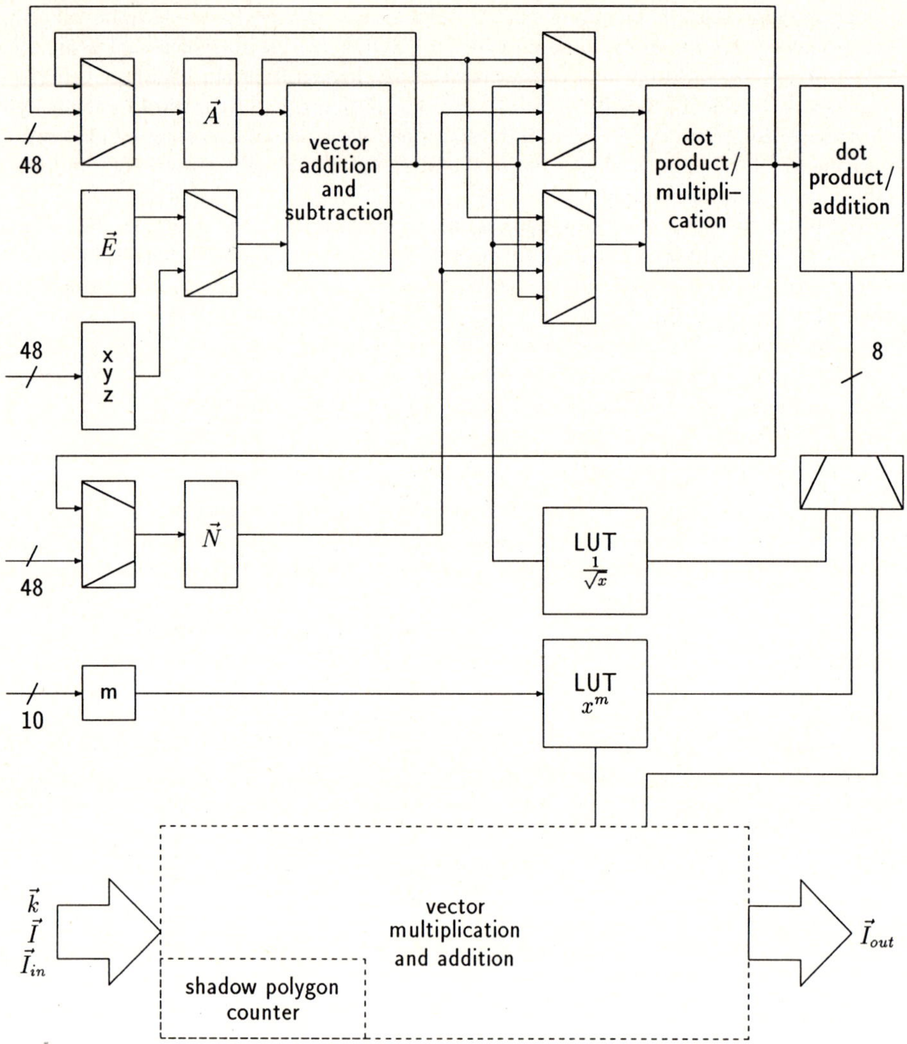


**Fig. 2**. The extended datapath for the shading processor with normalization and the treatment of shadow polygons

**Table 4.** Number of cycles that are needed to compute the different components of the illumination equation including loading

| processor | | without normalization | including normalization |
|---|---|---|---|
| ambient | computation of the ambient component | 4 | 4 |
| light source | computation of the ambient component and normalization of the interpolated normal | — | 6 |
| directional | diffuse component | 6 | 6 |
| light source | specular component | 7 | 7 |
| positional | diffuse component | — | 12 |
| light source | specular component | — | 13 |
| all | treatment of shadow polygons | 2 | 2 |

**Table 5.** Computation of the number of shading processors needed for a certain configuration. $\Delta t$ denotes the cycle time of a processor, $R$ the number of directional light sources, and $P$ the number of positional light sources. $o$ denotes the average number of objects per pixel and $M$ the number of pixels per frame. The number of frames per second is assumed to be 30.

| | | processor without normalization | processor including normalization |
|---|---|---|---|
| maximum time per pixel | $\Delta t_{Pixel}$ | $7 \cdot o \cdot \Delta t$ | $13 \cdot o \cdot \Delta t$ |
| maximum throughput time per pipeline | $\Delta t_{tp}$ | $(14R + 4) \cdot o \cdot \Delta t$ | $(14R + 26P + 6) \cdot o \cdot \Delta t$ |
| due time per pixel | $\Delta t_{due}$ | $\frac{1}{30 \cdot M} s$ | $\frac{1}{30 \cdot M} s$ |
| number of parallel pipelines | $p = \frac{\Delta t_{Pixel}}{\Delta t_{due}}$ | $\frac{30 \cdot M \cdot 7 \cdot o \cdot \Delta t}{s}$ | $\frac{30 \cdot M \cdot 13 \cdot o \cdot \Delta t}{s}$ |
| number of shading processors needed | $L$ | $p(2R + 1)$ | $p(2R + 2P + 1)$ |

An example demonstrates the number of processors that are needed to perform a real-time Phong shading. Assume 30 frames per second and 1 M pixels, hence

$$\Delta t_{due} = 33 \text{ ns}$$

which is less than the cycle time of a processor! Compared with the time that is needed to render $R = P = 5$ light sources for one pixel ($o = 3$),

$$\Delta t_{pixel} = 1950 \text{ ns},$$

the result is that $p \approx 60$ parallel pipelines, or 1260 processors would be needed.

## 5 Discussion and Conclusion

Though the concept of the shading processor developed in this paper seems to be promising, for example with regard to the hardware support of PHIGS PLUS, its implementation in the PROOF environment is quite expensive. Beyond the fact that spot light sources cannot be treated, perspective transformation is not handled correctly either.

Furthermore, it is questionable if the amount of hardware is justifiable if preprocessing methods like the highlight shading method could lead to a similar quality without the need for any shading stage in the system.

Last, but not least, in commercially available processors like the Intel i860, most of the parts that are needed for the illumination computation are already implemented. Furthermore, this processor already is available with a clock frequency of 40 MHz. Consequently, the shading processor can only be seen as a case study, that hopefully leads to new concepts for shading hardware.

## Acknowledgements

This work was partly supported by the Commission of the European Communities through the ESPRIT II project 2484, SPIRIT.

## References

[1] Bishop, G. and Weimer, D. M.: Fast Phong shading. *ACM Computer Graphics*, 20(4):103–106, 1986.

[2] Claussen, U.: On reducing the Phong shading method. In F.R.A. Hopgood and W. Straßer, editors, *Proceedings of the Eurographics'89*, Elsevier (North-Holland), Amsterdam, 1989.

[3] Claussen, U.: Parallel subpixel scanconversion. In A.A.M. Kuijk and W. Straßer, editors, *Advances in Graphics Hardware II*, Springer, Berlin, 1988.

[4] Claussen, U.: *Verfahren zur schnellen Beleuchtungs- und Schattierungsberechnung*. PhD thesis, Universität Tübingen, 1990.

[5] Deering, M., Winner, S., Schediwy, B., Duffy, C. and Hunt, N.: The triangle processor and normal vector shader: a VLSI system for high performance graphics. *ACM Computer Graphics*, 22(4):21–30, 1988.

[6] Kuijk, A. A. M. and Blake, E. H.: Faster Phong shading via angular interpolation. *Computer Graphics Forum*, 8(4):315–324, 1989.

[7] Newman, W. M. and Sproull, R. F.: *Principles of Interactive Computer Graphics*. McGraw-Hill, 1981.

[8] Romanova, C. and Wagner, U.: A VLSI architecture for anti-aliasing. 1989. Presentation at the Eurographics Hardware Workshop 1989 in Hamburg.

[9] Schneider, B.: A processor for an object-oriented rendering system. *Computer Graphics Forum*, 7(4):301–310, 1988.

[10] Schneider, B. and Claussen, U.: PROOF: an architecture for rendering in object space. In A. A. M. Kuijk, editor, *Advances in Graphics Hardware III*, Eurographics, Springer, Berlin, 1989.

[11] Shantz, M. and Lien, S.: Shading bicubic patches. *ACM Computer Graphics*, 21(4):189–196, July 1987.

[12] van Dam, A.: PHIGS+ functional description revision 3.0. *ACM Computer Graphics*, 22(3):125–218, 1988.

# A Multipurpose Hardware Shader

Josef Pöpsel, Eckard Tikwinski

ABSTRACT For the last few years the state of the art in producing three-dimensional Gouraud shaded graphics has been the use of Gouraud shading hardware. Combined with z-buffering it enables graphic workstations to provide real time display. The disadvantages of this approach are the relatively poor quality of Gouraud shaded images and its still very high cost, which so far prohibit real-time applications running on standard PCs. This article describes a universal approach to provide a very powerful graphic unit using minimal hardware at very low cost. This graphic unit will not only support Gouraud shading, but also such methods as 2D-texturing [3], solid texturing [10], normal (bump) texturing [2], shadow mapping [15, 13] and Phong shading [11] as well as a combination of these methods (shade trees [5]).

## 1 Introduction

In parallel with the increase in hardware power within the last 20 years, graphics quality has been enhanced. The simple line drawings which were common some years ago have been succeeded by today's standards for shaded objects (PHIGS+/PEX) [6]. For real-time applications (e.g., simulation) only Gouraud shading [8] combined with the z-buffer algorithm are currently possible. Other algorithms (Scan-Line algorithm [9], Raytracing [14,1] or Radiosity [7]) cannot be used because of the tremendous computing power they require [4]. In contrast to Gouraud shading, which is distinguished by the very simple and steady algorithm it uses, the other methods mentioned above cannot (yet) be realized in hardware. However, the disadvantage of Gouraud shading is the poor quality that can be achieved (Machband effects, poor detailing level), which is far from photo realism. In recent years various methods have been published to evade this drawback:

- With 2D-texturing [3], a two-dimensional picture is 'glued' onto the shaded surface. Every single point of the picture of an object is, after the shading, modulated with the colour of the texture at the corresponding place. An advertising pillar is a good example for 2D-texturing.

- With 3D-texturing (solid texturing) [10] the displayed object is 'milled from the block'. After shading the object, the colour is modulated with a function which depends on the object's three-dimensional coordinates. A marble pillar is an example for 3D-texturing.

- With normal texturing (bump texturing) [2], the normal of a texture modulates the normal of a point of the object. Thereafter the point is illuminated. Modulating the normal produces optical effects such as a golf ball surface. It has to be pointed out here that normal texturing can only be used in combination with Phong shading [11], because the value of the normal vector must be known for each pixel.

- A very general method is provided by so-called shade trees [5], where a freely definable function is called for each point, which alters the appearance of the object. The input parameters of this function are calculated by linear interpolation inside the polygons of the object.

This list of special methods can be substantially extended.

In the end, all of these methods have something in common: they interpolate over a polygon a number of parameters (some use more, others less parameters) and call a more or less complex function to calculate the colour of the pixel.

## 2 Concept

If we define $C|_{x,y}$ as the colour of the pixel (x,y), then

$$C|_{x,y} = f(P_1(x,y), P_2(x,y), ..P_n(x,y))$$

where $f$ represents the function used by the displaying method. $P_i$ stands for the $i$-th of the $n$ input parameters, where $P_i(x,y)$ is determined by the values at the polygon corners.

Below, two examples are given for Gouraud shading with and without 2D-texture:

- For Gouraud shading with $n = 4$ $(r, g, b, z)$ we can write

$$C|_{x,y} = f\begin{pmatrix} r(x,y) \\ g(x,y) \\ b(x,y) \end{pmatrix}$$

$$\text{with} \quad f = \begin{pmatrix} r(x,y) \\ g(x,y) \\ b(x,y) \end{pmatrix} \quad \text{for} \quad z(x,y) > \textit{z-buffer(x,y)}$$

- For Gouraud shading with 2D-texture and $n = 6$ $(r, g, b, z, t_u, t_v)$

$$C|_{x,y} = f\begin{pmatrix} r(x,y) \\ g(x,y) \\ b(x,y) \end{pmatrix}$$

$$\text{with} \quad f\begin{pmatrix} k * r(x,y) + \overline{k} * TB_{r,g,b}(t_u,t_v) \\ k * g(x,y) + \overline{k} * TB_{r,g,b}(t_u,t_v) \\ k * b(x,y) + \overline{k} * TB_{r,g,b}(t_u,t_v) \end{pmatrix} \quad \text{for} \quad z(x,y) > \textit{z-buffer(x,y)}$$

where $TB_{r,g,b}(t_u, t_v)$ represents the colour of the texture at position $(t_u, t_v)$, $k$ and $\overline{k}$ are modulation constants $(k + \overline{k} \equiv 1)$.

If one separates the evaluation of the shading function $f$ from the interpolation, the calculation can be performed by low-cost signal processors with sufficient speed. However, a precondition is that the front-end hardware interpolator preprocesses the data especially for the signal processor to free the signal processor from address calculation and similar administration tasks. For very simple functions the signal processor is not required at all. Using Gouraud shading, for example, without any textures, the pixel colour is identical with the results of the interpolation. The required z-buffer comparison is performed by hardware.

# 3 The Universal Shader

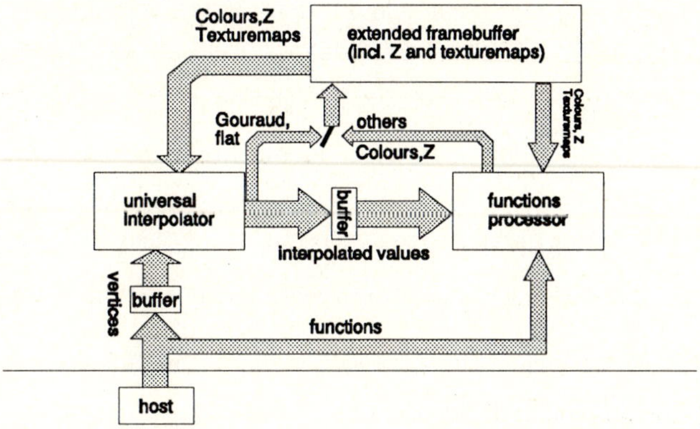


**Fig. 1.** Data flow of the universal shader

Figure 1 shows a data flow chart containing essentially four elements:

- host computer
- universal interpolator
- functions processor
- extended frame-buffer

1. The host computer transfers the polygon corner vertices to the universal interpolator as well as a particular shading function (as program code) to the functions processor. This shading function remains constant over a great number of polygons.

2. From the vertices of the polygon, the universal interpolator evaluates the parameters for all pixels inside the polygon by bilinear interpolation. These parameters and all necessary information are then passed on to the functions processor.

   There is also a direct link to the extended frame-buffer. Therefore, the interpolation results of the Gouraud and flat shading can be transferred directly to the frame-buffer, by-passing the functions processor.

   The universal interpolator can be realized in hardware (ASIC) with minimal effort. It mainly consists of a microprogram controlled arithmetic unit and control logic. The initialization and programming of the microcode is performed by another signal processor, which has to be regarded functionally as a part of the interpolator. The interpolator also has two identical interfaces to the frame-buffer to allow access to two different areas without the need to reload addresses when changing from one area to the other.

   Particularly for Gouraud shading there are four parallel adders, which can deliver the colour and z-value for one pixel per clock cycle.

3. The functions processor is a standard signal processor which calculates the shading functions.

4. The extended frame-buffer contains, in addition to the actual display memory (double-buffered, 24 bit), the z-buffer including z-comparator as well as memory space for texture-maps or, generally speaking, for two-dimensional arrays (e.g., normals for bump texturing). Using address shifting, this memory area can also be utilized as frame-buffer (hardware panning).

The links

$$\text{host} \rightarrow \text{universal interpolator}$$

and

$$\text{universal interpolator} \rightarrow \text{functions processor}$$

are realized using FIFOs, in order to be able to continuously load the individual function blocks.

For a better understanding of the universal shader we now go more into detail using the refined data flow shown in Figure 2.

The universal interpolator, which is the kernel of the universal shader, consists of three logical components:

- One microcode programmable, highly parallel processor, whose structure is optimized particularly for the many interpolation operations required (ASIC, four-level pipelined, 20 MHz)

- The initialization signal processor which provides the microcode program for the interpolation processor after transferring the required variable parameters evaluated from the corner point information of the polygons to be displayed.

- A span Gouraud shader, which can, on its own, interpolate n times in parallel r, g, b and z. In the contrary to the interpolation processor, which can perform only one interpolation per clock, the span processor needs only one clock per pixel. Using pure Gouraud shading, the span shader is used as accelerator (ASIC, 20 million pixels/sec).

There is a twofold link between the universal interpolator and the extended frame-buffer. Each interface has registers for R,G,B (with pre-boundary check and clipper for 0-255) and Z, as well as up and down counters for x and y. The doubled interface is particularly useful for source-destination operations like window move.Either of the two interfaces can be selected by the functions processor as well, instead of the universal interpolator, to give the functions processor full access to the extended frame-buffer. Both interfaces are integrated into the span shader ASIC.

The dual-ported RAM linking the universal interpolator and functions processor has a width of 32 bits and a depth of 1024 words.

### 3.1 The Interpolation Processor

The interpolation processor consists of an 80-bit wide, 1024 deep dual-ported RAM (combined microprogram memory and buffer), an arithmetic unit and a control unit. Every instruction is performed in one clock cycle with the exception of conditional jumps (2 clock cycles). One instruction performs up to six parallel operations. One microprogram word (80 bits) contains data as well as instruction code. The data part is split into the two segments DW1 and DW2 (each 32 bits wide). The remaining 16 bits represent the code for

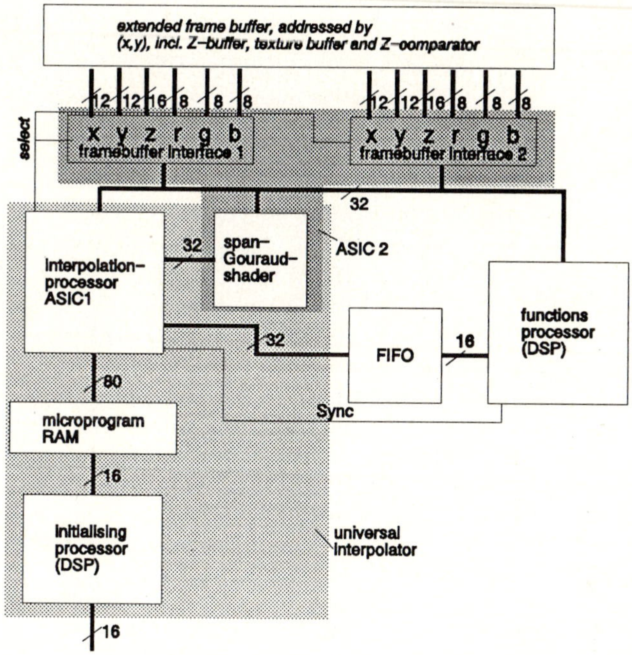


Fig. 2. Refined data flow chart of the universal shader

the available instructions, which are divided into six groups for the respective six parallel instructions.

The word format is shown in Table 1:

**Table 1.** Microprogram word format

| bits | 0..31 | 32..63 | 64..67 | 68 | 69..70 | 71..75 | 76..79 |
|---|---|---|---|---|---|---|---|
| contents | data word 1 | data word 2 | primary instruction | frame-buffer interface select | frame-buffer access type | interface register select | interface counter manipulation |
| name | DW1 | DW2 | PRI | FIS | FZA | IRS | ICM |

Primary Instructions (PRI, 4 bits):

The following primary instructions have been implemented so far:

| | |
|---|---|
| IP (interpolate) | performs 32-bit signed addition DW1:=DW1+DW2 |
| ISPC (interpolate span count) | if last IP instruction did not cause a carry from bit 15 to 16, same as IP, else DW1:=DW1+DW2-$10000 |
| MV (move) | copy data<br>if bit31(DW1) and bit31(DW2)<br>then program[DW1].DW2:=program[DW2].DW2<br>else if not bit31(DW1) and bit31(DW2)<br>then program[DW1].DW2:=program[DW2].DW1<br>else if bit31(DW1) and not bit31(DW2)<br>then program[DW1].DW1:=program[DW2].DW2<br>else if not bit31(DW1) and not bit31(DW2)<br>then program[DW1].DW2:=program[DW2].DW2 |
| WC (write constant) | if bit31(DW2)<br>then program[DW2].DW2:=DW1<br>else program[DW2].DW1:=DW1 |
| RX, RY, RZ, RR, RG, RB (read X,Y,Z,R,G,B) | read values from the interface selected in DW1 (starting from bit 16, bit 0-15:=0) |
| REP (repeat) | repeat function<br>DW1:=DW1-1;<br>if DW1 $\geq$ 0 then goto program[DW2] |
| SYNC1 | wait until the SYNC1 instruction is overwritten by the initializing signal processor (DSP). This is used for synchronization of the initializing DSP with the interpolation processor. |
| SYNC2 | sends the instruction to activate the sync-signal to the functions processor and waits for this event. This is used to synchronize the functions processor with the interpolation processor. |
| '-' | no primary instruction is performed. |

Frame-buffer interface select (FIS, 1 bit):

Possible values: 1,2

Selects first or second interface between the universal interpolator and extended frame-buffer, which will be used for succeeding operations.

Frame-buffer access type (FZA, 2 bits):

Possible values: FW, FWZ, FR, -

| | |
|---|---|
| FW | Writes the values of the selected interface into the frame-buffer. No z-comparison is performed. |
| FWZ | Same as FW, but z-comparison is performed. |
| FR | Reads the extended frame-buffer and writes to both (!) interfaces. |
| - | No frame-buffer access. |

Frame-buffer accesses, together with frame-buffer interface select, are always, without exception, executed as the first step in the microprogram (highest priority).

Interface register select (IRS, 4 bits):

Possible values: WX, WY, WZ, WR, WG, WB; SR, SG, SB, SZ, SDR, SDG, SDB, SDZ; SN; SN8; FP; -

| | |
|---|---|
| WX-WB | Writes DW1 into the respective registers of the interface selected by FIS, before (!) the primary instruction is executed. Only bits 16-32 (digits to the left of the decimal point) are transmitted. R, G, B are limited to the range of 0-$FF. |
| SR-SDZ | Writes DW1 into the respective registers of the span Gouraud shader, before (!) the primary instruction is executed. SR-SZ are the starting values of the span, SDR-SDZ represent the gradients of R, G, B and Z within the span. |
| SN | Transmits the number of pixels to be interpolated (=DW1) to the span shader. SN also synchronizes the interpolation processor with the span shader. Writing SN into the span shader causes n-times execution of the span interpolation, if the span shader is ready. Otherwise the interpolation processor will wait. This is executed before (!) the primary instruction. |
| SN8 | Used for fast erasing of the extended frame-buffer (80 million pixels/sec). DW1 blocks sized 4*2 pixels are written. The selected interface is used as frame-buffer address, where the values for SR, SG, SB, SZ are written to the pixels $(x*4, y)..(x*4+3, y), (x*4, y+1)..(x*4+3, y+1)$. The values for SR-SZ are not altered. |
| FP | Transmits DW1 to the buffer between interpolation processor and functions processor before (!) the primary instruction is executed. |
| '-' | No register is selected. |

The instructions FP and '-' are not coded with the four IRS-bits (lack of available bits), instead the four ICM-bits are used (see below).

Interface counter manipulation (ICM, 4 bits):

Possible values: X+, Y+, X-, Y-, XY+, XY-, X+Y-, X-Y+, -

The counters of the selected interfaces are increased respectively decreased after (!) execution of the primary instruction (lowest priority).

Thus a program step contains the instruction combinations shown in Table 2.

**Table 2.** Instruction combinations

| DW1 | DW2 | PRI | FIS | FZA | IRS | ICM |
|---|---|---|---|---|---|---|
| initial | increment | IP, IPSC | 1 | FW | WX, WY, WZ | X+, Y+ |
| value | | | 2 | FWZ | WR, WG, WB | X-, Y- |
| src addr | dst addr | MV | '-' | FR | SR, SG, SB | XY+, XY- |
| constant | dst addr | WC | | '-' | DSR, DSG, DSB | X+Y-, X-Y+ |
| repeat | jump | REP | | | SN, SN8 | '-' |
| counter | | | | | | |
| | | SYNC1 | | | FP | |
| | | | | | '-' | |
| | | SYNC2 | | | | |
| | | '-' | | | | |

Using the described instructions, it possible to generate optimized programs for the interpolation processor, which can become quite simple if the generation is supported by software. Those programs are stored in the initialisation processor and, when required, copied (by the initialization processor) into the 80-bit dual-ported RAM (after the variable data are entered). The initialization processor regards the dual-ported RAM as organized into 16-bit $\times 5120$, so that the data can be manipulated quite easily.

The overall hardware requirements are modest, compared with the achieved flexibility and execution speed. Apart from the frame- and z-buffer, which are always required, there are two ASICS, two low-cost standard DSPs, 10 kbyte very fast dual-ported RAM (20 ns) as microprogram memory and buffer, and 4 kbyte dual-ported RAM (50 ns) as buffer between interpolation processor and functions processor.

### 3.2 Examples

Finally, some sample programs are given to demonstrate the performance power of the interpolation processor. Data which are entered into the microprogram by the initialization processor are underlined.

Example 1: Draw a window with constant colour and constant Z

(Start with X,Y, width Nx, height Ny, colour (R,G,B), z-value Z)

| Line | Label | DW1 | DW2 | PRI | FIS | FZA | IRS | ICM |
|---|---|---|---|---|---|---|---|---|
| 1 | | R.0 | 0 | - | - | - | SR | - |
| 2 | | G.0 | 0 | - | - | - | SG | - |
| 3 | | B.0 | 0 | - | - | - | SB | - |
| 4 | | Z.0 | 0 | - | - | - | SZ | - |
| 5 | | X.0 | 0 | - | - | - | WX | - |
| 6 | Loop: | Y.0 | 2.0 | IP | 1 | - | WY | - |
| 7 | | Nx/4.0 | 0 | - | 1 | - | SN8 | - |
| 8 | | Ny/2.0 | Loop | REP | - | - | - | - |

Lines 1-4 write R,G,B and Z into the span shader

Line 5 writes x into interface 1

Line 6 writes y into interface 1 and then increments y by 2

Line 7 generates Nx/4 pixel blocks (4*2) next to each other in the desired colour

Line 8 causes Ny/2-times repetition. The functions processor stays idle during this action.

The above program can clear a 1280 × 1024 pixel screen within 1.6 ms.

Example 2: Window copying

Starting from (X1,Y1) to (X2,Y2), width Nx, height Ny. Windows may overlap, yet with restrictions.

| Line | Label | DW1 | DW2 | PRI | FIS | FZA | IRS | ICM |
|---|---|---|---|---|---|---|---|---|
| 1 | | Ny.0 | Rep2 | WC | - | - | - | - |
| 2 | | Y1.0 | 0 | - | 1 | - | WY | - |
| 3 | | Y2.0 | 0 | - | 2 | - | WY | - |
| 4 | Edge: | Nx.0 | Rep1 | WC | - | - | - | - |
| 5 | | X1.0 | 0 | - | 1 | - | WX | - |
| 6 | | X2.0 | 0 | - | 2 | - | WX | - |
| 7 | Span: | 0 | 0 | - | 1 | FR | - | X+ |
| 8 | Rep1: | 0 | Span | REP | 2 | FW | - | X+ |
| 9 | | 0 | 0 | - | 1 | - | - | Y+ |
| 10 | Rep2: | 0 | Edge | REP | 2 | - | - | Y+ |

The inner loop (lines 7,8) needs 3 clock cycles. Thus, using a 20 MHz clock cycle, a window of 100 × 100 pixels can be copied in 1.5 ms.

Example 3: Gouraud shaded triangle

(base line horizontal, top point above base line, top point colour (R,G,B), top point coordinates (X,Y,Z), height Yh, variations of the left edge dEX,dER,dEG,dEB,dEZ, variation of the triangle width dN, variations within a span dSR,dSG,dSB,dSZ (remains constant (!) within a triangle for all spans)).

| Line | Label | DW1 | DW2 | PRI | FIS | FZA | IRS | ICM |
|---|---|---|---|---|---|---|---|---|
| 1 | | dSR | 0 | - | - | - | SDR | - |
| 2 | | dSG | 0 | - | - | - | SDG | - |
| 3 | | dSB | 0 | - | - | - | SDB | - |
| 4 | | dSZ | 0 | - | - | - | SDZ | - |
| 5 | | Y.0 | 0 | - | 1 | - | WY | - |
| 6 | Edge: | Z.5 | dEZ | IP | - | - | SZ | - |
| 7 | | R.5 | dER | IP | - | - | SR | - |
| 8 | | G.5 | dEG | IP | - | - | SG | - |
| 9 | | B.5 | dEB | IP | - | - | SB | - |
| 10 | | X.5 | dEX | IP | 1 | - | WX | - |
| 11 | | 0.5 | dN | IPSC | - | - | SN | - |
| 12 | | Yh.0 | Edge | REP | - | - | - | Y+ |

Lines 1-4 load delta-registers of the span shader.
Line 5 sets Y start address.
Lines 6-10 write the starting values of the spans into the span processor and then perform the interpolation (edge interpolation).
Line 11 writes the number of pixels for the current span into the span processor and then starts the span interpolation. The functions processor stays idle during this action, as in the previous example.

One triangle containing 100 pixels (e.g., X=5, Y=0, Yh=10, dN=2.0, dEx=-1.0) is calculated within 116 clock cycles. If one assumes that the microprogram parameters for the next triangle can be generated by the initialization processor within this time, then the described hardware will be able to draw approximately 172 000 triangles/sec.

Example 4: Gouraud shading + transparency + texture

This example demonstrates how shading methods which, up to now, have had to be implemented in software (if at all), and therefore were very time-consuming, can be performed in considerably less time. A good example for such an application is a coloured air-balloon.

To simplify the matter, only the inner loop of a triangle is shown, which is required for one span.

| Line | Label | DW1 | DW2 | PRI | FIS | FZA | IRS | ICM |
|---|---|---|---|---|---|---|---|---|
| n | Span: | ZS. | dZS | IP | | | FP | |
| n+1 | | 0 | 0 | RZ | 1 | FR | WX | |
| n+2 | | texX. | dtexX | IP | 2 | | WY | |
| n+3 | | texY. | dtexY | IP | | | FP | |
| n+4 | | RS. | dRS | IP | | | FP | |
| n+5 | | 0 | 0 | RR | 1 | | FP | |
| n+6 | | 0 | 0 | RR | 2 | FR | FP | |
| n+7 | | GS. | dGS | IP | | | FP | |
| n+8 | | 0 | 0 | RG | 1 | | FP | |
| n+9 | | 0 | 0 | RG | 2 | | FP | |
| n+10 | | BS.0 | dBS | IP | | | FP | |
| n+11 | | 0 | 0 | RB | 1 | | FP | |
| n+12 | | 0 | 0 | RB | 2 | | FP | |
| n+13 | | NX | Span | REP | 1 | | | X+ |

| | |
|---|---|
| n | Z-interpolation, then, after transfer to the functions processor, reading of the z-value from the extended frame-buffer. Thereafter transfer to the functions processor. |
| n+1 | Reading of the z-value from the extended frame-buffer, then transfer to the functions processor. |
| n+2, n+3 | Writing the texture coordinates in interface 2, then interpolation of the texture coordinates. |
| n+4 | Transfer of the red component (Gouraud), then interpolation of 'red'. |
| n+5 | Reading of the frame-buffer (red component of the background), then transfer to the functions processor. |
| n+6 | Reading of the frame-buffer (red component of the texture), then transfer to the functions processor. |
| n+7..n+9 | Steps n+4..n+6 for green component. |
| n+10..n+12 | Steps n+4..n+6 for blue component. |
| n+13 | Repeat n..n+12 for all pixels within one span. |

The program, running on the functions processor to perform the span interpolation, looks like this:

```
read z1
read z2
if z1 > z2 then begin
      read rGour
      evaluate r:=rGour*k1
      read rBack
      evaluate r:=r+rBack*k2
      read rTexture
      evaluate r:=r+rTexture*k3
      ... the same steps for g
      ... the same steps for b
```

```
      write z1,r,g,b, into frame-buffer
end else begin
      read 9 parameters
end
```

Because the signal processor used can access memory parallel to executing arithmetic operations, and, furthermore, can perform the operation $x := x + k \times x\prime$ in one single clock cycle (MAC), it takes only 15 clock cycles (100 ns each) for one pixel. The universal interpolator needs 14 clock cycles (50 ns each) for the equivalent action. This leaves the functions processor as the bottleneck. However, using this quite costly shading method, it is still possible to achieve a pixel-rate of approximately 650000/sec (about 6500 triangles/sec).

The list of methods can be extended at will.

## 4 Summary

In this paper a circuit was introduced which makes it possible very flexibly and also very efficiently to draw polygons by any given, freely programmable shading function. This is achieved using a combination of special hardware and low-priced signal processors. Taking into account the advantages of ASICs, the circuitry can be realized in a PC-environment at very low cost. With the hardware described, de facto standards like RenderMan [12], which are very demanding concerning the flexibility of the hardware shader, can possibly run in real time.

## Acknowledgements

I wish to thank U. Claussen and Ch. Hornung for their ideas contributing to the development of the conception. Acknowledgements to K. G. Vits for the translation, and, last but not least, many thanks to B. Groth who created the necessary productive environment by the supply of coffee and biscuits.

## References

[1] Amanatides, J.: Ray tracing with cones. *Computer Graphics* 18(3): 129-135, July 1984.

[2] Blinn, J. F.: Simulation of wrinkled surfaces. *Computer Graphics* 12(3): 286-292, August 1978.

[3] Blinn, J. F. and Newell, M. E.: Texture and reflection in computer generated images. *Communications of the ACM* 19(10):542-547, October 1976.

[4] Claussen, U.: Verfahren zur schnellen Beleuchtungs- und Schattierungsberechnung. *Dissertationsarbeit*, Fakultät Physik, Universität Tübingen, Germany 1990.

[5] Cook, R. L.: Shade trees. *Computer Graphics* 18(3): 223-231, July 1984.

[6] van Dam, A.: PHIGS+ functional description revision 3.0. *Computer Graphics* 22(3): 125-218, July 1988.

[7] Greenberg, D. P., Cohen, M. F. and Torrance. K. E.: Radiosity: a method for computing global illumination. *The Visual Computer* 2: 291-297, 1986.

[8] Gouraud, H.: Continuous shading of curved surfaces. *IEEE Transaction on Computers* C-20(6):623-628, June 1971.

[9] Newman, W. M. and Sproull, R. F.: *Principles of interactive computer graphics*. Springer, 1986.

[10] Peachey, D. R.: Solid texturing of complex surfaces. *Computer Graphics* 19(3): 279-286, July 1986.

[11] Phong, B. T.: Illumination for computer generated images. *Communications of the ACM* 18(6): 311-317, June 1975.

[12] *The RenderMan Interface.* Pixar, San Rafael, CA, edition 3.0, May 1988.

[13] Reeves, W. T., Salesin, D. H. and Cook, R. L.: Rendering antialiased shadows with depth maps. *Computer Graphics* 21(4): 283-291, July 1987.

[14] Whitted, T.: An improved illumination model for shaded display. *Communications of the ACM* 23(6): 343-349, June 1980.

[15] Williams, L.: Casting curved shadows on curved surfaces. *Computer Graphics* 12(3): 270-274, August 1978.

# Some Practical Aspects of Rendering

Andreas Schilling

ABSTRACT The scan conversion of simple primitives, e.g., vectors and triangles has been worked on in many different ways. General descriptions of algorithms often do not consider 'minor' problems, that can be difficult to solve in practical implementation. Some of these problems are addressed in the following and ways to solve them are presented[1].

The paper consists of two parts. The first part deals with the scan conversion of triangles, the second part describes the implementation of two vector drawing algorithms.

- Drawing Triangles: Calculation of Parameters for Incremental Algorithms

  1. Polygons can be represented by edge functions, that are negative on one, and positive on the other side of the edge. This representation is used in rendering hardware like PROOF [5], Pixel Planes [3] or in software algorithms like the one described by Pineda [4]. The parameters can be chosen in such a way, that the function represents the distance between pixel and edge. In this case the function value can be used to determine the subpixel mask. To get these parameters, the function has to be normalized [1], which usually requires the calculation of a square root. But there is an elegant way to avoid the square root.
  2. Color increments (Gouraud shading) and $z$ increments, that are used to interpolate the colors and depth can become very large, if they are calculated in the conventional way, which is described e.g. in [2]. This can cause the color ($z$) value of edge pixels to be computed wrong or even to overflow. It is shown, how this occurs and how the problem can be solved.

- Drawing Lines

  Line drawing without antialiasing is performed with the Bresenham algorithm, which can be implemented on the triangle render hardware.

  A simple antialiasing is performed with an algorithm, that is not much more complex than the Bresenham algorithm.

[1]The experiences, described here were gained in a research project, partly supported by the Commission of the European Communities through the ESPRIT II-Project SPIRIT, Project No. 2484 [6,7].

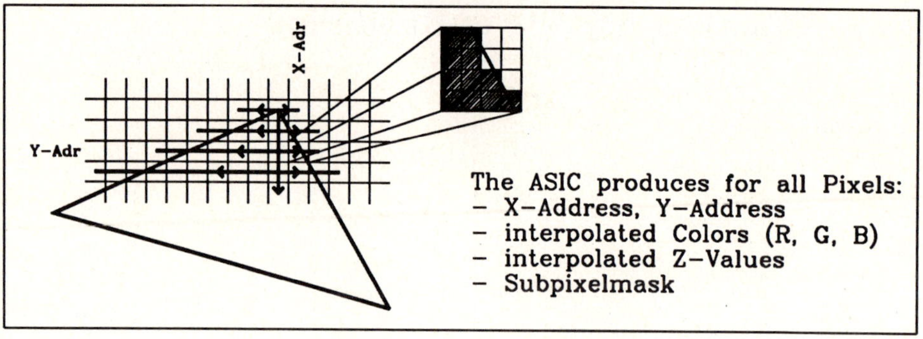


**Fig. 1.** Functions of the ASIC

# 1 Drawing Triangles: Calculation of Parameters for Incremental Algorithms

The rendering chip in the SPIRIT workstation is able to render triangles and lines. The first information that is needed for the rendering of triangles (see Fig. 1) is the information, which pixels belong to the triangle. How to get these pixels is the topic of the first section.

## 1.1 A Practical Distance Measure — the Square Distance ($L_1$ Norm)

For the scan conversion, we use an algorithm like the one described by Pineda in [4]. A presumption for this kind of algorithms is an edge function, that behaves like the one shown in Fig. 2. It is positive on one side and negative on the other side of the edge. With three units that can calculate such edge functions, we can now decide, whether a certain point lies inside the triangle or outside. If all three edge functions are positive, the point is inside, otherwise it is outside.

*How Can We Get Such a Function?*

The easiest way is to choose a linear function

$$E(x, y) = (x - X)de_x + (y - Y)de_y$$

with the condition:

$$de_x \Delta X + de_y \Delta Y = 0$$

If we use

$$de_x = \Delta Y$$

as $X$ increment and

$$de_y = -\Delta X$$

as increment in $Y$ direction, we get the formula suggested by Pineda with the advantage that the calculation is very simple. The edge units can be built of only adders, without multipliers, as we only have to add the increments proceeding from one pixel to its neighbor.

We can scale the above formula by an arbitrary factor. So if we need the Euclidean distance, we can normalize the increments by dividing the values by the Euclidean length of the vector ($L_2$ norm). We then get the following increments:

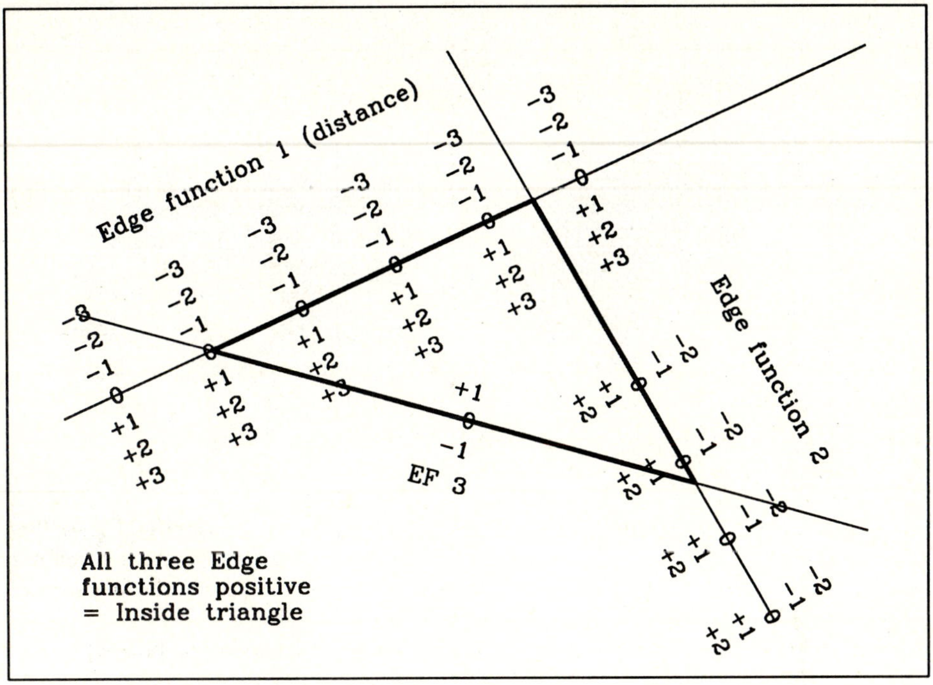


**Fig. 2.** Example of edge functions for rendering

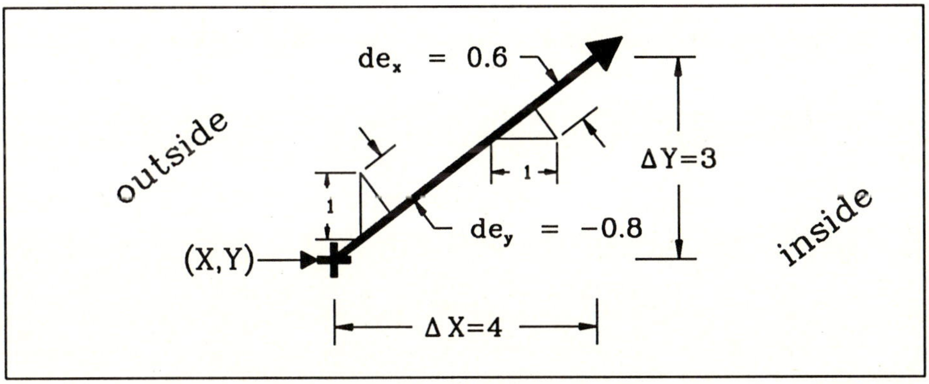


**Fig. 3.** *X* and *Y* increments of the edge function

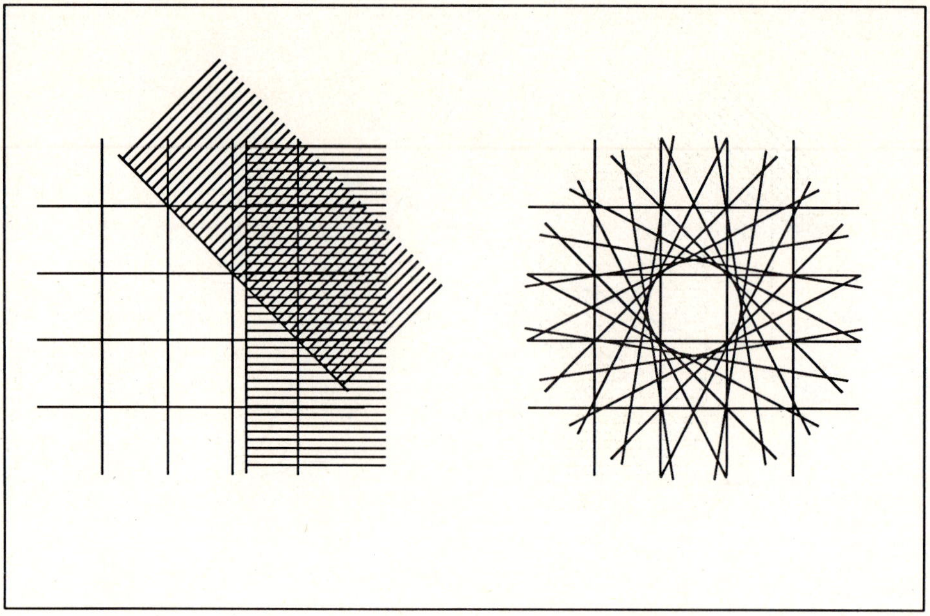

**Fig. 4.** Circular distance

$$de_x = \frac{\Delta Y}{\sqrt{\Delta X^2 + \Delta Y^2}}$$

and

$$de_y = -\frac{\Delta X}{\sqrt{\Delta X^2 + \Delta Y^2}}$$

and we can still use the same edge units, because the distance is a linear function in $X$ and $Y$ (see example edge in Fig. 3).

*Why Do We Need This Distance?*

Until now, we used only the sign of the edge function for the decision if we are in or out. So the value of the distance is of no interest. But if we want to calculate subpixel information for later antialiasing, we need exact data about the edge. The distance, together with the slope information is enough to look up the subpixel mask, i.e. the information, which part of the pixel is covered (see Fig. 1). One little detail has to be noticed. We now have to consider not only pixels with their center inside the polygon (positive edge function), but also pixels that are covered less than half (edge function between 0 and –0.something). We cannot give a fixed distance, because it is different for edges with different slopes ($1/\sqrt{2}$ for edges with a slope of 45°, $1/2$ for vertical or horizontal edges). So if we take all pixels not more than $1/\sqrt{2}$ away from the edge into consideration, we will get too many pixels, but that is better than losing pixels that we wanted to get. In Fig. 4 can be seen, why we call this distance the circular distance. All edges that have a given distance from the pixel center form a circle.

Now there is a formula for the increments that solves several problems at one time. If we look at the most demanding part of the increment calculation above, we see the square root in that formula. Now the simplest solution is to omit the root and take the

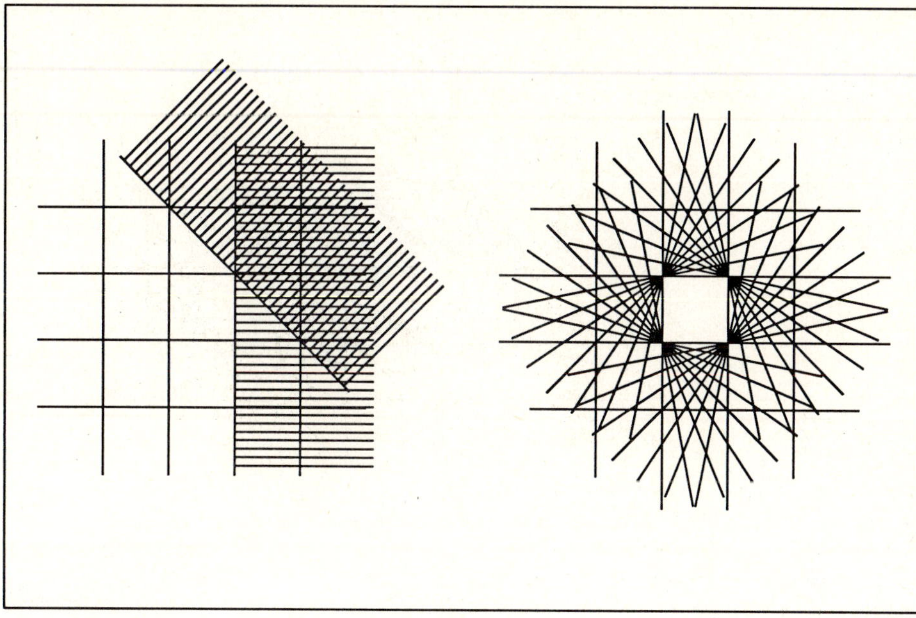

**Fig. 5.** Square distance

sum of the absolute values of $\Delta X$ and $\Delta Y$ instead. Speaking in mathematical terms that means, we divide by the $L_1$ norm or Manhattan distance instead of the $L_2$norm. The new increments are:

$$de_x = \frac{\Delta Y}{|\Delta X| + |\Delta Y|}$$

and

$$de_y = -\frac{\Delta X}{|\Delta X| + |\Delta Y|}$$

The distance is not independent of the angle anymore. But if we don't want to do a more complex filtering (like convolution with sine(dist)), than we need something like a rectangular box filter. A circular filter never would result in a homogeneous coverage of the screen. So this formula is not only more easy to calculate, but also a more desired result. We call this definition of distance the square distance (see Fig. 5).

For the calculation of the subpixel mask, the square distance is as useful as the circular one, because all information about the edge is contained in the distance and the increments (for the slope of the edge).

## 1.2 Color and $z$ Increments

*Why Do We Need Increments?*

Let's explain it with the calculation of the depth. We have a plain triangle in the $x$-$y$-$z$ space. We could calculate the depth from the $x$ and $y$ coordinates with a linear formula like $z = dz_x \times x + dz_y \times y + z_0$. But normally we render neighboring pixels one after the

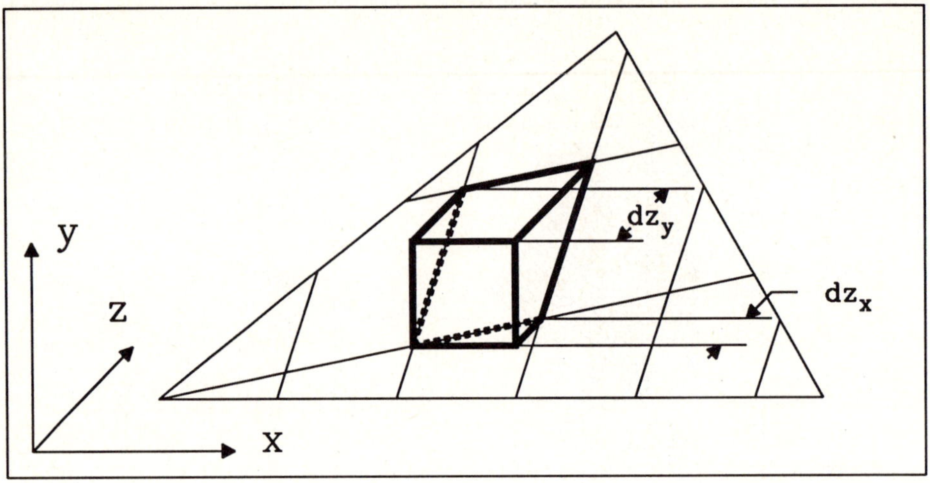


**Fig. 6.** Calculation of $z$ with an incremental algorithm

other, so we can save the multiplication and add only $dz_x$ or $dz_y$ as we go from one pixel to the next (see Fig. 6).

*How Can We Calculate the Increments?*

Because we have the three vertices of the triangle with their $x$, $y$ and $z$ values, it is as simple as solving a system of linear equations.

The formula for $dz_x$ for example is:

$$dz_x = \frac{z_1 y_2 - z_2 y_1}{x_1 y_2 - x_2 y_1} = \begin{vmatrix} z_1 & z_2 \\ y_1 & y_2 \end{vmatrix} \bigg/ \begin{vmatrix} x_1 & x_2 \\ y_1 & y_2 \end{vmatrix}$$

(If vertex $V_0$ is not located at the origin, we move it to the origin by subtracting $x_0$, $y_0$ and $z_0$ from the coordinates of the vertices $V_1$ and $V_2$)

But let's have a closer look at what we really do (Fig. 7). First the two-fold area of the triangle in the $x$-$y$-plain is calculated ($A_{xy} = \begin{vmatrix} x_1 & x_2 \\ y_1 & y_2 \end{vmatrix}$). Then the two-fold area of the triangle in the $y$-$z$-plain is divided by the first value. ($A_{zy} = \begin{vmatrix} z_1 & z_2 \\ y_1 & y_2 \end{vmatrix}$). The result is the increment in the $x$-direction. The values for the $y$-direction and the color increments for both directions are obtained analogously. Because the area in the $x$-$y$-plain may be very small, the increments can become very large.

*What Is the Problem with Large Increments?*

First of all, big increments don't fit into our registers. Second, and that is the main problem, we can get very wrong $z$ values or colors. Fig. 8 shows, how this happens. The problem is, that with our equations we calculate the $z$ or color at the pixel center. So if we need the $z$ value or color of a pixel, that lies on the border of the triangle with the center outside of it, we get a value that can be even outside of the allowed range.

In order to avoid this, we apply the following rule: The area $A_{xy}$ is divided by the longer side of its bounding box. If the result is smaller than 1, this means that in the average in every line (column) less than half a pixel is covered. Surely not more than one pixel

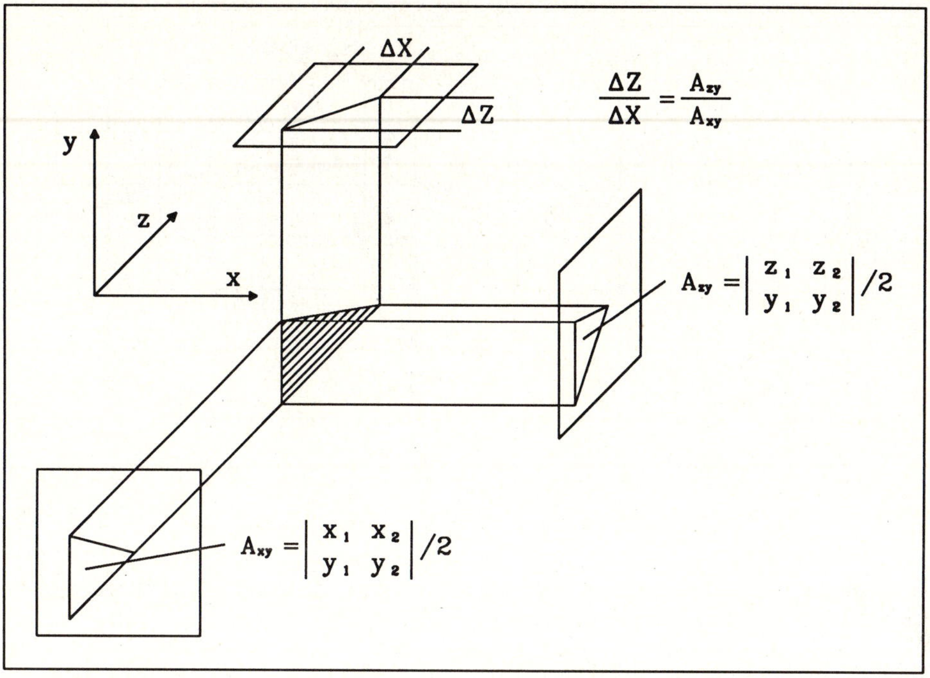


**Fig. 7**. Calculation of increments

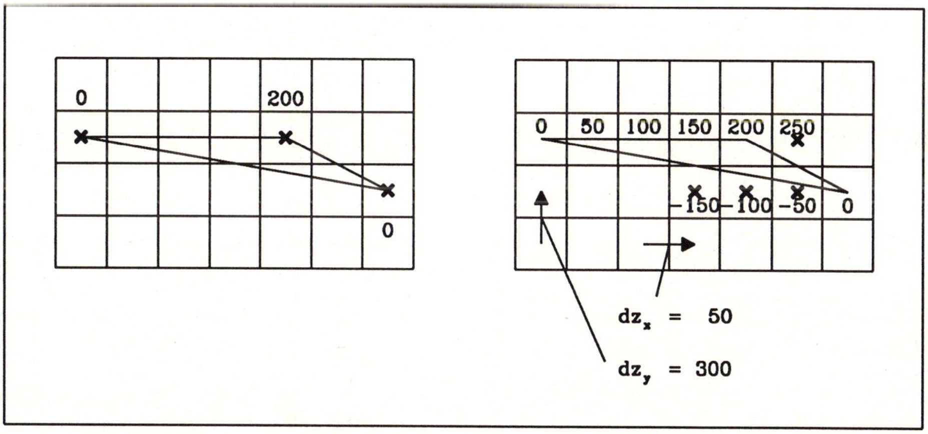


**Fig. 8**. Overflow problem with conventional increments

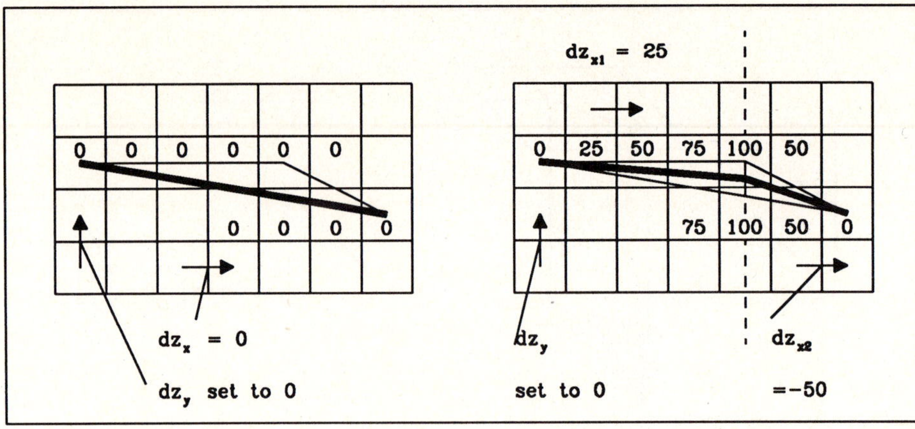


**Fig. 9.** Solutions for the overflow problem—lines of interpolation are emphasized

per line (column) is covered. So it doesn't make sense to calculate the increments in the direction perpendicular to that longer side. These increments are set to 0. The increments in the other direction are calculated as the ratio of the edge values of $z$ (respectively $r$, $g$ or $b$) and the length of the bounding box. By using this method, the increment values can become not larger than the maximum values of $z$, $r$, $g$ and $b$. With this simple method we introduce other errors by omitting the information of the third vertex. If we want to be totally correct, we can obtain it by interpolating along a line within the triangle as shown in Fig. 9. The formula for the increments looks like $dz_x = (z_1/y_1 + z_2/y_2)/2$ for the first part of the triangle and $dz_x = (z_1/y_1 + z_2/y_2)/2$ for the second part. The disadvantage of the second method is, that the triangle usually must be rendered in two parts.

In both cases we need only 2 protection bits for the digits left of the decimal point (one for overflow, one for underflow). Clipping the output at the minimum and maximum values of the colors or $z$ is still required for the triangles rendered in the normal way.

## 2 Vector Drawing

Two algorithms are used for vector drawing. Both are implemented on the same hardware, that is used to calculate the edge functions for triangles. For fast lines without antialiasing, we use the Bresenham algorithm. The second algorithm performs the drawing of thin, smoothened vectors, which consist of only two pixels per row (resp. column).

### 2.1 Fast Vectors

The Bresenham algorithm is easy to perform with the same hardware, that is used for the calculation of the edge functions for the triangles. It is explained using a vector with a slope $0 <= m <= 1$ as an example. Using the Bresenham algorithm a modified distance is calculated. It is the Euclidean distance multiplied by the two-fold length of the vector. However, this distance is calculated one pixel in advance in order to be able to decide how to proceed. Moreover, the calculated value is the (scaled) distance from a point located 1/2 pixels higher than the point exactly right of the current pixel. By this the sign of this value can be used to discern whether to proceed to the right or in the upper right direction.

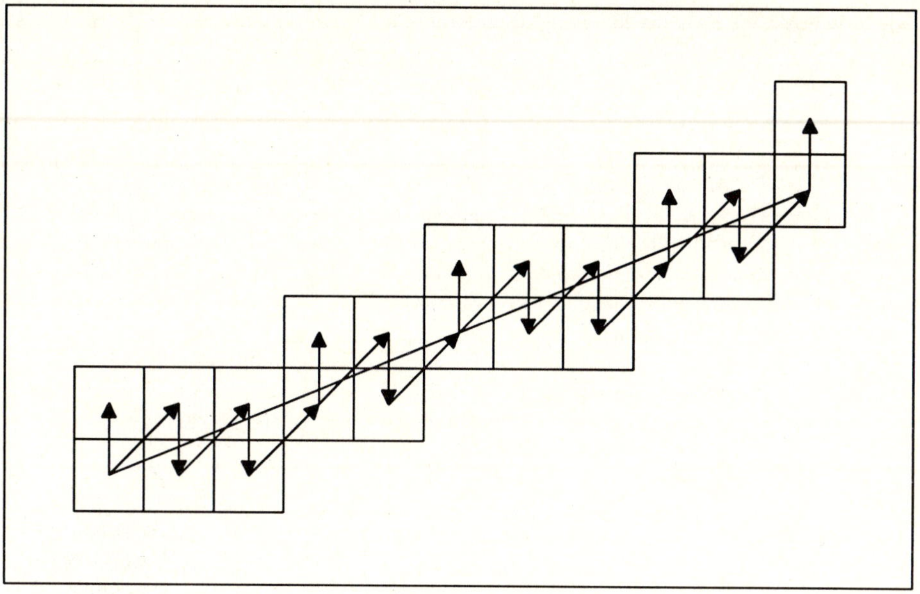

**Fig. 10.** Thin smoothened vector

So the distance is initialized with a value of $e_0 = \Delta Y - \Delta X/2$, then the increments for the $X$-direction ($de_x = \Delta Y$) and for the direction 45 degrees up to the right ($de_x + de_y = \Delta Y - \Delta X$) are loaded. The control logic controls — according to the sign of the current distance — whether to increment only $X$ or $X$ *and* $Y$. Our hardware only allows to load increments up to an absolute value of 1. Therefore the above mentioned increments are divided by an arbitrary power of two, which means, that the number is simply loaded; the hardware does not use the position of the 'decimal'-point. With the Bresenham algorithm only those pixels are calculated that are really needed.

## 2.2 Thin Vectors with Fast Antialiasing: the Fineline Algorithm

A cheap antialiasing method for vectors uses only two pixels per row resp. column. The brightness values assigned to these two pixels add up to 100% of the desired brightness for the vector. To get such 'antialiased' lines, we can also use the same hardware as for the calculation of the triangle edges. As example we take again a vector with a slope between 0 and 1. Possible directions for the next pixel to calculate are diagonally up to the right, upwards and downwards (see Fig. 10). The values for the distance, the colors and the $z$-value are stored every time after a step downwards or up to the right. So always the lower of the two pixels of a column is chosen. By this we can ensure, that proceeding to the upper right again leads to a hit.

The brightness of the pixels is distributed in such a way, that the values of one column add up to 100%. For that purpose the up-down-distance from the vector for Pixel $i$ is calculated as:

$$e_i = e_0 + (X_i - X_0) * de_x + (Y_i - Y_0) * de_y,$$

which is achieved with the following parameters:

$$de_x = -\frac{\Delta Y}{\Delta X}$$

and

$$de_y = 1$$

This linear formula implies, that the distance function $e$ for a neighboring pixel can be computed by simply adding or subtracting $de_y$ or $de_y + de_x$ resp. for diagonal neighbors. The starting value of the distance $e_0$ is 0, when the starting point $(x,y)$ of the vector is in a pixel center. Otherwise, $e_0$ has to be calculated:

$e_0 = Y - y + (X - x) * de_x$,

where $x$ and $y$ are the coordinates of the vector starting point, and $X$ and $Y$ are the (integer) pixel coordinates of the starting pixel.

The resulting distance is used to calculate the color $C$ of the pixels from the original color $C_{org}$:

$C = C_{org} * (1 - abs(e))$

When proceeding to a new column, the first pixel is always set. The sign of $e$ determines, whether the second pixel is above or below the first one.

The ASIC works as a state machine. Fig. 11 and 12 show the state diagrams for the Bresenham machine and the Fineline machine. The value $e$, that is used for the decision, is the distance or error term, described above. The bold arrows indicate the directions, in which the machine proceeds for the case of a line with a slope between 0 and 1. The words PUSH and POP show, where the current value of the error term (or edge function) and colors/$z$ are stored and retrieved in order to proceed from a previously reached point rather than from the current point. Note that the Fineline machine needs only 2 states more than the Bresenham machine. This is not complex compared to the state machine for the Pineda algorithm, which is shown in Fig. 13 for comparison.

Like with the Bresenham algorithm, with the Fineline algorithm normally only those pixels are calculated, that are really needed. This means, that the efficiency remains the same; the Fineline algorithm is exactly two times slower than the Bresenham algorithm, because the number of pixels that have to be drawn has doubled.

## 3 Conclusion

Some special problems in rendering have been shown and solutions were presented. They represent only a small fraction of the large class of problems, that are generally not addressed in the literature.

# References

[1] Fuchs, H., Goldfeather, J., Hultquist, J. P., Spach, S., Austin, J. D., Brooks, F. P., Eyles, J. G. and Poulton, J.: Fast spheres, shadows, textures, transparencies, and image enhancements in pixel-planes. *Computer Graphics*, 19(3):111–120, July 1985.

[2] Fuchs, H. and Poulton, J.: Pixel planes: A vlsi-oriented design for a raster graphics engine. *VLSI Design*, 3:20–28, 3rd Quarter 1981.

[3] Fuchs, H., Poulton, J., Eyles, J., Greer, T., Goldfeather, J., Ellsworth, D., Molnar, S., Turk, G., Tebbs, B. and Israel, L.: Pixel-planes 5: A heterogeneous multiprocessor graphics system using processor-enhanced memories. *Computer Graphics*, 23(3):79–88, July 1989.

[4] Pineda, J.: A parallel algorithm for polygon rasterization. *Computer Graphics*, 22(4):17–20, August 1988.

[5] Schneider, B.: *Eine objektorientierte Architektur für Hochleistungs-Display-Prozessoren.* PhD thesis, Eberhard-Karls-Universität Tübingen, 1990.

[6] Slater, M.: The graphics subsystem of the Spirit workstation. Presentation given at the Eurographics Conference., September 1989.

[7] Zabolitzky, J. G.: The matter of Spirit. Presentation given at the Eurographics Conference., September 1989.

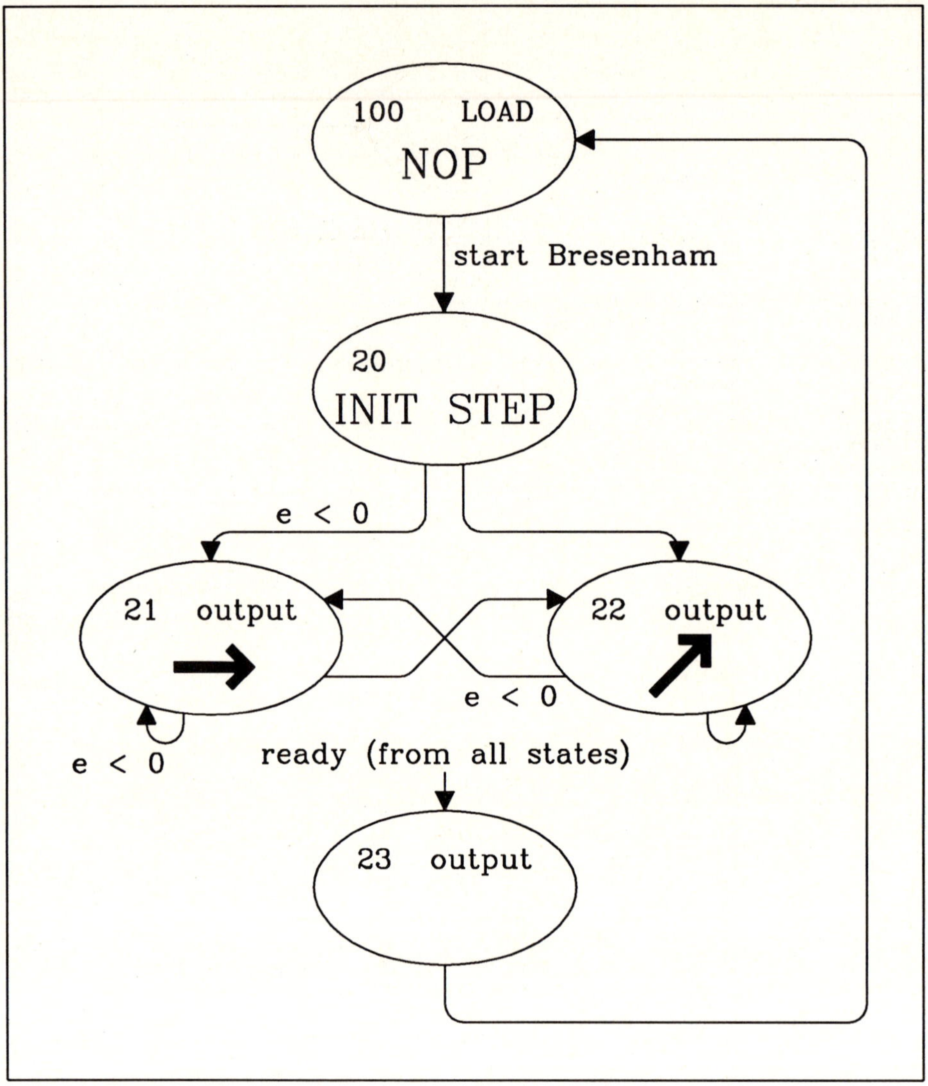


**Fig. 11**. State diagram for Bresenham vector drawing

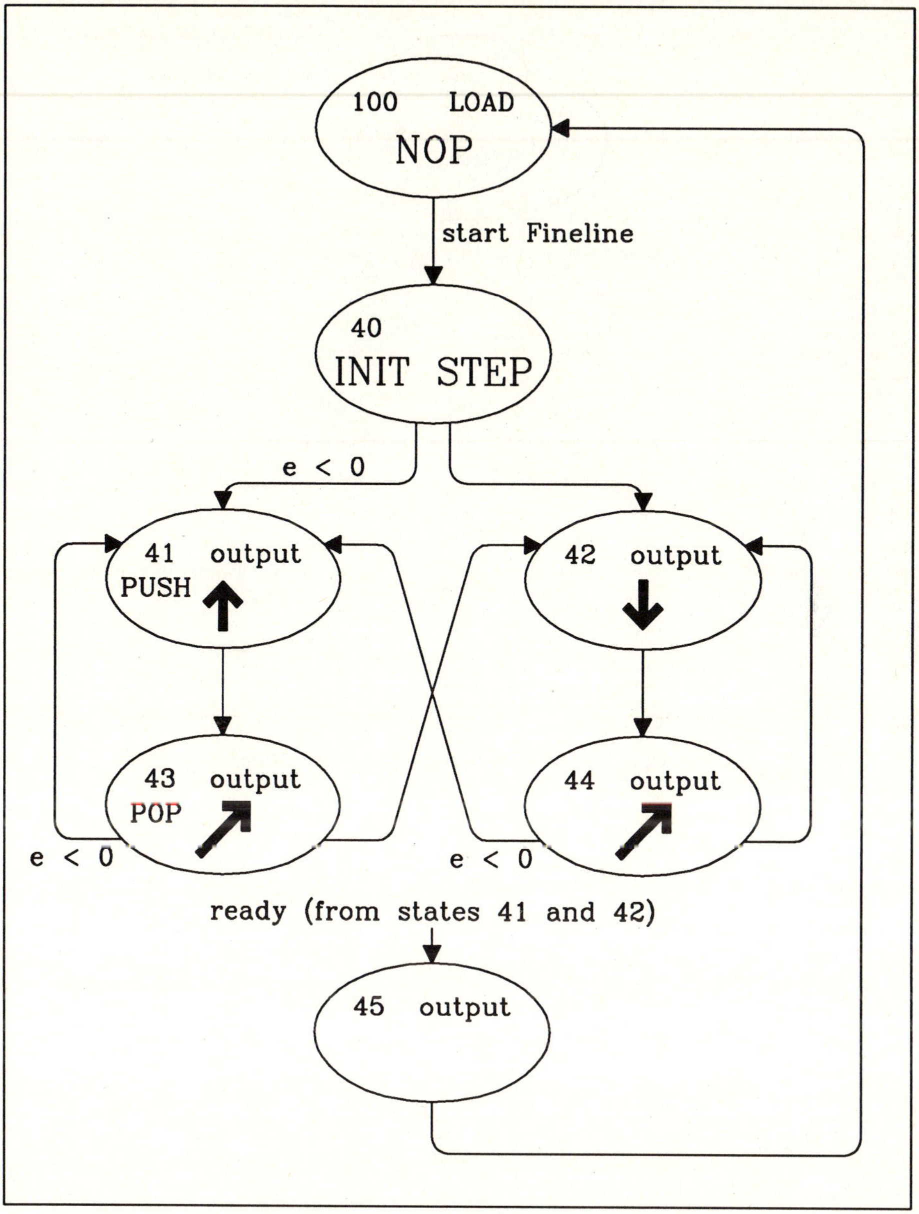


**Fig. 12.** State diagram for 'antialiased' vector drawing

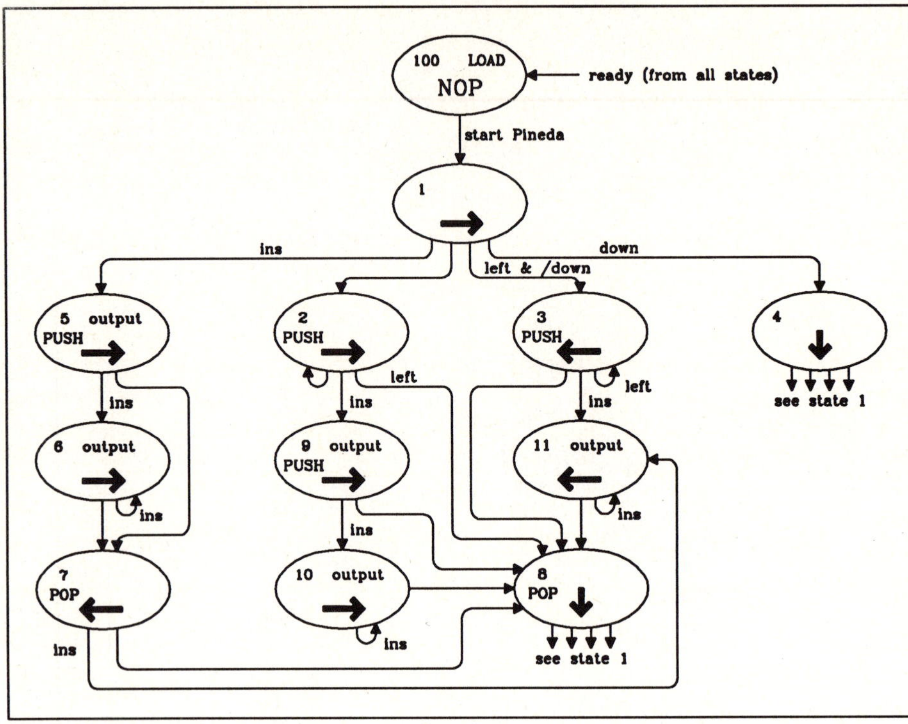


**Fig. 13**. State diagram for the Pineda algorithm

# Part II

# Ray Tracing

# MARTI—A Multiprocessor Architecture for Ray Tracing Images

M-P. Hébert, M. D. J. McNeill, B. Shah, R. L. Grimsdale and P. F. Lister

ABSTRACT Multiprocessor systems are well suited to ray tracing, since each ray can be traced independently. However, the large databases required to model complex scenes create problems of data access. In this paper we propose a multiprocessor architecture for ray tracing which removes the need for duplication of the database at processor level. The database is held on a group processor basis, and resides in shared memory. Many of these groups, or *clusters*, can be replicated to form a highly parallel multiprocessing system. Results of a software simulation of the architecture are promising, indicating that a large number of processors per cluster is possible.

## 1 Introduction

Ray tracing has emerged as one of the most photorealistic methods of rendering, particularly when combined with a sophisticated lighting model. In the ray tracing model primary rays are cast from the eye through each pixel into the scene, where intersection tests are performed on objects. Once the intersection between a ray and the closest object has been found, further rays are cast to the lights in the scene and in the reflection and refraction directions, where more intersection tests are performed [17]. Thus several secondary rays are cast for each primary ray. Since high quality graphics monitors typically display around one million pixels, it is easy to see that many millions of rays are generated during a rendering, particularly when improvement techniques such as antialiasing are included. Scenes can contain thousands of object primitives, so a brute force technique where every ray is intersected with every object is computationally too expensive. It is well known that most of the computational power is required for the intersection tests [17], and therefore speed-up techniques which remove the need to intersect every ray with every object have been developed [6,7,10]. The rendering time is dramatically reduced, although the algorithm still requires many minutes or hours of conventional processing time.

The solution to the problem of unacceptably long rendering times has been to parallelize the process. Ray tracing is well suited to parallelization, since every ray can be traced independently, although there are many problems introduced by such a solution—handling of the database, inter-processor communication and efficient use of system resources. Algorithms have been proposed based on architectures such as transputers [8], where the database is distributed across the network of processors, and on more dedicated hardware in which the database is duplicated in each processor [13]. In this paper we propose a scheme where the database is held on a group processor basis, minimising inter-processor communications but avoiding the need for a fully distributed system with its associated overheads.

The structuring of data in object space is a favourite speed-up technique, usually employed as a pre-processing step, since this can be performed in a view-independent way. In this paper we present a method by which the data structure can be built as an integral part of the rendering process, which not only encourages a more complete analysis of the algorithm, but raises issues of changing scenes and efficient use of a multiprocessor system.

In sections 2 and 3 data structures exploiting coherency and antialiasing issues are discussed. In section 5 we propose the architecture, and section 6 describes the simulation technique used in its evaluation. Results are presented in section 7.

## 2 Octree Structure

### 2.1 Ray Tracing Octrees

Spatial subdivision techniques, such as octrees, are well known for reducing the computational expense of ray tracing algorithms. It is well known that a ray can access the cells of a grid [6] more quickly than those of an adaptive subdivision structure (such as an octree [7] or a Binary Space Partition (BSP) tree [10]). However, in a grid cell, more intersections between rays and objects may be computed as objects may be unevenly distributed among the cells. Moreover, areas with a high density of objects are usually the 'interesting' parts of the scene and thus many rays will intersect these heavily loaded cells. If the grid is finely subdivided in order to diminish the computational cost, then more memory is required than for an adaptive subdivision structure. For instance, an octree usually has a depth greater than 10. A grid of $8^{10}$ cells requires at least four gigabytes of memory. This is a problem in a multiprocessor architecture, where a shared resource such as memory can be considered to have a lower effective bandwidth than a local, privately owned resource.

The BSP defined by Kaplan [10] is very similar to the octree. Instead of dividing a parallelepiped in eight child nodes, the subdivision is performed in three successive stages. On the one hand, it could be argued that a BSP needs less leaf nodes than an octree for achieving the same efficiency. On the other hand, the number of branch nodes increases in a BSP. Empirical data show that no one structure is best suited for all scenes, and that the number of nodes is similar for all structures in most sample scenes.

Our choice for the octree structure was motivated by the possibility of using the HERO algorithm [1]. Compared with other octree traversal methods, HERO decreases the number of floating point operations and the number of manipulations of pointers addressing nodes. In order to reach the next hit voxel from the current one, a common ancestor technique [14] is traditionally used. HERO avoids all ascents to the common ancestor by using recursion. Moving to a parent node only requires a value to be popped from a stack. Recursion also enables the intersection between rays and the boundary planes of nodes to be computed only once per ray and per plane. The coordinates of the boundary planes can be determined by mid-point subdivision. Precision problems do not occur as the octree depth is much smaller than computer word lengths. Thus, these coordinates do not need to be stored; this diminishes the size of the octree structure dramatically.

### 2.2 Building Octrees

Most nodes belong to the lower levels of the octree. However, these nodes are rarely accessed during the ray tracing process (see Figure 1). For the Utah teapot database modelled with 9120 polygons, the four deepest levels of the octree contains 56.5% of the nodes but only 2.2% of accesses concern this nodes. The remaining 97.8% of accesses occur in the upper part of the octree which contains 43.5% of the nodes. This suggests that the lower levels of the octree should not be built. However, if these lowest levels are not built, the cost in terms of floating point operations increases fourteenfold for the teapot image, due to the additional computed intersections. We have therefore investigated a dynamic building of the octree. During a preprocess the top levels of the octree are built. Due to the adaptive nature of the octree structure, lowest level nodes, if required, can be easily added to the tree during the ray tracing process. Only those nodes which are useful are created. The size of the data structure is therefore reduced, yet the number of arithmetic operations does not increase. Dynamic octree building is particularly efficient for very large data bases.

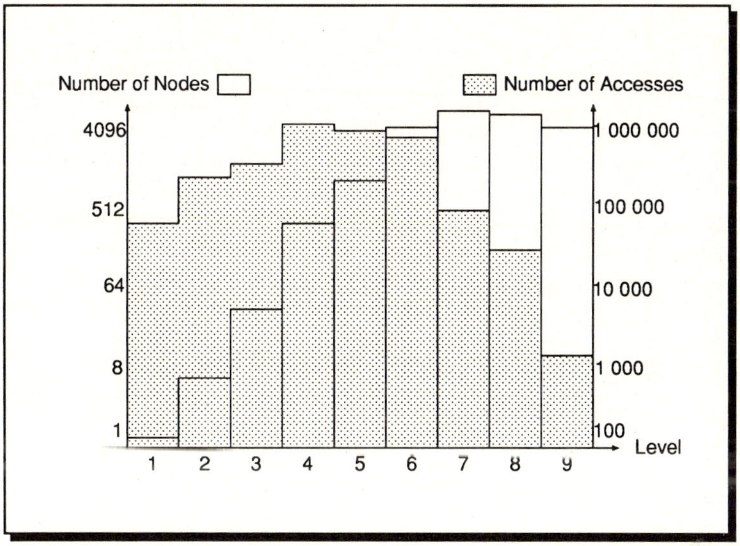


**Fig. 1.** Number of accesses and number of nodes per level of octree

Typically a data structure such as an octree is built for a particular scene and stored on disc. This file is then accessed by the renderer and pixel values are either stored on disc or displayed on the screen. Since the data structure can be used for many viewing positions the build time is negligible. For many scenes, when rendering is performed by a single processor, the build time for the octree is less then 10% of the total rendering time. However, when multiprocessor systems are considered, this build time can become significant in the rendering process due to several factors. Firstly, when hundreds or thousands of processors are employed to render an image, the percentage of time taken to build the data structure increases. Secondly, once rendering times are reduced to an acceptably small time—and we consider this to be within the bounds of current hardware performance—application developers and users will want to move away from the idea of a static scene and develop instances of moving objects and lights. This may perhaps lead to the data structure being re-built for each frame. It is therefore sensible to use the available processors to build the data structure. Subtrees of an octree can be built in parallel and then ordered. A similar algorithm to static building is used for building and ordering subtrees dynamically.

# 3 Antialiasing

Being a point sampling method, ray tracing is prone to aliasing. According to the Shannon theorem, aliasing can only be reduced by either filtering out the high frequency components of the image or by increasing the sampling density. The simplest way to antialias an image is to supersample the whole image or to pass it through a low pass filter. However, a lot of computational effort is wasted in regions of low frequency pattern changes and the reduction in aliasing at high frequency pattern changes is not significant. Hence adaptive supersampling methods need to be used. Antialiasing in ray tracing can be performed in image, object or ray space.

## 3.1 Antialiasing Algorithms

*Image Space Antialiasing*

Most antialiasing algorithms are based on image space. Whitted [17] introduced the idea of adaptive oversampling, whereby rays are traced through the four corners of the pixel. If the intensity values vary more then some threshold value, the pixel is subdivided. The contribution of each subpixel is weighted by its area, and the final pixel intensity is obtained by the summation of the subpixel values. However, whatever the oversampling rate, regular aliasing defects will appear. To avoid this problem, Mitchell [12] and Dippé and Wold [5] suggest algorithms based on non-uniform sampling, which distorts the aliasing effects, thus making them less conspicuous to the eye. Mitchell uses multistage box filters, whereby different regions of the image are sampled at different densities. The eye perception model is used to evaluate the threshold values. These values form the criteria to determine the sample densities. Dippé and Wold implement an adaptive stochastic sampling algorithm, which uses the Poisson function and jittering to determine the error estimates, error bounds and the sampling rates.

*Object Space Antialiasing*

Algorithms based on object space antialiasing use information available in the object space to prefilter the image before being sampled. Amanatides [3] introduced a cone tracing algorithm which traces cones into the environment, and antialiases the image by filtering across the cross-section of the cones in object space. However, the cost of tracing cones greatly outweighs the advantages in image quality.

Thomas [16] introduced the method of edge detection. Edges are detected by observing how the ray passes through covers, built around the surfaces. Only rays which pass near a surface edge are filtered using a low pass filter.

*Ray Space Antialiasing*

Akimoto [2] present a method based on adaptive undersampling. Representative pixels in a region are raytraced and their ray trees stored. Intermediate pixel intensities are obtained by interpolating between these pixels. This method, however, is expensive in terms of memory requirements and for very complex scenes the regions have to be pixel wide to ensure small objects are not missed.

## 3.2 Edge Detection Algorithm

The algorithm used at Sussex has been developed with multiprocessing systems in mind, and incurs no additional communication overheads. When a ray passes close to an edge, the corresponding pixel is supersampled. Since we use polygonal databases only, proximity of a ray from an edge is detected as part of the intersection algorithm. This requires only a single additional comparison. If the edge and the intersection point do not lie in the same node, then pointers to the node containing the edge and the following leaf nodes which the ray crosses up to the intersection point are stored. The pixel identifier and the leaf node list are passed to the antialiasing routine, which traces the subpixel rays through the nodes in the list, thereby reducing the overhead of the subpixel rays crossing the octree. Results have shown that on average only 25% of pixels need to be antialiased.

# 4 Texturing

An important feature of any renderer is the ability to provide textured objects. Although one-, two- and three-dimensional mapping takes place, a widely used technique in ray tracing is to map a two-dimensional texture onto a three dimensional object. Texture can be applied procedurally, such as wood effects, where there is little implication for the architecture, or by color mapping, where the intersection point of the ray and the surface is used to index into a stored color map.

## 4.1 Distribution of Texture Data

The inclusion of texturing on a large scale—tens or hundreds of color maps requiring many megabytes of storage space—presents the problem of data access. Texture information can be stored with the object/surface, with each object containing only the texture-id and the address of the entry into the color map. When a textured surface is hit by a ray, plane constants can be worked out and stored with the surface for future use. Once the intersection point of the ray and the surface is found, the tracing processor calculates the index into the color map before requesting the required entry.

## 4.2 Antialiasing in Texturing

Antialiasing textured surfaces is necessary when a surface lies at an oblique angle to the observer, since one pixel may cover perhaps hundreds or thousands of texture pixels, or texels. The problem is how to approximate the color of the area covered by the pixel. Antialiasing therefore needs to be performed not just near an edge, but in every case where a ray intersects a textured surface.

The following algorithm was developed to work in conjunction with the antialiasing algorithm discussed in section 3. When a ray hits a surface and the intersection point is not near the edge of the surface, additional rays can be cast in order to approximate the color by supersampling, followed by filtering. Note that these rays need only to be intersected with the surface and do not need to be traced through space, since the intersection is not near the surface edge. For the case where the ray intersects the surface near an edge then these additional rays need to be traced through the stored voxels as outlined in section 3. Once the parameters are worked out for the particular intersection point on the surface the appropriate index can be calculated and the color requested.

# 5 Description of the Architecture

## 5.1 Architecture Overview

Although searching through an octree structure reduces the rendering time dramatically, ray tracing is still a computationally expensive algorithm. Processor power must therefore be fully exploited. Algorithms using image parallelism compute a pixel intensity fully in one processor. On the one hand, it makes maximum use of the processors by incurring a minimum of overheads. On the other hand, each processor needs to be able to access the whole database. Databases are so large that it is unrealistic to duplicate the scene data for every processor. Resources must then be shared among processors. MARTI—a Multiprocessor Architecture for Ray Tracing Images—is based on observations of the ray tracing algorithms.

MARTI is made up of independent units, called *clusters*, which consist of a number of general purpose, fast floating point, programmable microprocessors tracing rays using image parallelism (see Figure 2). Using microprocessors as opposed to specialized hardware enables the implementation of various types of primitives and lighting models, in addition to the evolution of the algorithm. Processors are grouped in such a way that each cluster is seen as only one unit. An interface node deals with all interfaces between MARTI and external devices. All clusters, the host processor and the display are linked through an interconnection network.

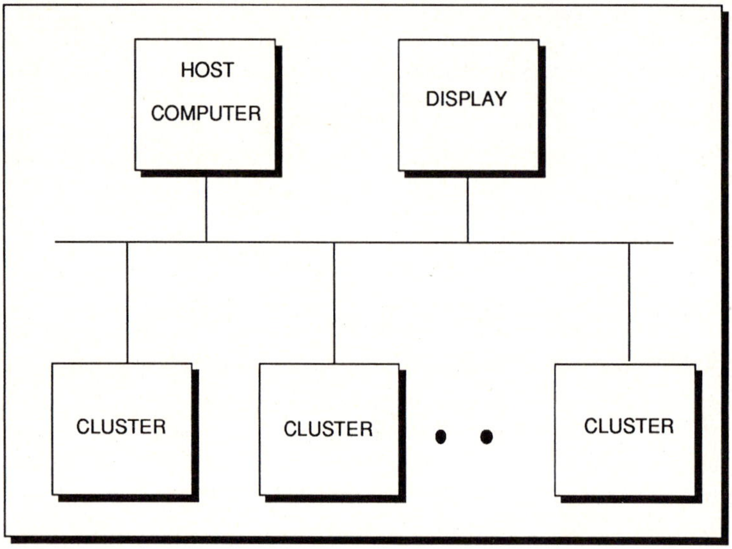


**Fig. 2.** Architecture overview

## 5.2 Cluster Architecture

*Sharing Memory*

The choice of powerful processors with local memories diminishes inter-processor traffic. A shared memory allows a few processors to access the database with very short delays, due to the high locality of reference for ray tracing algorithms, and straightforward memory management. The database is stored in the *cluster memory*, which is shared among all processors of the cluster. A bus links the cluster memory to the processing nodes.

*Master/Slave Operation*

A master node supervises the cluster. It waits for interrupts, controls job execution and interfaces the cluster to the interconnection network. When a cluster is idle, it can request a task from the job queue of the host processor. For instance, during the ray tracing process, the location and size of a tile on the screen is fetched, and the intensity of every pixel of the tile is computed by the cluster. By managing a cluster job queue, the master node knows when a cluster has finished its task and can send an 'end of process' message to the interface node. Although no deadlocks occur in our implementation, the master node can prevent such an event from occurring in another software implementation.

The control of the master node avoids disturbing a processing node which does not request any service, whenever an external device or another node interrupts. It also enables the internal management of the cluster to be transparent to the rest of the architecture.

*Processing Nodes*

Every processing node includes a processor and local memory. Processors are computationally powerful in order to reduce management overheads. As ray tracing requires a lot of floating point operations, they must include a fast floating point arithmetic unit. Programmable processors allow the rendering of any type of scene models and also algorithm development.

Programs are duplicated in every local memory. Data requested by a processor are copied from the cluster memory to its local memory. Due to the high locality of reference of ray tracing algorithms, most data requests will be local; no delays will occur for accessing cluster memory (see section 7 for results).

Figure 3 sums up the cluster architecture. Each cluster has a shared memory, a master node and several processing nodes made up of a processor and local memory.

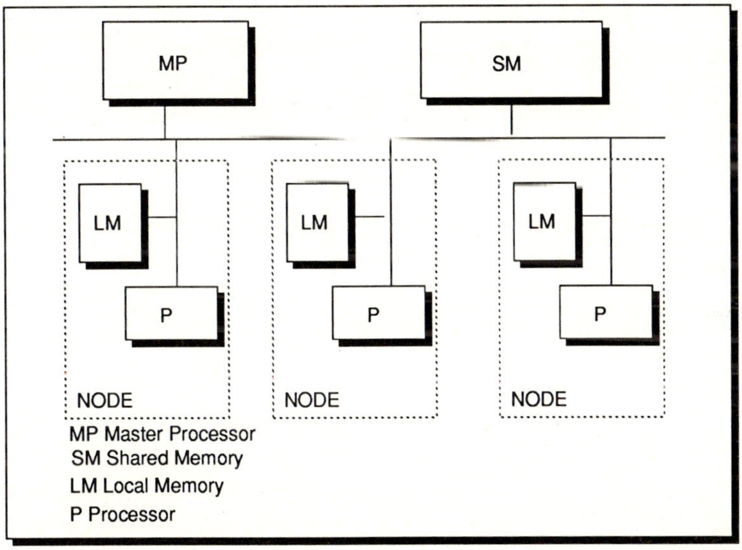


**Fig. 3.** Cluster Architecture

### 5.3 Ray Tracing with MARTI

*Initialization and Preprocessing*

The host computer sends programs and data to MARTI. The clusters can then start to build the octree. The master node distributes disjoint subtrees to the processing nodes requiring nodes. The processing nodes build the subtrees and write them to shared memory.

*Ray Tracing*

In each cluster, the master nodes requests patches of tiles from the host and makes tiles available to processing nodes. Each processing node requires scene data to compute pixel intensities. If these data are not held in the local memory, then shared memory is accessed and the data are copied locally. Once a processing node has achieved its task, it writes pixel intensities to the shared memory, and fetches a new job from the job queue. The master node requests a new task from the host processor when the job queue is empty.

During the calculation of a pixel intensity, a voxel pointing to a large number of objects may be reached. In that case, dynamic octree building is performed. The ray tracing process then continues normally. There is no data consistency problem as the data are computed and never modified. The worst case is when the same computation is performed several times by different processors.

Fragmentation of objects into several nodes of an octree implies redundant ray-object intersections. A mailbox [4] can be efficiently used since a ray is fully processed in one processor. As a cluster computes only a part of the image, dynamic octree building is an efficient data management technique for a cluster.

*Aliasing*

The intensity of a pixel is computed fully inside a single processor. Hence there is no communication overhead associated with the antialiasing routine. It is also reasonable to assume that the whole ray path is stored in the local memory in the first pass and therefore there is no need for shared memory accesses for the subpixel rays.

Pixels which need to be antialiased require longer to trace, but since tiles are read by a processor on request, no additional load imbalance problems will arise due to antialiasing.

## 6 Simulation

### 6.1 Multiprocessing in a Unix Environment

The BSD socket abstraction provides the means whereby processes can communicate with each other within a communications domain. Sockets are derived from BSD 4.2 and will also be included in future releases of AT&T Unix[1] System V. Apollo DOMAIN/OS, incorporating BSD4.3, SYSV.3 and AEGIS environments allow the use of sockets in both its BSD and System V environments. Sockets are implemented on top of the reliable transmission control protocol (TCP), which provides a robust environment for interprocess communication.

The basic building block for interprocess communication is the socket, an endpoint for communication. Each socket has a type and one or more associated processes. Sockets exist within communication domains—abstractions introduced to bundle common properties of

[1]Unix is a registered trademark of AT&T in the USA and other countries

processes communicating through sockets. Each socket is identified uniquely by a socket address. This is a structure that specifies the socket's *Address Family*, *Network Address* and *Port Number*.

Standard routines are provided by Unix for mapping host names to network addresses, network names to network numbers, protocol names to protocol numbers and service names to service numbers, and the appropriate protocol to use in communicating with the server process. With these support routines, an application program rarely has to deal directly with addresses. Thus, services can be developed in a largely network-independent fashion.

## 6.2 Motivation

Simulating the various architectural considerations benefits from a distributed multiprocessor tool for several reasons.

- The use of the socket abstraction allows a robust and transparent way of logging of all inter-process communication. Processes can represent individual processor action, groups of processors, buses, or indeed any action on data the programmer desires. Data flow into and out of the process is again under programmer control; data can be input to and output from the process via file, standard input or socket—another process. The ability of a process to poll its connected sockets for incoming data—listen for input on all its connections—allows processes to emulate the action of a bus. A library of routines can be built to implement the inter-process connections in a generic way, so making the use of sockets transparent to the user, and allowing simulations to be built easily and quickly, without the need to re-compile code for different connection topologies.

- The ability to run several processes in parallel. Although it is not necessary to simulate the architecture wholly, executing two or more processes synchronized, in parallel, and logging their data flow overcomes the drawback of simulation using sequential algorithms, namely execution time and the unrepresentative nature of the simulation.

- The processor bound nature of the ray tracing algorithm. The simulation requires isolating the various parts of the code conforming to different processors in the architecture, running sections of the code in parallel and also transferring possibly large amounts of data between processes. To do this sequentially on a single machine would increase the already long time needed for the algorithm by an unacceptable amount. Implementing transparent support for the Internet communications protocols allows the extra power of networked processors to be utilized.

- The ability to run all or part of the simulation on a specialized architecture. Since the use of the Internet communications protocols allows processes to be executed on hosts other than Apollo Domain workstations, the simulation can include all or part of the algorithm executing on a specialized type of architecture, e.g. a shared memory machine such as the Sequent Symmetry.

Since programming with sockets allows generic access to various protocol suites, the extra time involved in the construction of a distributed simulation tool was considered worthwhile. With the portability afforded by the C language [11] and the socket abstraction the simulation has access to a wide range of equipment, as well as indicating how well the ray tracing algorithm performs in a distributed environment.

The use of the socket abstraction in this way provides a representative method of profiling parallel processes. Although the initial coding involved is not insubstantial, it is an easy concept to grasp, and the transparency and portability afforded by such an abstraction are good justifications for proceeding along this path.

A framework, allowing simulation of the proposed architecture was therefore written using C in the Unix environment. Details of how the simulation was implemented are beyond the scope of this paper. The Distributed Ray Tracer is currently in use tracing images at Sussex.

### 6.3 Simulation of Cluster Level

A commonly used paradigm in constructing distributed applications is the client/server model. Processes can act as either *clients*, *servers*, or both. Client applications are the controlling processes, which make requests for service from server processes.

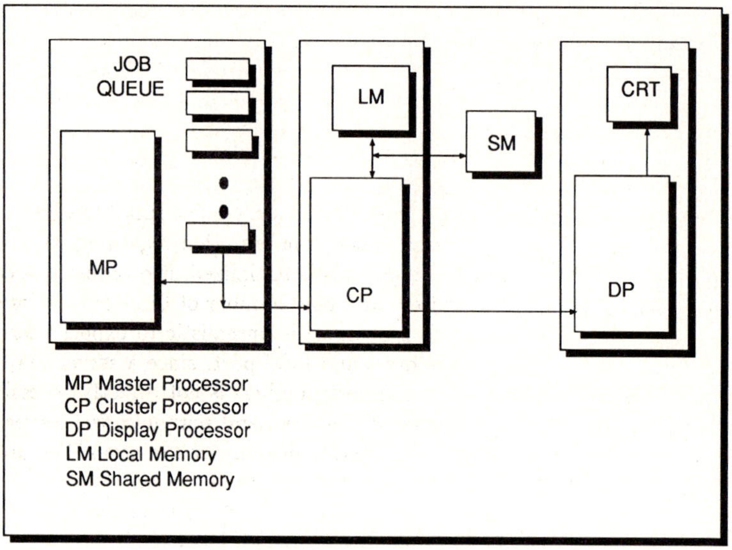


**Fig. 4.** Functionality of the Cluster Architecture

The client/server model is well suited to many areas of the architecture simulation. Consider the cluster level. The controlling process, the *client*, is the master processor, which after initialization sends tiles to the processing nodes. The processing nodes act as *server* processes, providing the service of tracing rays through pixels. They also act as client processes, however, since they require the service of the local frame buffer to accept rgb data. Since software processes are under programmer control, local memory can be modelled in software, and requests for data on the cluster bus—data not held locally—can be logged. Individual *processes*, then, can represent a master node, processing node, display processor, or cluster bus (see Figure 4).

The simulation is initialized by a managing process, which reads a user-defined data file containing details of the required configuration of the simulation. This managing process starts each process, and listens for signals from the process to indicate their status. If a process should become corrupted, the manager can kill the process and redistribute the task to another process. When a server process is initialized, it uses Unix system calls

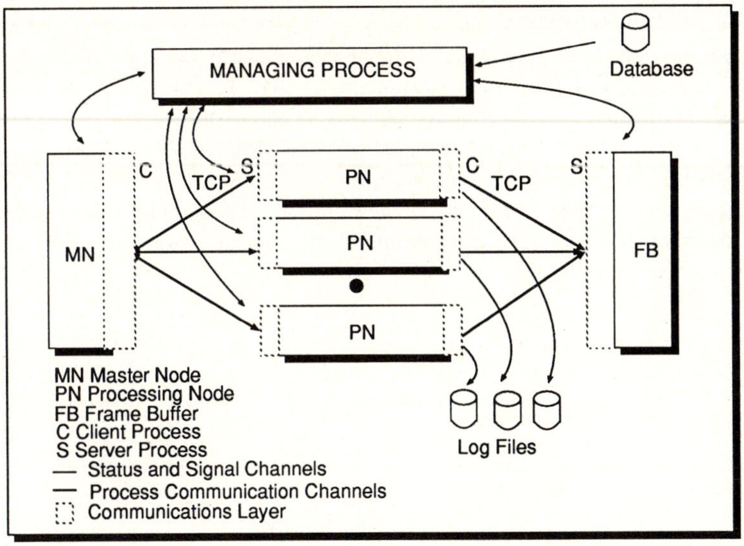


**Fig. 5.** Simulation Architecture

to establish a local address at which to offer its service. Once a suitable address and port number have been established, the server returns information regarding its whereabouts to the managing process. When a client process is initialized, it establishes a connection to the server (see Figure 5). The address and port number of the server is forwarded to the client at startup by the managing process. It is unrealistic to expect user programs to know proper values for the local address and local port, since a server may reside on multiple networks and the set of allocated port numbers is not directly accessible to the user. By using system calls to choose a valid address and port number, server processes rely on the local system to provide a valid communications endpoint and the programmer needs no detailed knowledge about the (possibly remote) environment.

The simulation has enabled us to investigate at process level the behaviour of the ray tracing paradigm in a multiprocessor architecture. The flexibility of the system has allowed for investigation of different software and hardware models. In particular several areas of interest have been closely modelled for different scenes which have suggested specific hardware and software solutions.

## 7 Performance

Fast access to shared resources and load balance are typical issues in multiprocessor architecture.

### Load Balance

Since pixel parallelism is intrinsically load balanced, a good balance is achieved by processing nodes and clusters. The master node only manages the cluster job queue and sends messages to the host and display node. Its task is negligible compared with that of processing nodes, thus it is able to cope with many processors per cluster. Sending tile instead of pixel intensities to the display node diminishes the management task of the display node, so no bottleneck should occur here.

**Accessing Shared Resources**

Within a cluster, all processors share the cluster bus and the shared memory. The communication on the cluster bus was determined by simulating a cluster, as explained in section 6.3. Results have been collected for two scenes: one is the gears picture [9] with 1170 polygons, the other is the Utah teapot modelled with 9120 triangles. The tiles are of $5 \times 5$ pixels. A cluster computes 2500 tiles. No antialiasing was implemented for these tests; however, as subsamples are computed in the same processing node, antialiasing does not increase the amount of communications. Results for four and nine processors in a cluster are shown in Figures 6 and 7.

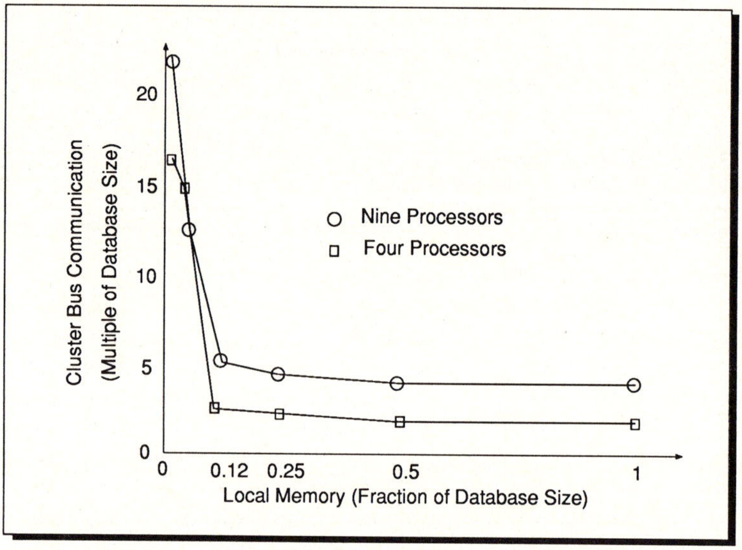


**Fig. 6.** Cluster bus communication for the gears database

The size of the local memories greatly influences the amount of communication on the bus, when it falls under one eighth of the size of the database. Over this size, the communication on the bus does not increase; thus there is no need for duplication of the database at a processor level. The number of accesses to the shared memory versus size of local memory (see Figure 6) behaves as the number of cache misses versus the size of cache memory [15]. This is an expected result as the local memories copy data as a cache memory does.

Note than in the worst case—the teapot picture with processing nodes having a local memory for data of only 3.125% of the size of the data base (about 87 Kbytes)—the communication on the cluster bus is 4.7% of the communication between a unique processor and memory computing the same tiles. In this simulation, the communications due to messages are about 200 Kbytes. There are no contention problems on the cluster bus even with small local memories. Therefore it is possible to add many more processors; the exact number is technology dependent.

Table 1 shows the ratio of the shared memory access to the local memory access when ray tracing the gears database and the teapot database with nine processors.

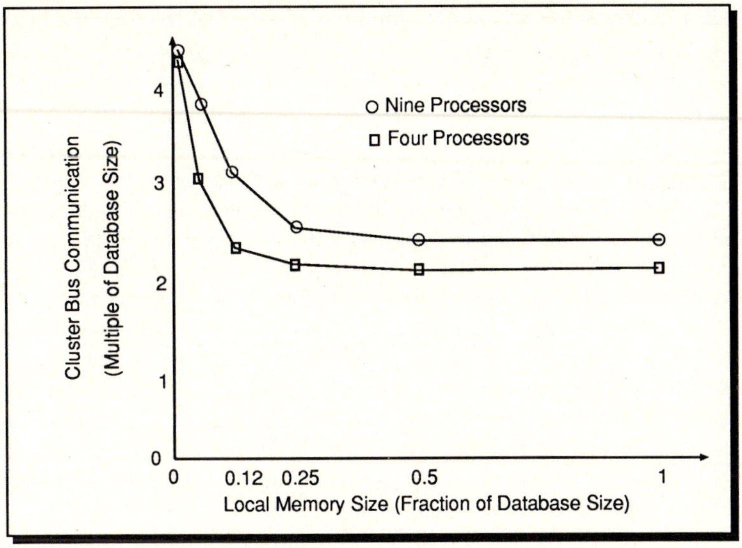


**Fig. 7.** Cluster bus communication for the teapot database

**Table 1.** Ratio of Shared Memory Accesses to Local Memory Accesses

| Local Memory Size (Database Unit) | Gears Database | Teapot Database |
|---|---|---|
| 1/4 | 0.005 | 0.027 |
| 1/8 | 0.006 | 0.035 |
| 1/16 | 0.015 | 0.038 |
| 1/32 | 0.027 | 0.047 |

Although only scene data are considered, we can say that the locality of reference is significantly high to allow many processors per cluster. For instance, with local memory size equal to one thirty-second of the size of the database, our results predict that thirty-seven processors per cluster will be acceptable, when only considering object and octree dataflow.

This is due to the fact that MARTI benefits from:

- image coherence by using image parallelism,
- space coherence as the number of accesses to data diminishes dramatically by use of the octree structure and the HERO algorithm. Only data of those objects and octree nodes which lie near the ray paths are accessed. Thus less data are required for every ray and data are not overwritten in the local memory from one pixel computation to the next.

If the database is duplicated in every cluster, there is no communication between clusters. The only communication on the interconnection network connecting clusters, display node and host is due to the distribution of tiles and of the writing of tile intensity to the the cluster node.

## 8 Conclusion

The architecture proposed, in particular the allocation of memory to the clusters, offers certain advantages for the ray tracing paradigm. The use of image space parallelism allows for inherent load balancing. The use of space and image coherence maintains low traffic on buses. The development of a general purpose hardware system combined with a integrated software model encourages maximum use of resources. The generality of the hardware is such as not to preclude the use of other algorithms. Results have shown that the locally available database to a group of processing nodes provides effective support for the ray tracing algorithm, while remaining scalable.

Future research will concentrate on increasing the communication bandwidth between clusters, in order to ray trace scenes without duplicating the data in every cluster. By benefiting from the high coherence of ray tracing, an architecture with an interconnection network of low complexity should be effective.

We also propose a trade-off between the efficiency of the space subdivision technique and its size. The dynamic octree building should be particularly efficient for animated ray tracing.

## Acknowledgements

The authors wish to thank Andrew D. Nimmo, Steven R. Evans, Martin White and Graham J. Dunnett for their contribution to this work. This project is supported by the U.K. Science and Engineering Research Council.

## References

[1] M. Agate, R.L. Grimsdale, and P.F. Lister.: The HERO algorithm for ray-tracing octrees. In *Advances in Computer Graphics Hardware IV*. Springer-Verlag Berlin Heidelberg New York, 1991.

[2] T.K. Akimoto, K. Mase, A. Hashimoto, and Y. Suenaga.: Pixel selected ray tracing. In *Proceedings of the Eurographics 89*, pages 39–50, 1989.

[3] J. Amanatides.: Ray tracing with cones. *Computer Graphics*, 18(3):129–135, July 1984. SIGGRAPH'84 (Minneapolis, Minnesota, July 23-27, 1984).

[4] B. Arnaldi, T. Priol, and K. Bouatouch.: A new space subdivision method for ray tracing CSG modelled scenes. *The Visual Computer*, 3:98–108, 1987.

[5] M.A.Z. Dippé and E.H. Wold.: Antialiasing through stochastic sampling. *Computer Graphics*, 19(3):69–78, July 1985. SIGGRAPH'85 (San Francisco, California, July 22-26, 1985).

[6] A. Fujimoto, T. A. Tanaka, and K. Iwata.: ARTS: Accelerated Ray Tracing System. *IEEE Computer Graphics and Applications*, pages 16–26, April 1986.

[7] A.S. Glassner.: Space subdivision for fast ray tracing. *IEEE Computer Graphics and Applications*, 4(10):15–22, October 1984.

[8] S. Green, D. Paddon, and E. Lewis.: A parallel algorithm and tree-based computer architecture for ray-tracing computer graphics. In PM Dew and TR Heywood RA Earnshaw, editors, *Parallel Processing for Computer Vision and Display*, 1989.

[9] E. Haines.: A proposal for standard graphics environments. *IEEE Computer Graphics*, 7(11):3–5, November 1987.

[10] M.R. Kaplan.: Space tracing, a constant time ray tracer. In *SIGGRAPH'85 tutorial on the uses of spatial coherence in ray tracing*, July 1985, San Francisco, CA.

[11] B. Kernighan and D. Ritchie.: *The C Programming Language*. Prentice-Hall Software Series. Prentice-Hall, 1988.

[12] D.P. Mitchell.: Generating antialiased images at low sampling densities. *Computer Graphics*, 21(4):65–69, July 1987. SIGGRAPH'87 (Anahcim,California, July 27-31, 1987).

[13] T. Naruse and M. Yoshida.: SIGHT - a dedicated computer graphics machine. *Computer Graphics Forum*, 6(4):327–334, 1987.

[14] H.Q. Samet.: *Applications of Spatial Data Structures: Computer Graphics, Image Processing and GIS*. Computer Series. Addison Wesley, 1989.

[15] H.S. Stone.: *High-Performance Computer Architecture*. Electrical and Computer Engineering. Addison-Wesley Publishing Company, second edition, 1990.

[16] D. Thomas, A. Netravali, and D. Fox.: Anti-aliased ray tracing with covers. *Computer Graphics Forum*, 8:325–336, 1989.

[17] T. Whitted.: An improved illumination model for shaded display. *Communications of the ACM*, 23(6):343–349, June 1980.

# A Cellular Architecture for Ray Tracing

Abdelghani Atamenia, Michel Meriaux, Eric Lepretre, Samuel Degrande and Bruno Vidal

ABSTRACT We propose in this paper a massively parallel machine dedicated to image synthesis by discrete ray tracing techniques. This machine is a four-stage pipeline, the last stage being a bidimensional cellular array with one cell per pixel. Two main phases describe its behaviour:

- Loading into the cellular array of the objects of the scene to be displayed, after having been transformed into sets of planar polygons, and then into voxels.
- Cellular ray tracing over the fully distributed scene.

The first phase allows us to see this machine as a massively parallel (not realistic) rendering unit: at the end of the loading phase: objects are fully identified pixel per pixel in the cellular array. Then, we have only to display the computed visual features (by means of Gouraud or Phong-like incremental methods during the loading phase).

The second phase increases the image quality by executing the ray tracing algorithm in a very special way, i.e., completely distributed all over the many cells of the array. In that phase, objects are seen as split into voxels into a virtual 3D memory space. The machine is an attempt to bring a dramatic answer to the problem of performance, taking into account not only the computational power required for image synthesis by using a massive parallelism, but also the realization costs by using very regular structures, which make it a VLSI-oriented architecture.

## 1 Introduction

The aim of this paper is to describe a VLSI-oriented machine dedicated to ray tracing. This machine uses the massive parallelism of a cellular network in order to achieve the amount of computation required by computer image generation.

Cellular networks are usually built for solving specific problems, such as linear algebra [6], [9]. Some attempts have appeared in the fields of image synthesis or image processing ([12], [5], [10]), but none of them has dealt with ray tracing yet. Some experimental work is currently being done on the Cube-3 Machine, at the University of New-York.

Let us quote, however, two models which are not so far from what we propose here:

- $CM^2$ [4] is a multicomputer machine based on a regular subdivision of the object space in order to limit the number of computations of ray-object intersections to the objects belonging to the volume where the ray actually is. But its extension to a very large number of processors would cause a lot of costly repetitions of (parts of) objects in the processors.

- VOXAR is a Transputer-based multicomputer machine with a hypertorus structure [3]. Every processor handles a metavoxel space, every metavoxel being composed of voxels. The 3D space is subdivided into voxels crossed by rays, until they meet one voxel occupied by an object. Rays in different metavoxels are processed in a parallel way in different processors. Rays are traced analytically (according to the 3DDA algorithm proposed fro ARTS [8]) through the voxels of the same metavoxel.

## 2 Proposed Architecture

The architecture we propose here aims at using massive parallelism for ray tracing (several thousands of elementary processors), instead of the low or medium parallelism of the previous attempts.

### 2.1 Global Description

The architecture is a 4-stage pipeline. The first one, namely the 'geometry' subsystem, is concerned with geometric computations, and outputs objects in screen coordinates. The *geometry subsystem* is supposed to be able to, on the one hand, solve the usual geometric problems, mainly those about the complex scene modelling, and on the other hand, be fast enough to feed the downstream states [2].

The 3 following states, *precomputation, distribution* and *RC*, handle the voxel part of the image synthesis process, which has to discretize the objects of the scene into voxels and to load those voxels into a memory space fully distributed all over the network. This will allow further shading computations.

### 2.2 Precomputation

Precomputation essentially splits the polygons into trapezes with horizontal parallel sides and computes the true normals to their vertices. The choice of this special type of polygon, which has the drawback of artificially increasing the number of faces, is due to the fairly better performances we get under a pipeline mode while loading the polygons into the network ([11]).

### 2.3 Object Distribution

The objects are distributed to the cells of RC by using the left edge of the network. They go across the network like a wavefront, and are at the same time converted into surface elements (voxels), which are stored in the virtual 3D memory space associated with the physical 2D network.

### 2.4 Cellular Network

RC is the main module of this architecture. It is a 2D matrix with one cell per pixel. RC obviously belongs to the class of image-space partitioning machines.

The aim of RC is:

- To store the objects as surface or volume elements in the virtual 3D memory space.
- To execute the ray tracing algorithm in a cellular way in order to compute the shadows and shadings of all the visible objects.

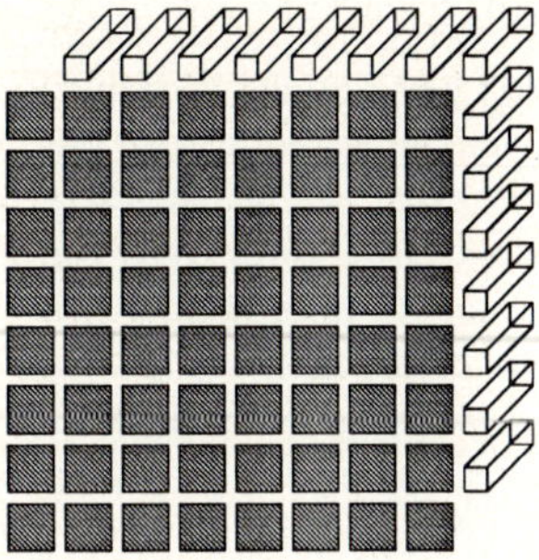

New problems about programming and control appear when using a cellular network. These are essentially due to the large size of the array (512 × 512 or 1024 × 1024) and to the need for an efficient communication tool allowing for easy cooperation between the cells.

The greatest interest of such an architecture, apart from its obvious massive parallelism, lies in the special loading of the scene into the network: it appears to be a kind of splitting of the database, which allows, on the one hand, to suppress the usual bottleneck when accessing at this database, and on the other hand, to drastically reduce the complexity of the ray-object intersection computation, by only making a very easy comparison between one ray coming into a given cell and what this one contains.

For architectural reasons as well as computational complexity ones, the network we use is only 4-connected.

## 3 Modes of Operation

There are two modes corresponding to the two phases of scene loading and ray tracing.

### 3.1 Scene Loading

The loading phase makes each cell know what objects, split into voxels, it has to handle, and give it the relevant information about light sources and the viewer's position.

The objects are split into trapezes and normals at the vertices are computed in the precomputation unit. The trapezes are then injected in a distribution pipeline and split into horizontal lines or 'spans'. Lastly, each horizontal span is split into voxels in the multipipelines of the RC network.

Every cell will receive the features of the objects, such as object type, proper color, coefficients for further shading computations, etc., followed by the sequence of polygons belonging to the object.

| | |
|---|---|
| Xl, Xr | left and right limits of a span |
| Z, DZx | depth and depth variation along x |
| N, DN | normal and normal variation along x |

### 3.2 Ray Tracing Execution

It is well known that the ray tracing algorithm can be highly parallelized because the computations are independent in one pixel from another. This remark fully justifies the use of cellular networks for ray tracing.

From a global point of view, a ray tracing algorithm builds and evaluates a forest of intersection trees, each one being associated with a pixel. Cellularly speaking, the forest can be seen as distributed all over the network, with one root per cell. Indeed, the image computation is the evaluation by every cell of the corresponding distributed tree.

The tree construction is started by every cell, which, given the viewer's position, searches its own memory space for an intersection; if it is the case, secondary rays are cast. When a given ray goes out of the memory space of the cell, i.e., $x$ or $y$ changes, a request is transmitted to one of the neighbours in the right direction. This new cell will then have either to route the ray if there is no intersection, or to send again secondary rays, thus building a sub-part of the initial tree. When receiving a ray which intersects some object, a cell has to compute the light intensity which must be sent back to the emitting cell. This computation consists of storing the received ray, computing the new rays, sending them, and waiting for them to come back.

Every cell will thus compute the sub-tree it has generated and will transmit the computed values to the node which has sent it the request (the ray). The execution of the algorithm, started by the cells of the screen (i.e., the cells with $z=0$), mainly consists of drawing rays in the virtual 3D network and trying to find intersections in the cells crossed by the rays. In order to decide whether there is intersection, one only has to compare the current depth of the ray with the depths of the various voxels composing the objects the cell has to deal with. The ray propagation is exactly an analytic drawing of the half-line in 3D, given its direction ([18], [1]).

However, the rays carrying the intensity information back to the root of a sub-tree already know their destination: so we can use a more straightforward way of routing them through the network. This is also the case for ways toward the light sources.

### 3.3 Other Problems

#### RC Size

As the cellular structure is finite, the question arises whether the chosen size (screen size) is correct. Some problems appear, due to the fact that we are only able to discretize that part of the scene which is inside the virtual 3D cube. So we cannot deal with objects or parts of objects outside the cube; moreover rays going outside the cube are lost. A minimal solution to this important problem is to suppose that the whole scene is inside the cube. Another solution would be to add some processors executing a classical ray tracing outside the cube.

#### Viewer's Position

The viewer's position has only an importance on the primary rays. If the viewer is located at a finite distance, it is necessary to send oblique primary rays. However some aliasing effects may appear when he is close to the screen.

#### Shadowing

A question arises about the best solution between the two following ones:

- should we cast rays from the voxels toward the sources, every cell being supposed to know their positions?
- should we, in a first step, try to illuminate all the voxels from every source, and keep in every cell information about the sources which can reach it? In the second step, it would thus be unnecessary to send secondary rays toward the sources.

It appears that a good storage/communication load balance leads us to choose the last solution, i.e., pre-casting the source rays.

## 4 The Basic Cell

A cell is a processor with a special communication tool and some reduced computational power. This is a compromise between a higher integration rate—allowing for a lower cost—a shorter image generation time and a better quality.

### 4.1 Computational Power

A cell must be able to identify objects and commands it receives. It has to manage coming and going rays. A coming ray may generate 2 rays. The cell has to determine their directions from the coming ray and the local normal, and evaluate the light intensity according to a given shading model, e.g. Whitted's or Phong's. It is clear that the most time- or silicon-consuming parts are the computations of the reflected or transmitted rays, requiring complex operations like square root (for normalization) or division, and the evaluation of the intensity model, requiring exponentiation. it appears that approximations can be used without any important consequence on the resulting image.

We have chosen to use a standard 20 bits ALU with a RAM microprogram in the first implementation of the cell, helped by specialised operators.

### 4.2 Storage Size

A cell has to store some rays (say M), including the primary one at the beginning of the ray tracing process. But M is rather hard to evaluate; however it is quite important because it could cause the deadlock of the communication system. In case of such a deadlock, we propose to destroy one or more sub-trees and to postpone the corresponding computations.

A cell must store in its memory:

1. viewer's position
2. visible light sources positions and features
3. ambient light intensity
4. each voxel it has to deal with, and its visual features (including true normal).

Thus, every cell is able to compute the data necessary for generating new rays or evaluating light intensity.

The most important part is obviously the voxel storage: our study shows that about 40 bytes are necessary per voxel. This will be implemented in the first prototype in standard cell for 16 voxels. In a full custom implementation, we intend to store only the occupied voxels, by using an index table. If the occupancy rate is 10 per cent, the voxel storage would cost about 5 Kbytes if the depth is 1024, which is quite compatible with current full custom technology.

### 4.3 Communications

Communications are unidirectional and asynchronous. They use buffers shared by neighbouring cells. To every buffer is associated a mutual exclusion flag indicating its current state (full or empty).

A cell has to get a message only when the corresponding output buffer is free in the case of simple routing, or when the message has to be processed locally (i.e., in case of intersection).

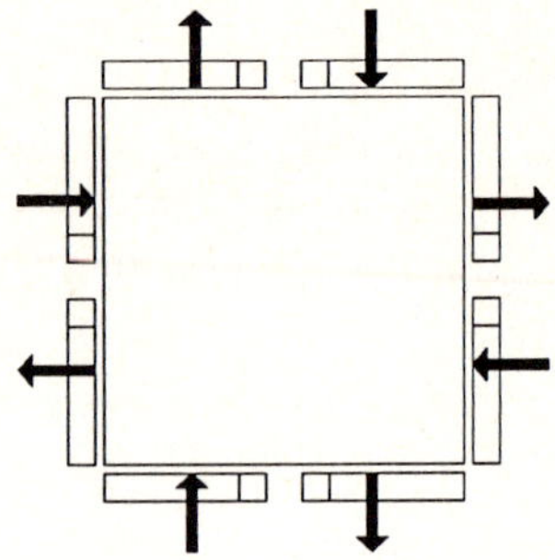

## 5 Simulation

This architecture has been simulated on a 17 Transputer network: the distribution stage and RC are implemented on a $4 \times 4$ network, and a first Transputer with more memory acts as precomputation and data construction unit. It appeared quickly that we could not successfully simulate large networks on this array. We are now simulating the machine on a Parstec Multi-Cluster with 32 T800, with 2 Megabytes per Transputer. This allows us to simulate a $128 \times 128$ cellular network with 64 depth levels.

## 6 Conclusion

The fully distributed approach that we propose appears to be realistic: the first simulation results we have got for the ray tracing phase are very positive and go along the same line as the theoretical and practical results we had for the first loading phase. We are now studying more accurately the architecture of the basic cell for a VLSI semi-custom implementation. Such a basic cell should be operating at mid-1990, allowing the building of a $16 \times 16$ prototype (but with coordinate range over 0-1023 in $x$, $y$, $z$) by mid-1991. Other theoretical studies remain to be done, e.g., about deadlock cases, correct processing of non trivial light sources, or antialiasing.

## References


[1] Amanatides, A., et al: A Fast Voxel Traversal Algorithm for Ray Tracing. *Eurographics '87*, pp. 3-12.

[2] Atamenia, A.: Architectures Cellulaires Pour La Synthèse d'Images. *Thèse de Doctorat*, Lille, June 1989.

[3] Caubet, R., et al.: Le suivi analytique de rayons: un algorithme incremental rapide pour la machine Voxar, *MICAD '89*, Paris, pp. 653-664.

[4] Cleary, J.G., et al.: Multiprocessor Ray Tracing. *Computer Graphics Forum*, vol. 5, no. 1, March 1986, pp. 3-12.

[5] Deering, M., et al.: The Triangle Processor and Normal Vector Shader : A VLSI System for High Performance Graphics. *Computer Graphics*, vol. 22, no. 4, August 88, pp. 21-30.

[6] Drake, B.L., et al.: SLAPP: A Systolic Linear Algebra Parallel Processor. *Computer*, vol. 20, no. 7, July 1987, pp. 45-49.

[7] Eyles, J., et al.: Pixel-Planes 4: A Summary. *Advances in Computer Graphics Hardware II.* EurographicSeminars. Springer, 1988, pp. 1833-207.

[8] Fujimoto, A., et al.: ARTS: Accelerated Ray-Tracing System. *IEEE Computer Graphics and Applications*, April '86.

[9] Kung, S.Y., et al.: Wavefront Array Processors—Concept to Implementation. *Computer* vol. 20, no. 7, July 1987, pp. 18-33.

[10] Lattard, D. and Mazaré, G.: Une nouvelle architecture cellulaire pour la reconstruction parallèle d'images. *Proceedings of PIXIM 88*, Paris, pp. 193-207.

[11] Lepretre, E.: Algorithmes Parallèles et Architectures Cellulaires Pour La Synthèse d'Images. *Thèse de Doctorat*, Lille, June 1989.

[12] Martin, P., et al.: Circuit systolique pour la synthèse d'images. *COGNITIVA 87*, Paris La Villette, 18-22, May 87, pp. 112-117.

[13] Meriaux, M.: Contributions a l'imagerie informatique: Aspects algorithmiques et architecturaux. *Thèse d'état*, Lille, 1984.

[14] Meriaux, M.: A Cellular Architecture for Image Synthesis. *Microprocessing and Microprogramming*, 1984, vol. 13, pp. 179-187.

# An Efficient Parallel Ray Tracing Scheme for Highly Parallel Architectures

Didier Badouel and Thierry Priol

ABSTRACT The production of realistic image generated by computer requires a huge amount of computation and a large memory capacity. The use of highly parallel computers allows this process to be performed faster. Distributed memory parallel computers (DMPCs), such as hypercubes or *transputer*-based machines, offer an attractive performance/cost ratio when the load balancing has been balance and the partition of the data domain has been performed. This paper presents a parallel ray tracing algorithm for DMPC using a Shared Virtual Memory (SVM) which solves these two classical problems. This algorithm has been implemented on a hypercube iPSC/2 and results are given.

## 1 Introduction

The ray tracing technique is well known both for its ability to provide high quality images and its requirement in memory and computation power. Despite recent research for improving ray tracing algorithms, they are still too slow. The use of highly parallel computers is one way to decrease synthesis time. These machines offer memory and computing resources which can be scaled. Intel and DARPA have announced the Touchstone project for the development of a highly parallel computer (2000 processors) with a peak performance of 150 Gflops. IBM has a similar research project with the VULCAN parallel computer that will deliver a peak performance of 1.2 Teraflops in the 90s. Inmos (SGS-Thomson) in Europe is also involved in research to develop a high performance RISC processor (H1) that will replace the Transputer for building parallel computers. These new architectures will outperform supercomputers like CRAY or FUJITSU. However, the lack of tools and environments for these new architectures discourage potential users.

This paper advocates the use of a new portable environment based on a shared virtual memory for DMPCs. This environment provides an easy way to efficiently parallelize the ray tracing algorithm. The shared virtual memory is used for accessing data manipulated by the ray tracing algorithm. The paper is organized as follows: Section 2 gives a brief background on ray tracing, highly parallel computers and how they can be programmed. Section 3 describes our algorithm and shows why emulating a SVM is not so paradoxical. A real implementation on an iPSC/2 hypercube allows us to present several encouraging results. Section 4 describes two approaches to efficiently implement a SVM on DMPCs.

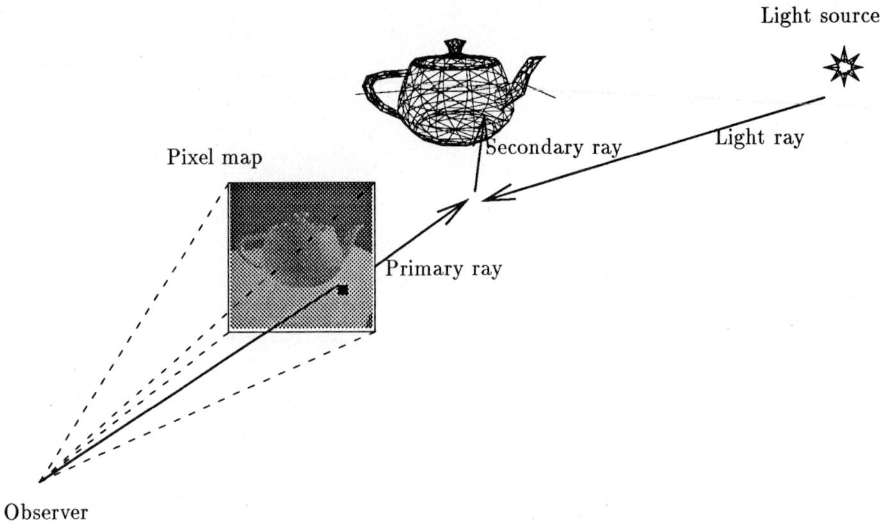


**Fig. 1.** The ray tracing principle

# 2 Backgrounds

## 2.1 The Ray Tracing Principle

The ray tracing algorithm is used in computer graphics for rendering high quality images. It is based on simple optical laws which take effects such as shading, reflection and refraction into account. It acts as a light probe, following *light rays* in the reverse direction (Figure 1). The basic operation consists in tracing a ray from an *origin* point towards a *direction* in order to evaluate a light contribution. The closest intersection (*impact* point) between the ray and the scene determines the object, if one exists, which contributes to this evaluation. The computation of each pixel of a simulated screen plane consists in shooting a ray from an *observer* through this pixel (*primary* rays). When an impact point is found, the contribution of various light sources to the intensity of the pixel are computed by shooting rays (*light* rays) from this point to each light source to determine if the relevant point is shadowed. According to the photometric properties of the intersected object, new rays are shot from the impact point, in order to take into account the contribution of the neighboring objects [12,21,35]. If the object is transparent (reflective) a ray is shot in the refracted (reflected) direction (*secondary* rays).

*Geometric computations* are used to find the closest intersection point between a ray and the objects in the scene. Their number increases with the *photometric* complexity of the scene (i.e., with the number of rays) and with the *geometric* complexity of the scene (i.e., with the number and the shape of the objects). Computing realistic images requires several million of rays and several hundred thousand objects. It is this large number of ray/object intersections which makes ray tracing a very expensive method. Several attempts have been proposed to minimize the number of ray/object intersections. These solutions are based on what we call an *object access structure* which allows a fast search for objects along a ray path. These structures are based on a tree of bounding

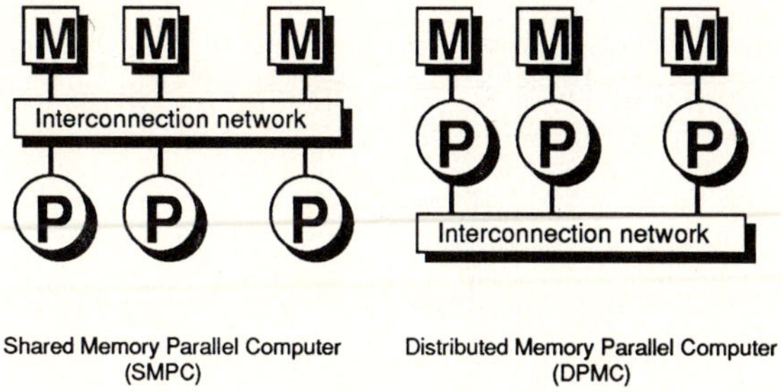


**Fig. 2.** MIMD architectures

boxes [24,33] or on space subdivision [2,8,14,15,23]. A parallelization of the ray tracing algorithm must address the problem of using a object access structure.

### 2.2 Highly Parallel Computers

Large improvements in computing speed can be obtained by highly parallel computers which are made up of many microprocessors (more than a hundred). They can be either Single Instruction Multiple Data (SIMD) architectures like the well known *Connection Machine* or Multiple Instruction Multiple Data (MIMD) machines such as arrays of *transputers* or hypercube computers. As this paper focuses on the use of MIMD architectures, we describe them briefly. Highly parallel MIMD computers may be split in two categories depending on how the processors are connected to the memory units (Figure 2).

Shared Memory Parallel Computers (SMPCs) constitute the first category. Processors which share a single address space are connected to local memories through an interconnection network. Each processor can physically access any local memory. The network can be either a bus (e.g., SEQUENT and ENCORE computers ) or a multistage network (e.g., BBN and IBM RP3 computers). Since the bandwidth of a bus is limited, the multistage network is the only way to make highly parallel shared memory computers. The cost of such a network is prohibitive for large numbers of processors. Moreover, caches for speeding up remote memory accesses and for avoiding *hot spots* in the multistage network cannot be implemented easily.

Machines in the second category avoid these problems. The design of Distributed Memory Parallel Computers (DMPCs) is very simple. Furthermore, they are scalable. Processors are connected together by the interconnection network, which allows the exchange of messages between processors. A large number of DPMCs are available commercially. They are differentiated by their interconnection network. Hypercube topologies are used in the Intel iPSC and the NCUBE2. Transputer-based machines like the Telmat T-Node and the Parsys SN1000 are based on a reconfigurable interconnection network in order to simulate a large number of topologies.

However, there is another side of the picture : programming a DPMC is more difficult than programming a SMPC because programmers must take data management into account. They must partition data used by the algorithm and add message-based primitives for remote data access. The next section describes some programming methodologies for DMPCs.

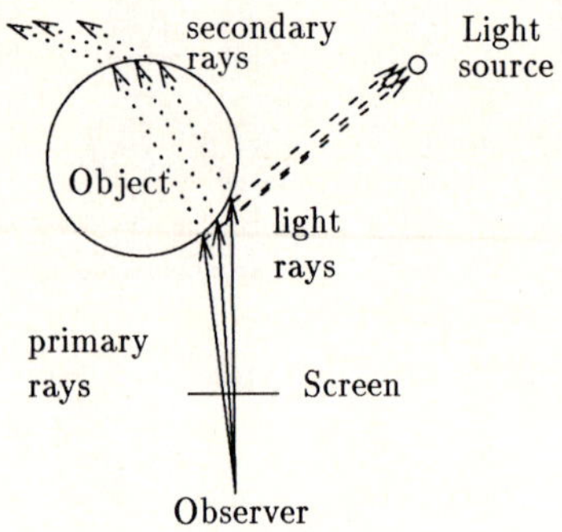


**Fig. 3.** Ray coherence property

### 2.3 Parallel Programming Methodologies for DMPCs

The programming of DMPCs consists of subdividing the problem to be solved into a set of communicating tasks. The lack of *general purpose* automatic parallelization tools makes this work difficult. However, several programming methodologies exist and can be applied to the ray tracing algorithm. The first approach focuses on the parallelization of loops. Loops are analyzed in order to discover dependencies. A set of tasks are created that represents a subset of iterations. Communication primitives are added when a task needs remote data. This approach is called *control oriented* parallelization. The second approach consists in partitioning the data domain of the algorithm. Each sub-domain is associated with a processor. Computations are assigned to processors which own the data used by these computations. They are sent to processors by mean of messages. In fact, this is the dual approach of the first one, and is called *data oriented* parallelization.

Parallel ray tracing algorithms published in the literature can be grouped according to these two approaches. Algorithms based on *processing without dataflow* [9,28,30,34] or *with object dataflow* [3,17,18,19,31] have been parallelized with the first technique whereas those based on *processing with ray dataflow* [10,11,13,16,22,25,29,32] have been parallelized with the second technique. A survey of these methods is given in [4].

## 3 A Paradoxical Approach

Ray tracing is intrinsically parallel since the evaluation of one pixel is independent from others. The difficulty in exploiting this parallelism is to simultaneously ensure that the load be balanced and that the database be distributed evenly across the memory of the processors. The parallelization of such an algorithm raises a classical problem when using distributed parallel computers: how to ensure both a data distribution and a balanced load when no obvious relation between computation and data can be found? This problem can be illustrated by the following schematic ray tracing algorithm:

**for** $i = 1, xpix$ **do**
  **for** $j = 1, ypix$ **do**
    $pixel[i,j] = \Sigma(contrib(\ldots, space[f_x(\ldots), f_y(\ldots), f_z(\ldots)], \ldots))$
  **done**
**done**

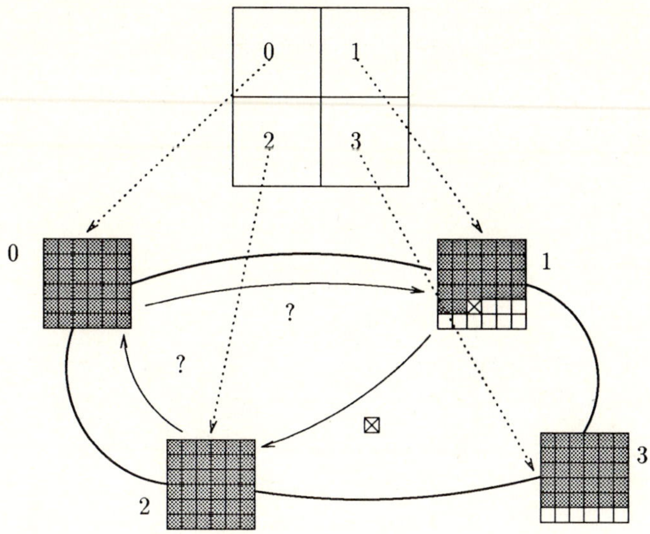


**Fig. 4.** Pixel map distribution and dynamic load balancing

The computation of one pixel $pixel[i, j]$ is a sum of various light contributions $contrib()$ according to the photometric model. Indeed, the recursive nature of the photometric model induces a dependency between the computation for the various contributions to one pixel. Searching all the data $space[a, b, c]$ used for the evaluation of one pixel is equivalent to the ray tracing itself.

We cannot afford to duplicate the database in every node as it will involves a severe limitation on the size of the database we can render. When choosing parallel architectures, the goals are both to speed up the execution and to be able to use larger databases.

The study of models of parallelism which can be implemented on DMPCs [3,32] leads us to advocate the use of a Shared Virtual Memory (SVM) for the parallelization of the ray tracing algorithm. In fact, this paradoxical approach for DMPCs can ensure a efficient distribution of the data while allowing all the nodes to access the entire database. Then, as described in the next section, the load can be balanced dynamically during the execution phase. This approach is classified as a *control oriented* parallelization. In the Section 3.2, we describe how the data is distributed and the management accesses to the SVM which contains the database.

### 3.1 Distributing Computations

In this section we consider the distribution of computation. This distribution must ensure that each processor does roughly the same amount of work. This can be done by distributing pixels among processors. Two approach can be used. The first (called *static scheduling*) consists in subdividing the screen in as many parts as processors. Each processor is responsible for computing all pixels belonging to its part of the screen. This approach is not satisfying because the computation time for every pixel is not the same and consequently the amount of work associated with each processor is not identical. The other approach (called *dynamic scheduling*) consists in assigning pixels to idle processors. As soon as a processor has finished computing a pixel, it asks a server for a new

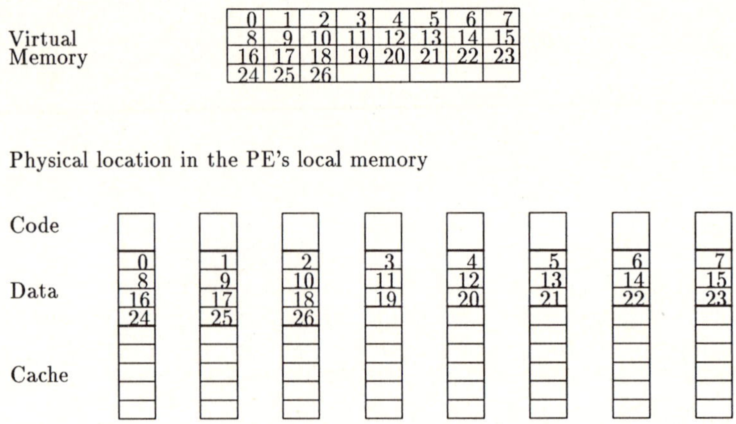


**Fig. 5.** Distribution of a virtual memory

pixel. This solution ensures a balanced load however it does not take into account the ray coherence property which can be used to improve remote data accesses described in the next section. The ray coherence property is showed in Figure 3: two rays shot from the observer through two adjacent pixels have a high probability of intersecting the same objects. This property is also true for all the rays spawned from the two primary ray. The dynamic scheduling technique does not ensure that the same processor treats neighboring pixels. Consequently we advocate the use of a mixture of the two techniques. The static scheduling technique improves the remote data accesses whereas the dynamic scheduling technique solves the load balancing problem.

As shown in Figure 4, each node owns a part of the pixel map. For example, if we use 4 nodes to compute an image with a $512 \times 512$ resolution, each node manages a $256 \times 256$ sub-pixmap. We use a square (or nearly square) sub-pixmap in order to exploit as much as possible the ray coherence property. When a node completes the computation of its sub-pixmap, it sends a request to get a *work item* (i.e. a set of pixels) from a node still working on its own sub-pixmap. This request moves along a ring topology. If this request goes back without satisfaction, the node knows that the image computation is achieved. This local termination detection is sufficient for our application.

In order to insure a balanced load, the only parameter to be determined is the size of this *work item*. If its size is minimal (i.e. work item = one pixel), then we have the best load balance we can obtain, assuming that the computation of one pixel is indivisible over the set of nodes. However the communication cost is high. In balancing the load, we must not generate more work in communication activity than in computation. Experimental results show that a work item about $3 \times 3$ pixels is a good compromise.

### 3.2 Distributing Data

The use of a Shared Virtual Memory for a DMPC was first investigate by K. Li [27]. The large number of nodes allows the use of the combined local memories to store a SVM. In this distributed context, we observe two levels of data access : for each node, the set of node memories represents a larger address space than its own local memory but with slower access. As a remote data access is quite expensive with respect to a local access a cache mechanism must be used in order to increase the ratio of local data accesses.

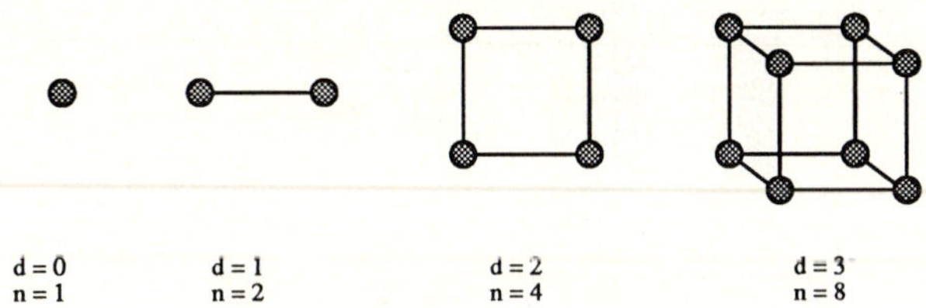


**Fig. 6**. The hypercube topology

In the ray tracing algorithm, the shared database contains the photometric and geometric parameters of the objects of the scene, together with the object access structure. The mechanism we use to manage the virtual shared memory is called *Object Paging* where an *object* (a polygon, a voxel of the grid ... etc) is an item of a *page*. A page is the unit for the data exchange between local memories. The paging mechanism allows uniform virtual memory management independent of the type of objects shared in this memory. An object belongs to one and only one page, and thus its memory location is contiguous.

In our algorithm, the database is first evenly distributed over the set of nodes without any particular strategy. Therefore each node's memory almost contains the same number of pages. Each local memory is divided in three parts: the process code, a part of the database, and the cache memory. The two last parts are divided into pages to allow memory management (Figure 5).

During the synthesis task, the application can potentially access the entire database through a memory management routine. For each node, when a cache miss is detected (i.e., the page is neither in its local database nor in the cache memory) then a request is sent to the node responsible for this page. When the node receive the page, it stores it in its cache memory according to a LRU (Least Recently Used) policy. This search is done during the communication of the new page, and thus causes no extra cost.

The use of these classical mechanisms, data paging and cache memory, has two main advantages: first, they dynamically exploit the data access locality of an algorithm such as ray tracing where data accesses can not be statically determined. This is an improvement parallelization factor. Second, they provide a portable environment which simplifies the parallel code and which can be used as a basis for parallelizing other algorithms.

## 3.3 Experimental Protocol

Results described in Section 3.4 were obtained on an Intel iPSC/2. Processors are linked together according to a hypercube topology (Figure 6). This kind of topology is characterized by a dimension $d$ which is related to the number of processors N by the formula $N = 2^d$. Figure 6 shows how the processors are connected for different values of $d$.

*Architecture of the iPSC/2*

The iPSC/2 system consists of two main components: the cube and the system resource manager (Figure 7).

The cube houses all the nodes which are connected by the hypercube network. It consists of several cabinets (up to 4). Each of them houses up to 32 computational nodes. Each node consists of one Intel 80386 microprocessor augmented by an 80387 floating point co-processor and 4 Mbytes of local memory. It is equipped with the Direct Connect Module (DCM) for high speed routing message between nodes. These communication

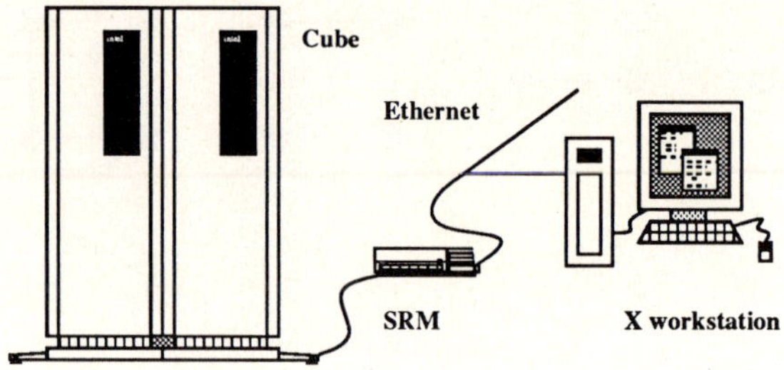


**Fig. 7.** The hypercube iPSC/2

processors allow programmers to view the network as a complete communication graph. Each processor can send a message directly to any other processors. This is very useful for implementing our shared virtual memory because the communication graph is not known in advance.

Software development tools are available on the System Resource Manager (SRM), which is connected via a special link to node 0. The SRM performs compilation, program loading and I/O operations for the cube. A process running on the SRM can act as an X-windows client which allows the display of images on an X-windows server on the ethernet network.

*The NX/2 Operating System*

The operating system of the iPSC/2 is made up of two parts. The first part runs on the SRM and consists of several UNIX processes. Several users can run their programs simultaneously. The operating system splits the cube into sub-cubes. Each of them is assigned to a user. Several commands have been added to allow the management of sub-cubes or parallel processes. The second part is a small kernel called NX/2 which runs on each processor of the cube. This kernel implements an asynchronous communication paradigm. Communication libraries have been added to C and FORTRAN to allow the exchange of messages between nodes and the management of parallel processes. Communication can be blocking, non-blocking or interrupt driven. This latter method is used in our parallel ray tracing algorithm for implementing the virtual shared memory. When a processor receives a request for a page, an interrupt is sent to the user process and a user handler is executed. This handler satisfies the request by sending the page to the processor which requested it.

*Experimenting on Other DMPCs*

Implementing our parallel ray tracing on other DMPCs requires that messages can be sent from a processor to all other processors. This can be done by a communication processor like the iPSC/2 or by the operating system using a *store and forward* message passing mechanism. The virtual shared memory can be implemented either by a communication interrupt driven like the iPSC/2 or by *lightweight* processes. In the latter case, two such processes are needed, one for computing pixels and one for receiving and satisfying page requests. These requirements can be found in a majority of DMPCs and show that our approach is well suited for DMPCs.

*Teapot*

*Mountain*

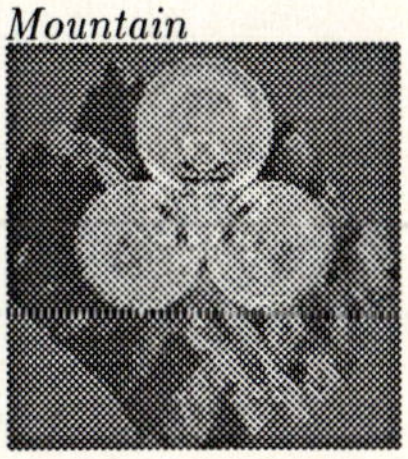

*Rings4*

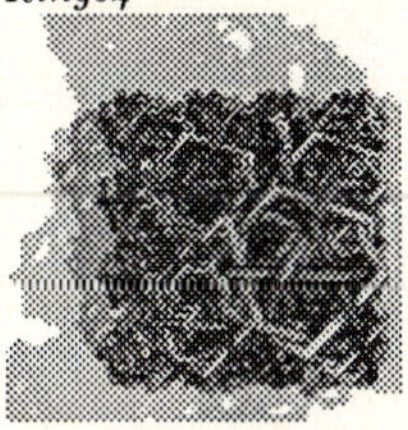

*Tetra10*

| Database | # polygons | # rays | Shared memory size | average pages/pixel |
|---|---|---|---|---|
| *Teapot* | 3 754 | 1 397 473 | 793 Kbytes | 58.19 |
| *Mountain* | 9 920 | 1 722 415 | 2 031 Kbytes | 61.94 |
| *Rings4* | 18 002 | 1 872 991 | 4 632 Kbytes | 125.91 |
| *Tetra9* | 262 144 | 303 239 | 36 189 Kbytes | 17.45 |
| *Tetra10* | 1 048 576 | 300 962 | 138 851 Kbytes | 33.00 |

**Table 1**. Databases characteristics and the rendering result

| 1 | 2 | 4 | 8 | 16 | 32 | 64 | |
|---|---|---|---|---|---|---|---|
| 3h12mn2s | 1h39mn57s | 51mn32s | 26mn05s | 13mn06s | 6mn35s | 3mn20s | *Teapot* |
| 4h45mn3s | 2h30mn38s | 1h17mn06s | 39mn10s | 19mn45s | 10mn00s | 5mn07s | *Mount.* |
| | 4h58mn46s | 2h33mn24s | 1h17mn35s | 38mn56s | 19mn41s | 10mn04s | *Rings4* |
| | | | | 4mn55s | 2mn26s | 1mn18s | *Tetra9* |
| | | | | | | 3mn46s | *Tetra10* |

**Table 2**. Synthesis times for an image resolution of 512 × 512 pixels

### 3.4 Results

Our experiments have been performed using a set of scenes called *Standard Procedural Databases* (SPD) provided by Eric Haines [20] and the famous *Teapot* from the university of Utah. These databases are presented in Table 1. Because of their geometric and the photometric diversity, they constitute a representative test set.

Synthesis times are shown in Table 2. A first result is that the distribution of the database enables the rendering of scenes like *Tetra10* which lies far beyond the memory capacity of one node. However as a result it is difficult to analyze the behavior of the algorithm for such large databases which cannot be executed with a small number of node. For small databases, the measurement of the parallel efficiency is straightforward while for the large databases it requires the use of a profile analysis to estimate the parallel overhead. For the test set, using up to 64 nodes, we always obtain an efficiency better than 78%. This work is presented in [3].

Following up on this encouraging result, in this paper, we will focus on an experiment which has given some interesting information concerning the behavior of our algorithm: We present some measurements of algorithm behavior as a function of cache size (the size of a page is 1Kbytes). These results are given in Figure 8. They illustrate the efficiency, the miss ratio and the page communication for various sizes for the cache memory. On these graphs, we represent 50% as a threshold below which the efficiency can be (arbitrarily) considered insufficient. Using a cache memory, when the number of pages becomes very small, it results a large cache fault ratio (or miss ratio) which entails a large number of page communications (Figure 8).

Between the different tested databases, *Rings4* and *Tetra9* represents the two extremes behavior: *Tetra9* uses a small average number of pages per pixel (17.45) and thus can be efficiently rendered with a small size for the cache, while *Rings4* which uses the greatest average number of pages per pixel (125.91) requires a larger cache memory to keep above the efficiency threshold (50%).

Concerning the evolution of the miss ratio, we notice that when using all the node memory capacity (about 3.2 Mbytes/node for the shared virtual memory management), we are far from the miss ratio corresponding to the critical threshold, and thus far from the network saturation. This saturation has been obtained with the *Rings4* database when using only 204 pages for the cache (Figure 8.3). Bomans [7] have shown that the peak communication rate on the iPSC/2 is 0.9 Mbytes/sec when using message size of 1 Kbytes (our page size), while the absolute peak communication rate is 2.75 Mbytes/sec. Thus we notice that the peak performance we have measured corresponds to about 70% of the network for this message size (and around 23% with respect to the absolute peak communication rate).

If we reduce the cache size once more, the communication performance decreases: this phenomenon corresponds to a network congestion similar to the *Hot Spot* which appears when using shared memory architectures [1].

## 4 Implementing a SVM on DMPCs

The SVM described in this paper is implemented inside the ray tracing algorithm, therefore it is easily portable on other DMPCs. However, the management of pages, the use of high level communication primitives and satisfying page requests add substantial overheads. In order to minimize these overheads, SVM can be incorporated in the operating system or can be implemented by designing special VLSI devices.

### 4.1 An Operating System Approach

Incorporating the SVM inside the operating system allows the use of fast, low-level communication primitives and the Memory Management Unit (MMU) available in each node. In a paper by K. Li and R. Schaefer [27], a SVM for an iPSC/2 is presented. They use the MMU of the Intel 80386 to yield a large virtual address instead of physical addresses for memory references. The virtual address space is a set of pages, each of which has a size of 4096 bytes. A 128 nodes iPSC/2 with 16 Mbytes of local memory allows a virtual shared address space up to 2 Gigabytes. Their results show that a kernel implementation can provide at least 23% improvement. We are working on such an implementation. Our approach differs in that it uses very low-level communication primitives which bypass the NX/2 protocol.

Unfortunately, this approach cannot be implemented on transputer-based machines due to the lack of a memory management unit.

### 4.2 A Hardware Approach

The implementation of a SVM requires that each processor is able to respond as soon as possible to page requests coming from other processors. Therefore, user tasks are often interrupted for replying to these requests. Special VLSI devices can be designed for doing this task. This approach is similar to the one which consists of implementing the routing

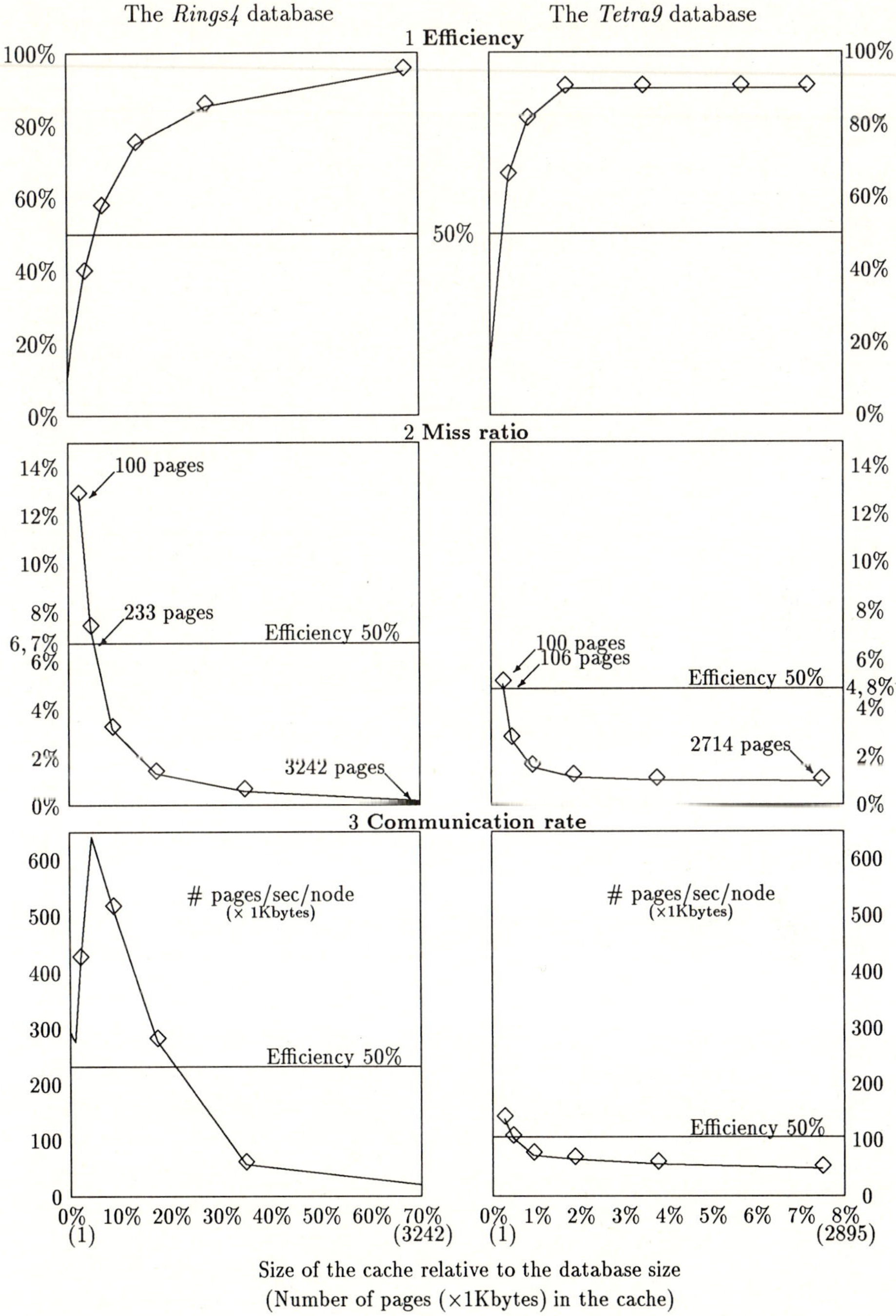


**Fig. 8**. Efficiency, cache miss, and page communication curves with respect to cache size

algorithm in VLSI router chip. In recent papers, R. Bisiani and M. Ravishankar present the PLUS machine [5,6] which is a distributed memory architecture. Global memory mapping and coherence management are performed by a hardware module implemented with PLD's and PAL's. The topology of the PLUS machine is a mesh. Routing is performed by a mesh router from Caltech. This architecture will offer the advantage of DMPC (simple design, scalability) and SMPC (easy programming).

## 5 Conclusion

In this paper, we have described a parallel scheme which appears quite paradoxical for a DMPC: the use of a Shared Virtual Memory to manage a distributed database. In fact, this mechanism efficiently exploits all the distributed resources of these architectures : computation, storage and communication resources.

Our current work concerns the implementation of the SVM in the kernel of the NX/2 operating system [26]. This implementation is based on the hardware MMU of the node processor (Intel 80386) which supports a virtual address space. We hope to obtain better absolute synthesis times by exploiting the fact that the virtual to physical address translations which were made by software will be faster using the MMU.

## Remarks

Concerning distribution, VM_pRAY (the ray tracing algorithm described in this paper) can be obtained by anonymous FTP on *irisa.irisa.fr (131.254.2.3)* in the directory iPSC2/VM_pRAY. Scenes in NFF format are available in iPSC2/NFF. A copy of VM_pRAY may also be obtained by sending electronic mail to either : `badouel@irisa.fr` or `priol@irisa.fr` for those who do not have access to `fnet`.

## References


[1] G. Almasi and A. Gottlieb.: *Highly Parallel Computing.* ISBN 0-8053-0177-1. Benjamin Cummings, 1983.

[2] B. Arnaldi, T. Priol, and K. Bouatouch.: A new space subdivision for ray tracing CSG modelled scenes. *The Visual Computer*, 3(2):98–108, August 1987.

[3] D. Badouel.: *Schémas d'exécution pour les machines parallèles à mémoire distribuée. Une étude de cas : le lancer de rayon.* PhD thesis, Université de Rennes I - IFSIC, Rennes, October 1990.

[4] D. Badouel, K. Bouatouch, and T. Priol.: Ray tracing on distributed memory parallel computers: strategies for distributing computations and data. In S. Whitman, editor, *Parallel Algorithms and architectures for 3D Image Generation*, pages 185–198. ACM Siggraph'90 Course 28, August 1990.

[5] R. Bisiani and M. Ravishankar.: Plus: A distributed shared-memory system. In *17th International Symposium on Computer Architecture*, May 1990.

[6] R. Bisiani and M. Ravishankar.: Programming the PLUS Distributed-Memory System. In *Fifth Distributed Memory Computing Conference*, 1990.

[7] L. Bomans and D. Roose.: Communication Benchmarks for the iPSC/2. In F. André and J.P. Verjus, editors, *Hypercube and Distributed Computers*, pages 93–103, Rennes, France, October 1989. INRIA.

[8] K. Bouatouch, M. O. Madani, T. Priol, and B. Arnaldi.: A new algorithm of space tracing using a CSG model. In *Eurographics'87*, August 1987.

[9] C. Bouville, R. Brusq, J. L. Dubois, and I. Marchal.: Synthèse d'images par lancer de rayons: algorithmes et architecture. *Acta Electronica*, 26(3-4):249–259, 1984.

[10] E. Caspary and I. D. Scherson.: A self balanced parallel ray tracing algorithm. In *Parallel Processing for Computer Vision and Display*, UK, January 1988. University of Leeds.

[11] J. G. Cleary, B. Wyvill, G. Birtwistle, and R. Vatti.: Multiprocessor ray tracing. Research Report 83/128/17, University of Calgary, October 1983.

[12] R. L. Cook and K. E. Torrance.: A reflectance model for computer graphics. *ACM Transactions on Graphics*, 1(1):7–24, January 1982.

[13] M. Dippé and J. Swensen.: An adaptative subdivision algorithm and parallel architecture for realistic image synthesis. In *SIGGRAPH'84*, pages 149–157, New York, 1984.

[14] A. Fujimoto, T. Tanaka, and K. Iwata.: ARTS: Accelerated ray_tracing system. *IEEE Computer Graphics and Applications*, 6(4):16–26, April 1986.

[15] A. S. Glassner.: Space subdivision for fast ray tracing. *IEEE Computer Graphics and Applications*, 4(10):15–22, October 1984.

[16] J. Goldsmith and J. Salmon.: Automatic creation of object hierarchies for ray tracing. *IEEE Computer Graphics and Applications*, pages 14–20, May 1987.

[17] S. Green and D. Paddon.: Exploiting coherence for multiprocessor ray tracing. *IEEE Computer Graphics and Applications*, 6:12–26, November 1989.

[18] S. Green and D. Paddon.: A highly flexible multiprocessor solution for ray tracing. *Visual Computer*, 5(6):62–73, March 1990.

[19] S. Green, D. Paddon, and E. Lewis.: A parallel algorithm and tree-based computer architecture for ray traced computer graphics. In *Parallel Processing for Computer Vision and Display*, UK, January 1988. University of Leeds.

[20] E. Haines.: A proposal for standard graphics environments. *IEEE Computer Graphics and Applications*, 7(11):3–5, November 1987.

[21] R. Hall and D. Greenberg.: A testbed for realistic image synthesis. *IEEE Computer Graphics and Applications*, 3(8):10–20, November 1983.

[22] D. Jevans.: Optimistic multi-processor ray tracing. In em Computer Graphics 1989 (Proceedings of CGI'89), pages 507–522, Leeds, 1989.

[23] M. Kaplan.: Space-tracing, a constant time ray tracer. In *SIGGRAPH'85 tutorial on the uses of spatial coherence in ray tracing*, 1985.

[24] T. Kay and J. Kajiya.: Ray tracing complex scenes. *ACM Computer Graphics*, 20(4):269–278, August 1986.

[25] H. Kobayashi, T. Nakamura, and Y. Shigei.: A strategy for mapping parallel ray-tracing into a hypercube multiprocessor system. In *Computer Graphics International'88*, pages 160–169. Computer Graphics Society, May 1988.

[26] Z. Lahjomri.: Mise en œuvre d'une mémoire virtuelle distribuée sur l'iPSC/2. Rapport de DEA. Institut de Formation Supérieure en Informatique et Communication (IFSIC). Rennes, September 1990.

[27] K. Li and R. Schaefer.: A hypercube shared virtual memory system. In *1989 International Conference on Parallel Processing*, pages 125–132, 1989.

[28] T. Naruse, M. Yoshida, T. Takahashi, and S. Naito.: Sight : A dedicated computer graphics machine. *Computer Graphics Forum*, 6(4):327–334, 1987.

[29] K. Nemoto and T. Omachi.: An adaptative subdivision by sliding boundary surfaces for fast ray tracing. In *Graphics Interface'86*, pages 43–48, May 1986.

[30] H. Nishimura, H. Ohno, T. Kawata, I. Shirakawa, and K. Omuira.: Links-1: A parallel pipelined multimicrocomputer system for image creation. In *Proc. of the 10th Symp. on Computer Architecture*, pages 387–394, 1983.

[31] M. Potmesil and E. Hoffert.: The pixel machine : A parallel image computer. In *SIGGRAPH'89*, Boston, 1989. ACM.

[32] T. Priol.: *Lancer de rayon sur des architectures parallèles : étude et mise en œuvre*. PhD thesis, Institut de Formation Supérieure en Informatique et Communication, Rennes, June 1989.

[33] S. Roth.: Ray casting for modeling solids. *Computer Graphics and Image Processing*, 18(2):109–144, February 1982.

[34] T. Takahashi, M. Yoshida, and T. Naruse.: Architecture and performance evaluation of the dedicated graphics computer : SIGHT. In *COMPINT'87*, pages 153–160. IEEE, November 1987.

[35] T. Whitted.: An improved illmination model for shaded display. *Computer Graphics and Image Processing*, 23(6):343–349, June 1980.

# Part III

## Visualization Systems

# Building a Full Scale VLSI-Based Volume Visualization System

Reuven Bakalash, Arie Kaufman and Zhong Xu

ABSTRACT The hardware realization of an advanced prototype of the Cube volume visualization system, Cube-3, is presented. The primary hardware component of Cube is a viewing and rendering multiprocessor with distributed 3D voxel memory. Cube-3 design is based on our experience with two earlier prototypes: Cube-1 realized in hardware using printed circuit board technology and Cube-2 our first custom-designed VLSI implementation. Both prototypes are of reduced-size resolution ($16^3$) and can generate only orthographic views. Cube-3 is the next generation prototype of a full-scale resolution of $256^3$ voxels. It has been functionally extended to generate non-orthographic projections, 3D real-time transformations, and shading. The ability to project and manipulate volumetric images in real-time is attributed to a unique skewed memory organization, a generalized skewed mapping, a special ray projection bus, a congradient shading technique, and a new barrel-shifting mechanism. This paper specifically describes the latter mechanism.

## 1 Background

The Cube architecture [11] is a voxel-based architecture for 3D volumetric graphics. A volumetric object is typically represented as a large 3D grid of volume elements, or as they are called in short, *voxels*. The voxels may be derived from discrete samples of the physical phenomenon, from a scientific or engineering simulation, or they may be synthesized by the computer from a geometric model.

The voxel representation is very effective for the traditional applications employing sampled 3D voxel imagery, such as medical imaging (e.g., CT, MRI, and ultrasonography) [2, 4, 5, 7], geology (e.g., seismic data) [18], biology (e.g., confocal microscopy) [8, 9], and molecular systems (e.g., electron density maps [6]). Cube also caters to the traditional 3D graphics synthesis applications, such as computer aided design (e.g., solid modeling) [10], 3D simulation and animation (e.g., instrumentation simulation, flight simulation), and scientific volume visualization (e.g., fluid dynamics [16, 17]). The Cube approach is further effective when sampled data are intermixed with geometric data [13].

The Cube architecture is organized around a large 3D cubic frame buffer (CFB) of voxels and is comprised of three processors. These processors access the CFB to input sampled and synthetic data [14], manipulate [12], project [15], and render [3] the CFB images. In order to manage the huge quantity of voxels, the Cube architecture is equipped with several special features, such as parallel processing, incremental algorithms, a modular memory for parallel access, and a modular multiple-write bus for speeding up the viewing process. The viewing bus, called the Voxel Multiple-Write Bus (VMWB), selects the opaque voxel closest to the observer [11]. The selection time is proportional to the length in bits of the depth index, that is, $\log n$, where $n$ is the resolution. It is implemented as a multiprocessor of $n$ processing units.

A reduced-resolution hardware prototype, Cube-1, of $16^3$ resolution was realized first. It is a printed-circuit 16-board hardware assembly driven by an interface board which is hooked-up directly to an IBM-AT bus. The prototype has been operating successfully in true real-time, generating 20,000 orthographic projections per second and over 3,000 arbitrary 3D rotations per second [11].

## 2 Cube-2—The First VLSI Implementation

The modular nature of the Cube architecture is well suited for VLSI implementation. Such an implementation enhances the operating speeds, minimizes the physical dimensions, and lowers the hardware cost. The Cube-1 circuit design was used as the basis for the VLSI chip design of the Cube-2 VLSI prototype. Each Cube-1 board (i.e., module) was converted into a single Cube-2 chip. Each chip consists of a memory module with $16^3$ bytes, an addressing system with mapping and de-mapping mechanisms, a projection processing unit, a VMWB unit, translucency control, and depth sectioning. The circuit was redesigned to meet the special requirements of the VLSI.

Two major concerns that were met in the redesign of the Cube for VLSI are pin count and testability. In order to limit the pin count to 40, the I/O lines of the module were reduced by moving several functions from the interface board to the chip. It was done at the cost of replicating some of the interface logic circuits in all the modules. Testing the chip requires access to its internal functions: the memory, the addressing logic, the control status, etc., in addition to all the I/Os of the chip. This is in conflict with the pin count reduction. Therefore, nine test points were multiplexed with some input pins, with additional pin selecting test or input mode. Unlike the printed-circuit version of Cube-1, where the ID number of each module board has been set by proper wiring, in Cube-2 a special ID register has been added on the chip, which is initialized by a boot sequence.

The VLSI was designed on SUN workstations using Magic for the layout and simulation. The chips were fabricated by MOSIS in 2.0 micron double metal CMOS/Bulk technology, using a 40 DIP package. Each chip is comprised of a logic part, which occupies 40% of its space, and a $256 \times 8$ static memory on 60% of it. In total, there are about 14,000 transistors on the chip, with an overall area of $3.4 \times 4.6^2$mm. Figure 1 is a photo of the Cube-2 chip.

A special testbench has been constructed to test the basic functionalities of the chip. After correcting the first version and refabricating, we found that nine chips out of twelve were mostly functional. The final version of the VLSI chip is currently being fabricated. The whole Cube integrated circuit assembly occupies a single board, while the interface unit occupies another board. The Cube-2 system, located entirely on these two boards, will reside in an IBM-AT computer, which will be used as its host. The interface unit intermediates between the host and the Cube logic. It interprets commands given by the user and forwards them to the Cube logic board as control signals, initializes the identification numbers of the modules, creates scan sequences, and acquires the projection data from the CFB and moves it to the host. An operating environment, including software drivers and user interface, is being written on the IBM-AT, which uses its VGA graphics system to run the VLSI assembly as a satellite of an IBM-AT computer.

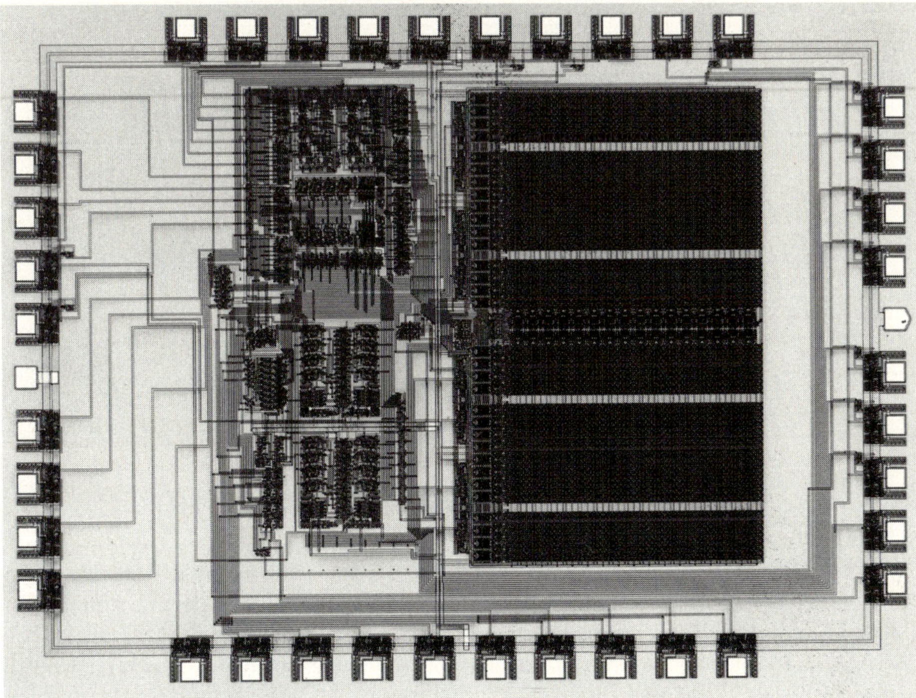

**Fig. 1.** Custom-designed VLSI chip of Cube-2

## 3 Cube-3—A Full-Scale Real-Time System

The next Cube generation is a VLSI-based prototype of a medium resolution of $256^3$, called Cube-3. Each chip of this prototype will be of medium size $(6.9 \times 6.8)^2$mm with 84 pins, and will include two processing units. Consequently, the prototype will require a total of 128 identical chips that will work in parallel.

The hardware of Cube-3 will run all our software systems and applications developed within the Cube research framework in real-time. The Cube-3 prototype will allow us to complete the development cycle of the system. Its purpose is threefold:

- to examine the feasibility of implementing in VLSI a volume visualization system with a working resolution of $256^3$, and to test it in real applications such as biomedical imaging, CAD, simulation, and scientific visualization;
- to measure the speeds attainable with such a resolution and to evaluate the system for interactive use;
- to test the hardware implementation of several new mechanisms developed recently for the Cube architecture.

The new mechanism includes: viewing from a non-orthographic direction using a generalized skewed mapping and parallel organization of the memory (see [15] for more details); transforming (e.g., rotating) 3D rooms (subcubes) by employing a barrel shifter; and discrete shading that employs a gradient-based table-driven technique [3].

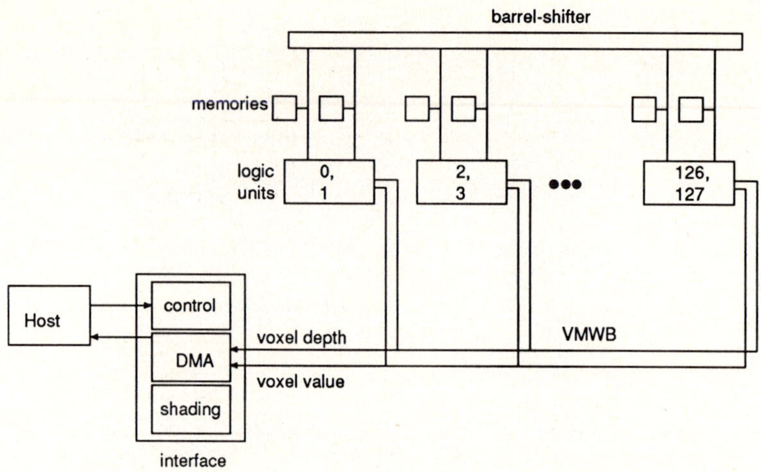


**Fig. 2.** The functional components of Cube-3

Cube-3 is a functionally extended version of Cube-2, which will include five basic components: interface, 256 logic modules, 256 memory modules, a barrel shifter, and a shading unit. The functional elements of the system are depicted in Figure 2. The interface, in addition to its basic intermediating function as in the previous versions, will control the barrel shifter and its data path, will manage a DMA communication with the host computer to speed up the transformation of the projected and shaded data, and will supervise the shading process.

Unlike Cube-2, the modular logic and the memory will be separated to minimize the cost, pin count, and chip area, and to increase reliability. The VLSI logic chips, two processing units on each, will include the addressing logic, the transparency and clipping controls, and the VMWB competition unit. The memory will be implemented using off-the-shelf standard $256^3$ byte chips.

The barrel shifter is a network interconnection between 256 pairs of processors and memories. A simultaneous shifting of 8 bits of data in any arbitrary distance among the 256 modules would normally require 256 buses or a large crossbar matrix of $256 \times 256$ paths, 8 bit each. Since both alternatives are not realistic because of their complexity, a special interprocessor communication network was developed [1]. A significant reduction in communication area was achieved by implementing bidirectional moves. In such a case, rotation to the right by $k$ units, when $k > 256/2$, can be performed with leftward rotation of $(256 - k)$ units. Another reduction was gained by dividing long rotations into smaller simultaneous rotational steps (but without the need for an intermediate reloading of the data). Thus, a rotation requires $k/s$ steps (clocks), where $s$ is the size of the step. The longest rotation is performed in $128/s$ clocks. Establishing such steps results in a desirable division of the entire communication network into small and modular building-blocks, implementable in VLSI.

The barrel shifter, shown in Figure 3, implements the divided modular mechanism based on a special flow-through network that interconnects among the modules. Its basic component is a modular barrel-switch unit (BSU) that is serving $s$ pairs of clients (processors and memories), receiving from each a single bit of data ($s$ bits in total) and shifting it on. A general width of $w$ bits of data requires $w$ duplicates of the BSUs at each group of

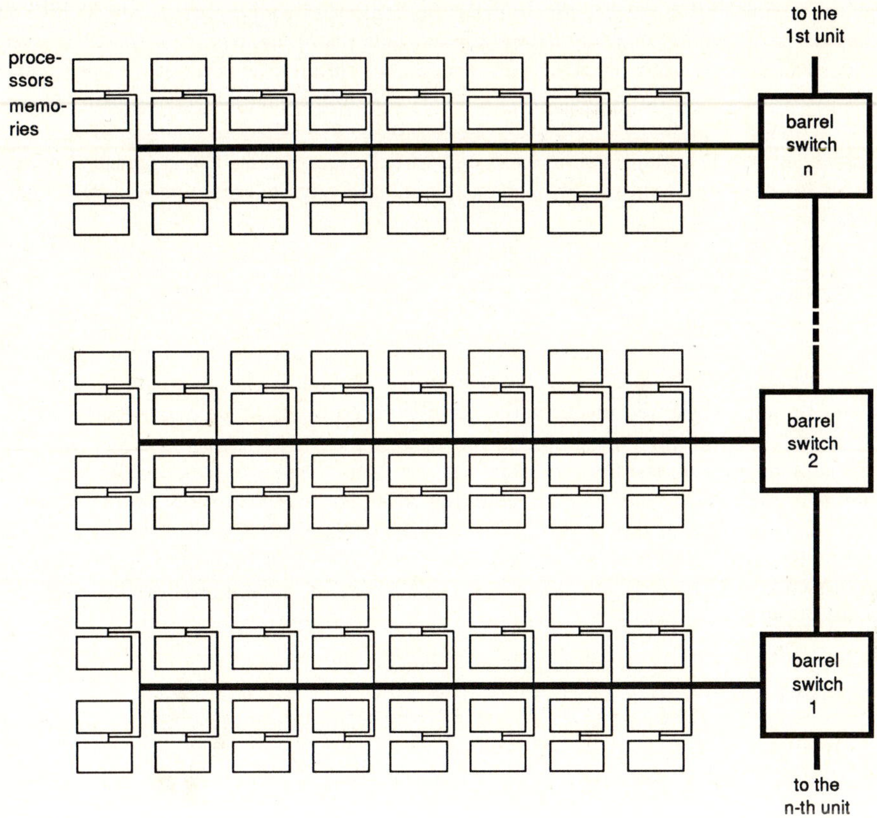


**Fig. 3**. The barrel-shift interconnection network

clients. This layout provides modularity and flexibility of the entire network. The network is extendible in its overall length, by serially connecting arbitrary numbers of BSUs, and in data width, by stacking up any number of BS units, one layer per data bit. The BSUs are organized in a simple and repetitive pattern of junction elements and connection paths, which is well suited for VLSI implementation. Each BSU will be implemented as a custom-designed VLSI chip. The barrel shift array counts about 2500 transistors. Adding the decoder, control circuits, and I/O pads to it totals 4000 transistors and 64 pins per chip.

Arbitrary data moves along the network have a unique meaning of real-time 3D graphics transformations. Typically, geometrical transformations in 3D systems are accomplished by a time-consuming matrix multiplication. In contrast, Cube employs the barrel shifter, a beam-based transformation in which intermodular data shifts along the beam result in a spatial transformation. For example, a 3D rotation about a primary axis is performed as a 2D rotation of beams parallel to the axis, where a beam is retrieved from the CFB, barrel shifted to reflect the rotation modulo 256 pertaining to the new location of the beam, and then pushed back into the CFB modules.

The real-time congradient shading [3], developed as part of the Cube project, will be implemented on the interface board. The hardware structure of the congradient shading includes a triple shift register, which holds the depth and color values of the voxel being processed and a whole scan-line before and a whole scan-line after it, so that the voxel's two horizontal and vertical neighbors are readily available for computing the gradient. The shift registers are implemented by memory and additional addressing logic. Congradient shading is a table-driven, depth-gradient, volumetric shading technique, which uses a predefined set of surface gradients stored in a look-up table. Congradient shading is suitable for real-time hardware implementation, operating as a pipeline with the viewing process.

## 4 Summary

We described the complete sequence of the Cube hardware realizations. The first implementation—Cube-1—$16^3$ resolution using printed circuit technology, verified the basic concepts of the unique skewed memory, the parallel access, and the parallel processing of an orthographic beam. Since the modular nature of the Cube architecture is well suited for VLSI implementation, the next natural step was a $16^3$ resolution custom-designed VLSI implementation. The experience accumulated with the two first prototypes has been applied to the design of the full-scale $256^3$ system, Cube-3, which is currently under development. Cube-3 will be able to run in real-time the interactive Cube software environment, the 3D user interface, and the applications (e.g., biological [9] and medical [2]), developed as part of the Cube project.

## Acknowledgements

This project has been supported by the National Science Foundation under grants MIP-8805130 and MIP-9049094 and grants from Hewlett Packard. We would like to thank David R. Smith for his invaluable advice concerning the VLSI design and testing.

## References

[1] Bakalash, R. and Xu, Z.: Barrel Shift Microsystem for Parallel Processing, *Proc. Micro 23, 23rd Symposium and Workshop on Microprogramming and Microarchitecture*, Orlando, Florida, November 1990.

[2] Bakalash, R. and Kaufman, A.: MediCube: a 3D Medical Imaging Architecture, *Computers & Graphics*, 13, 2 (1989), 151-157.

[3] Cohen, D., Kaufman, A., Bakalash, R. and Bergman, S.: Real-Time Discrete Shading, *The Visual Computer*, 6, 1 (February 1990), 16-27.

[4] Farrell, E. J., Yang, W. C. and Zappulla, R. A.: Animated 3D CT Imaging, *IEEE Computer Graphics and Applications*, 5, 12 (December 1985), 26-32.

[5] Goldwasser, S. M., Reynolds, R. A., Bapty, T., Baraff, D., Summers, J., Talton, D. A. and Walsh, E.: Physician's Workstation with Real-Time Performance, *IEEE Computer Graphics & Applications*, 5, 12 (December 1985), 44-57.

[6] Goodsell, D. S., Mian, S. and Olson, A. J.: Rendering of Volumetric Data in Molecular Systems, *Journal of Molecular Graphics*, 7, (March 1989), 41-47.

[7] Hoehne, K. H., Bomans, M., Tiede, U. and Riemer, M.: Display of Multiple 3D-Objects using the Generalized Voxel-Model, *Proceedings of SPIE, Medical Imaging II*, 914, (1988), 850-854.

[8] Jense, G. J. and Huijsmans, D. P.: Interactive Voxel-Based Graphics for 3D Reconstruction of Biological Structures, *Computers & Graphics*, 13, 2 (1989), 145-150.

[9] Kaufman, A., Yagel, R., Bakalash, R. and Spector, I.: Volume Visualization in Cell Biology, *Proceedings Visualization '90*, San Francisco, CA, October 1990, 160-167.

[10] Kaufman, A.: Voxel-Based Solid Modeling, *Proc. International Conference on CAD/CAM and AMT*, Jerusalem, Israel, December 1989, 1.1.3-1-3.

[11] Kaufman, A. and Bakalash, R.: Memory and Processing Architecture for 3-D Voxel-Based Imagery, *IEEE Computer Graphics & Applications*, 8, 6 (November 1988), 10-23.

[12] Kaufman, A.: The voxblt Engine: A Voxel Frame Buffer Processor, in *Advances in Graphics Hardware III*, A. A. M. Kuijk and W. Strasser, (eds.), Springer-Verlag, Berlin, 1989.

[13] Kaufman, A., Yagel, R. and Cohen, D.: Intermixing Surface and Volume Rendering, in *3D Imaging in Medicine: Algorithms, Systems, Applications*, K. H. Hoehne, H. Fuchs and S. M. Pizer, (eds.), June 1990, 217-227.

[14] Kaufman, A. and Shimony, E.: 3D Scan-Conversion Algorithms for Voxel-Based Graphics, *Proceedings ACM Workshop on Interactive 3D Graphics*, Chapel Hill, NC, October 1986, 45-76.

[15] Kaufman, A., Bakalash, R. and Cohen, D.: Viewing and Rendering Processor for a Volume Visualization System, in *Advances in Graphics Hardware IV*, R. L. Grimsdale and W. Strasser, (eds.), Springer-Verlag, 1991, 171-178.

[16] Shirley, P. and Neeman, H.: Volume Visualization at the Center for Supercomputing Research and Development, *Proceedings of the Chapel Hill Workshop on Volume Visualization*, Chapel Hill, NC, May 1989, 17-20.

[17] Upson, C. and Keeler, M.: V-BUFFER: Visible Volume Rendering, *Computer Graphics*, 22, 4 (August 1988), 59-64.

[18] Wolfe, R. H. and Liu, C. N.: Interactive Visualization of 3D Seismic Data: A Volumetric Method, *IEEE Computer Graphics & Applications*, 8, 7 (July 1988), 24-30.

# Correct Shading of Regularized CSG Solids Using a Depth-Interval Buffer

Jaroslaw R. Rossignac and Jeffrey Wu

ABSTRACT A convenient interactive design environment requires efficient facilities for shading solid models represented in CSG. Shading techniques based on boundary evaluation or ray casting that require calculations of geometric intersections are too inefficient for interactive graphics when CSG primitives with curved (parametric) surfaces are involved. Projective approaches, where the primitive surfaces are scan-converted using standard hardware-supported graphic functions are preferred. Since not all the points of the faces of a CSG primitive lie on the CSG solid, scan conversion must be combined with a procedure that tests the produced 3D surface-points against the original CSG expression. Point classifications against primitives defined by arbitrary curved boundaries may be performed, without geometric intersections, through depth-comparisons at each pixel. This approach has been implemented for the Pixel-Power machine by researchers at UNC. It deals with complex CSG trees by converting CSG expressions into sum-of-product form and repeatedly scan-converting the primitives of each product. The Trickle algorithm, which considerably reduces the number of scan-conversions in the general case has been developed at IBM Research and presented elsewhere. This paper discusses several recent improvements to the original Trickle algorithm. The overall algorithm has been simplified. The scan-conversion process and the point classification tests have been modified to correctly handle cases where several primitive faces coincide within an arbitrary numerical resolution. These enhancements are not only necessary for on/on cases in regularized Boolean expressions, but also for processing pairs of faces near their common edges. Finally, we point out that a simple two-pass extension of the trickle algorithm using an auxiliary shadow buffer suffices to compute directly from CSG shaded images with shadows.

## 1 Introduction

Mechanical parts commonly designed in CAD systems are seldom polyhedral and only in rare cases can be expressed as extrusions of 2D contours. Three-dimensional design techniques are thus necessary. The most popular technique for interactively designing models of 3D mechanical parts is Constructive Solid Geometry (abbreviated CSG), where designers construct solid models by combining sub-solids or parameterized primitive volumes through regularized Boolean expressions [1]. Such CSG specification is typically parsed and stored in a CSG tree, or more precisely a binary directed rooted acyclic graph. The internal nodes of the graph correspond to regularized set theoretic Boolean operators (union, intersection, or difference) and define sub-solids. The root defines the entire solid—typically a semi-algebraic three-dimensional r-set, which could be empty or composed of disconnected volumes. Terminal leaves of the graph represent parametric primitive shapes, which in traditional CSG-based systems were restricted to be intersections of planar or simple quadric half-spaces, such as cylinders or spheres. The graph is not Necessarily a tree since the same sub-solid may be used several times in the final Boolean expression. Although the graph can always be expanded into a tree, a systematic expansion should be avoided, especially when dealing with CSG definitions containing many instances of complex CSG sub-solids.

Often CSG graphs also contain linear transformations (often restricted to rigid body motions) that define the relative position of children nodes with respect to the parent node's local coordinate systems. The effect of these transformations are usually combined during tree traversal and propagated all the way down to the primitives to establish their final positions. The correct processing of these transformations is trivially combined with the approach described here and will not be discussed any further. We shall simply assume that the final position of each primitive instance is known whenever necessary.

CSG graphs can be conveniently edited by simply changing the Boolean expression or the primitives' type, position, orientation, or size parameters. Other representations, such as a boundary graph, are much more difficult to edit without endangering their validity. CSG is thus the preferred medium for performing an incremental (trial-and-error) design process. Interactive editing requires interactive feedback to guide the designers towards the desired solution. Interactive graphic from CSG is thus an essential component of the design process and shaded images have become the de facto standard for visualizing solid models. Several techniques for shading CSG solids have been reported.

### 1.1 Boundary Tesselation

CSG graphs may be converted into a boundary representation by boundary evaluation procedures [2] which computes edges and vertices by intersecting surfaces. Then, the bounding faces may, for example, be tesselated and rendered as a triangular mesh. The boundary evaluation is usually very time consuming, especially if higher degree implicit or parametric surfaces are involved. Tesselation is also delicate, because one must ensure that no cracks or overshooting occurs near the intersection edges.

### 1.2 Primitives' Tesselation

To avoid dealing with complex and expensive surface intersection and boundary tesselation procedures, many commercial solid modellers tesselate the primitives prior to the boundary evaluation. Good accuracy requires a large number of facets, and thus boosts up the cost of boundary evaluation, without even guaranteeing topological consistency. Furthermore, independent tesselations of coincident curved faces of different primitives may not be aligned properly creating models that topologically do not correspond to the designer's intent and that may even be invalid models for solids, due to numerical problems.

### 1.3 Ray-casting on CSG

Ray casting can be used directly on CSG, thus bypassing the expensive and delicate boundary evaluation, because the original 3D CSG expressions may be localized to each single ray, in which case it combines one-dimensional intervals obtained as intersections of the ray with the primitive solids [3]. Using these 1D models, the first point (along the viewing direction) on the ray that lies on the actual intersection of the ray with the solid can be easily computed. Efficient direct approaches for shading from CSG through ray-casting have been developed in software. They have been optimized for facetted models [4,5,6]. A hardware implementation exists for Boolean combinations of quadric half-spaces [7,8]. However, ray-casting involves computing a large number of ray/surface intersections and becomes particularly inefficient when higher degree algebraic or parametric surfaces are involved.

### 1.4 Projective Methods with Software Classification

Since, for parametric formulations, surface evaluation is faster than ray/surface intersection calculation, scan conversion techniques with (adaptive) tesselation of primitive surfaces have been used for shading boundary models. A hardware depth-buffer can be used for automatically selecting the visible faces. Because the faces of a CSG solid are not directly available, the depth-buffer visibility test must be combined with a trimming process that selects the portions of primitive faces that lie on the solid.

A software implementation of this selection has been combined with a depth-buffer test in [9] and works as follows. A point P on a front-facing face of a primitive A is first compared to the depth stored in the z-buffer of the corresponding pixel. If P is in front of what is stored in the z-buffer, it is 'classified', i.e., tested, against the CSG graph. Points on the boundary of the solid are rendered into the z-buffer. Outside points out are discarded. A point inside the solid will be automatically rejected by the z-buffer visibility test. Therefore, one can improve performance and avoid testing P against certain primitives in the graph, by classifying P against the I-zone of A, which is the intersection of a subset of the nodes of the original CSG graph [10]. If P lies inside the I-zone of A, it lies on the final solid or inside it. The software selection described in [9] classifies points against solid primitives by evaluating, at the tested points, the implicit functions that define the half-spaces bounding the primitive volumes. (Typically, a primitive is the intersection of such half-spaces. For example, a truncated cylinder is the intersection of one quadric half-space with two planar half-spaces.) These classification results are then combined up the tree according to the Boolean expression of the I-zone of the particular primitive on which the classified point lies.

### 1.5 Projective Methods with Z-buffer Classification

When sculptured primitives are used in the CSG expression (for example, primitives defined in terms of their boundary composed of trimmed NURBS surfaces), no set of implicit equations are available for classifying points against the primitive. As mentioned earlier, software implementation of such classification (for example through ray-casting [11]) would be far too expensive for graphics. A convenient alternative is to use depth comparisons and primitive boundary scan-conversion to classify points.

During scan-conversion, surface points are generated, which project onto individual pixels along the viewing direction. The depth of the 3D points (computed along the viewing direction away from the viewer) may be stored in the z-buffer memory associated with the corresponding pixel. A 3D point whose depth is stored in some pixel's z-buffer may be classified against a primitive by scan-converting the boundary of that primitive and computing the parity of the number of layers of the primitive's surface that are behind the point being tested. (One needs only to compare depth values of surface points projecting on the same pixel as the tested point with the value stored in the z-buffer. Each time the scanned point depth is larger than the stored one, a binary flag associated with that pixel is inverted.) Note that this process may be used to classify in parallel a large number of points, as long as they project on different pixels. This technique is described in [12] and mathematically justified in [13].

To classify a point against a CSG expression, it is not sufficient to classify the point against all the primitives. Point-primitive classification results must be combined according to a Boolean expression. For some simple Boolean expression, such as an intersection, no storage is necessary because the result can be formulated as the conjunction of Boolean results. The classification algorithm may process the primitives in any order and stop as soon as one of these results is FALSE. (This would be the case when, for example, the point was out of a primitive in a Boolean intersection.) If all the primitives are processed an no FALSE result is found, the point is inside the solid defined by the Boolean expression.

Unfortunately, the evaluation of more complicated CSG expression may require a large amount of temporary storage for intermediate binary results. Usually a stack mechanism is used for the temporary storage. The required stack depth may reach the depth of the CSG graph.

Since the amount of memory per pixel is limited, one cannot use a stack of arbitrary depth at each pixel. Yet, we want to perform classification operations in parallel for all pixels, so as to minimize the number of required primitive scan-conversions.

A technique that circumvents this memory limitation converts the CSG expression into a much larger (sum-of-product) form [14] in which primitive instances can be duplicated many times, appearing in several products. Techniques for eliminating redundant (empty) products have been discussed in [14].

Primitive faces are first trimmed against the appropriate products using repeated primitive scan-conversions. The resulting trimmed faces are then merged using a final depth buffer for selecting the front-most faces among all the products. Note that products can interfere and thus a front face of a product needs not lie on the solid. The z-buffer is used, as in [9], for both visible surface selection and for discarding faces interior to the solid.

This paper pertains to the implementation of this projective approach. It focuses on correct algorithms for computing the visible front-faces of a product, given that depth-buffer comparisons are performed with limited resolution and that one needs to correctly handle situations where faces of several primitives overlap or where the ray of a pixel intersect two adjacent faces very close to their common edge. In both cases, due to scan-conversion round-off errors, we cannot rely on the computed depth values, but must still produce a picture that corresponds to a regularized version of the CSG expression. A solid is regularized when it is equal to the topological closure of its interior with respect to the three-dimensional Euclidean space. Regularized solids have no dangling edges or faces. Thus, faces or edges that lie on several primitives, but are not bounding any three-dimensional volume in the final result, should not be displayed.

The next section presents a new algorithm for shading CSG solids and briefly discusses its historic evolution. Then we point out the accuracy and regularization problems and explain how we solve them. We also point out a simple extension of our algorithm that produces shaded images with shadows directly from CSG, without computing any silhouette edges that are usually required to define the limits of shadow volumes. In the final section, we demonstrate in detail the progress of the trickle algorithm on simple products with coincident faces. The appendix shows the content of the three buffers as the trickle algorithm progresses through the a real CSG object with many coincident faces and a non-convex primitive.

## 2 The Trickle Algorithm

Researchers at UNC [14] have implemented a hardware algorithm for trimming primitive faces by comparing them to all the front and back faces of all the primitives in a product. A variation of this approach was also reported in [4]. The comparisons are done independently at each pixel and involve depth tests, masks, counters, and logical bit operations at each pixel. The algorithm has been efficiently implemented on the Pixel-Power graphic system that has one processor with local memory at each pixel [14].

Researchers at IBM [15] have developed a more efficient algorithm for processing products, called the Trickle algorithm. It requires, in general, a much smaller number of primitive scan-conversions and of buffer-merging operations than the UNC algorithm and may be better suited for implementation on emerging commercial graphic workstations, because it only requires simple extensions of existing programmable depth-buffer functions. Both the UNC and the IBM algorithms handle non-convex primitives by producing and trimming the successive layers of a primitive's faces.

The strength of the trickle algorithm lies in the fact that it processes the primitive faces of a product in a front-to-back (away from the viewer) order independently at each pixel. This ordering permits to stop the processing of a product as soon as a visible point (or the background) has been reached at each pixel. Furthermore, while moving 'deeper' (away from the viewer) from one primitive-face layer to another at a given pixel, the trickle algorithm skips primitive-face layers that clearly cannot lie on the product because they are out of at least one primitive in the product.

A drawback of the trickle algorithm is that it uses three depth and intensity buffers (the standard depth and intensity buffers used for visible surface selection, plus a new depth-interval buffer, abbreviated DIB, composed to two depth buffers and two intensity buffers). Note that the UNC algorithm only requires two additional buffers and a counter. However, the trickle algorithm may be configured to run in four passes, once for each quadrant of the screen. Splitting the screen into four quadrants provides enough buffers for the trickle algorithm, even with the standard configuration of one depth and two intensity buffers commonly available on graphic workstations. Unfortunately, this four-pass approach requires that intensity buffers be sometimes used as depth-buffers, which is currently impossible with commonly available commercial graphic systems.

In this paper, we report a new version of the Trickle algorithm, which was originally published in [15]. A very high-level view of the trickle algorithm follows:

```
initialize buffer 1
for each product P do:
    compute the front of P in buffer 2
    merge the result into buffer 1 selecting the visible faces
```

Buffer 1 (depth and intensity) is used to select the visible surfaces of a union of products. The visible front faces of each product are computed one after the other using a DIB as summarized below. The result is stored in buffer 2.

```
initialize buffer 2 to the background
while not done, circulate through the primitives Q of P and do:
    compute into buffer 3 the next face of Q that lies behind buffer 2
    At pixels where the next face of Q is front-facing copy buffer 3 into buffer 2
```

The details and advantages of the Trickle algorithms are described in details in the companion paper [15]. We can only briefly mention that the trickle algorithm works because, when a point in buffer 2 immediately precedes in depth a front face of a primitive Q, it lies out of Q, and thus out of the product. Furthermore, the interval between the tested point and the corresponding front point on Q is also out of Q and thus out of the product (see Figure 1).

Z1, the point of the boundary of Q that lies immediately behind the point Z2 stored in buffer 2 is computed using buffer 3. If Z2 lies on a front facing portion of the boundary of Q, the segment separating Z1 and Z2 lies out of Q and the trickle algorithm advances buffer 2 to Z3 bypassing any point r that may lie between Z2 and Z3.

We propose below a pseudo-code presentation of a new version of the trickle algorithm. We have slightly simplified the algorithm of [15] by integrating the initialization steps into the main loop. The main improvement is in the carefully enhanced depth-tests that provide correct treatment of all singular (so called 'on/on') cases that involve coincident primitive faces and pixels in the vicinity of the projection of silhouette edges.

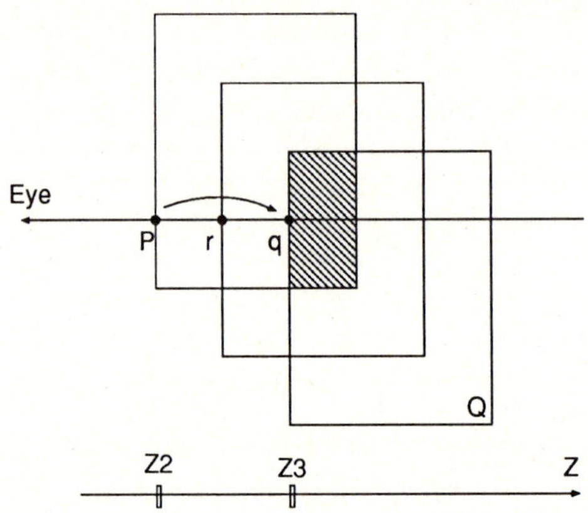


**Fig. 1.** Move forward: Point p lies on a primitive in the current product and its depth is stored in Z2. The primitive Q is scan-converted and the depth of point q on Q is stored into Z3 because point q is the first point on Q (in terms of depth) to be hidden by p. Point q is a front point for Q. Therefore, the segment (p,q) is out of Q and thus out of the product. The algorithm moves forward by storing the depth and intensity of p into Z2 and I2. Note that point r, on a different primitive in the product is skipped because it lies between p and q and thus is not on the product.

After an initialization of buffer 1, i.e., depth buffer Z1 and intensity buffer I1 are set to maximum depth and background color, (lines 1-3), the algorithm processes each product. For each product, buffer 2 is initialized to minimum depth and background color (lines 5-7). Then, the visible front faces of the product are computed and stored in the depth buffer Z2 and intensity buffer I2 (lines 9-31). Finally, the result is merged into buffer 1 (lines 33-35) wherever the current product's front is in front of previously processed products.

To compute the visible front faces of a product, we proceed as follow. A counter k is first initialized to -1 (line 9). It will be used to count how many primitives of the current product have been processed without affecting buffer 2. If there is only one primitive in the product, we need to scan it twice to properly produce the effect of regularization. If all primitives have been processed in this manner, there is no need for any further scan-conversion for this product, because we already have its visible faces in buffer 2 and we

```
FOREACH x IN pixels DO initialize final buffer
    {Z1[x] = infinity;          back plane
    I1[x] = black;}             background color
FOREACH P IN products DO
    {FOREACH x IN pixels DO initialize product buffer
        {Z2[x] = 0;             init buffer 2
        I2[x] = black;}

    k=-1;
    UNTIL(k==NumberOfPrimitivesIn(P)) REPEAT
        {k++;                   count useless passes
        change=0;               set if any pixel has changed
        Q= NextPrimitiveInTheCircularListOfPrimitivesIn(P);
        FOREACH x IN pixels DO initialize Z3, I3, and ff
            {Z3[x] = infinity;
            I3[x] = black;
            IF IsPositive(Q) THEN ff[x]=1 ELSE ff[x]=0;}
        FOREACH F IN faces(Q) DO
            {FOREACH x IN PixelsVisitedByScanconverting(Q) DO
                Z=DepthOfScanconvertedPointOn(F,x);
                I=IntensityReflectedByScanconvertedPointOn(F,x);
                IF (Z2[x] < Z - eps < Z3[x])
                    {Z3[x]= Z;
                    IF (IsFrontFacing(F)) I3[x]=I;}
                    IF (Z2[x] < Z - eps) ff[x]=!ff[x];}
        FOREACH x IN pixels DO move back if bad point
            {IF(ff[x] AND Z2[x] != Z3[x])
                {Z2[x] = Z3[x];
                I2[x] = I3[x];
                change = TRUE;}}
        IF (change) k= 0;}
    FOREACH x IN pixels DO merge into final z-buffer
        {IF(Z2[x] < Z1[x] + eps)
            {Z1[x] = Z2[x];
            I1[x] = I2[x];}}}
```

exit the UNTIL loop (lines 10-31). In the worst case, the trickle algorithm scan converts each primitive of the product roughly as many times as there is layers in all the primitives of that product. (Each layer may produce a tentative point for buffer 2, and it may be required to scan all but one primitives of the product to declare that the point in buffer 2 is out of the product.) However, in the average case, the algorithm stops the loop very early. Note that k is initialized to -1 (line 9) to ensure proper processing of products with a single primitive.

In the loop, we use a change flag (initialized line 12 and updated line 30) to see if we have advanced buffer 2 and if we should reset k to zero (line 31).

We execute the inside of the loop (lines 13-31) for primitives Q in the product. We circulate through the list of primitives in a consistent way (line 13). We first initialize buffer 3 and the front facing mask (lines 14-17). The mask is set to one if the current primitive is positive i.e., bounded. (We assume that each primitive has a bounded boundary. Primitives with a bounded interior are called positive. Others are called negative. In fact, if the leaves of the original CSG graph are bounded volumes, negative primitives correspond to leaves that have been subtracted an odd number of times.) The front facing flag ff is used to decide, at each pixel, whether the algorithm should advance buffer 2 or not (line 27).

Then we scan-convert faces of the current primitive Q (lines 18-25). For each pixel covered by the projection of Q, we update Z3 and I3 where appropriate using the depth and intensity of the scanned surface points (lines 22-24). The update takes place only if the scanned Z value lies between the depth stored in buffer 2 and 3 (line 22). The small *eps* value subtracted before the test is used to ensure correct treatment of coincident faces (see next section). Furthermore, I3 is only updated if the scanned surface is front-facing, so that we do not store intensities of back facing faces, should they overlap with front-facing ones near silhouette edges (see next section).

The front facing flag is flipped for each face of Q that passes behind Z2 (line 25). Again, the *eps* value is used to ensure that scan conversion accuracy and round-off errors do not lead to incorrect results.

Finally, once the entire primitive Q has been scan-converted, we advance by copying buffer 2 into buffer 3 wherever the front flag ff is set (line 27-31), i.e., wherever the points stored in buffer 2 are out of Q. Note that these points are replaced by front-facing points on Q (if any), which have been computed in buffer 3.

The additional condition, Z2[x] != Z3[x] (line 27), is necessary to ensure proper treatment of points outside of the projection of positive primitives. For these points ff=1, but Z2 and Z3 are both equal to the maximum depth, and the algorithm does not progress.

Line 33, an epsilon is used to prevent color mixing between overlapping faces of different products.

## 3 Treatment of Singularities

Singular situations occur when two different faces cover the same pixel and have the same—or almost the same—depth at points that project onto that pixel. Such situations occur in the mathematical (exact) model when faces of several primitives overlap. They also occur in the discretized graphic model near edges that connect a front and a back face or at constrictions (thin walls whose depth is less than the depth resolution of the z-buffer). A method for computing the correct picture in all these singular cases must be sufficiently robust to handle depth-errors due to the round-off errors of scan-conversion.

In this section, we discuss these singular cases and show how they are handled by our algorithm.

### 3.1 Silhouette Edges Yield on/on Cases

Different faces of the same primitive typically do not coincide. However, if a layer of the primitive has depth smaller than the depth resolution of the z-buffer, it will be processed as if it was flat. (Layers are more precisely defined in [15]. They correspond to the disjoint segments obtained by intersecting a ray parallel to the z-axis with the primitive's volume.) Furthermore, even for large primitives, we can locally have a situation where the primitive appears flat. For example, while approaching a silhouette edge, the abutting two faces of the same primitive (one front-facing and one back-facing) are arbitrarily close to each other in depth. At that edge both front and back faces have the same depth. If a pixel very close to the edge's projection on the screen is visited by the scan-conversion, both faces would have the same integer-rounded depth-value at that pixel. Thus, for that particular pixel, the primitive appears as a flat (zero-depth) degenerate solid. Since the trickle algorithm proceeds independently for all pixels, it must correctly handle such degenerate primitives, otherwise cracks or dangling edges may appear. The initialization (line 9) of the counter k to -1 ensures that products with a single primitives will be scan-converted twice, thus giving a chance for the trickle algorithm to produce a tentative point in buffer 2 during the first scan-conversion, and then to classify it as out during the second scan-conversion.

### 3.2 Need for Tolerance

Rotations used to position primitives introduce round-off errors in the coefficient of their bounding planes or vertices. Consequently, if for example primitives are rotated to align some of their faces, the surfaces containing faces that should overlap will usually not coincide, even though theoretically should. Furthermore, scan-conversion round-off errors may result in unpredictable depth-ordering of any two theoretically coincident faces at any pixel. Since the ordering based on pure depth comparisons would not be consistent across the entire overlap region of both faces, algorithm cannot rely on the result of depth tests for the covered pixels.

Therefore, in all computations that address the problem of coincident faces, we use a small tolerance value, called '*eps*' in our algorithm. This value will ensure that two depth values that were intended to be equal, will be considered equal.

Of course, choosing *eps* too large may result in treating as equal two values which were not intended to be equal. In such cases, the algorithm will produce a picture, that corresponds to a regularization 'modulo *eps*' of the solid, i.e., will remove shallow parts of the model and will display the correct faces everywhere else.

Treatment of on/on cases involves neighborhood evaluation [2]. Since we are testing faces front-to-back, only the neighborhood behind the face is relevant. (The neighborhood indicates whether there is material, with respect to the product, behind the face. If there were material in front of the face, the trickle algorithm would have stopped sooner at that pixel and would never have reached that face. Therefore, if there is material of the product behind the face, the face point is on the product and is the most-front point visible through the corresponding pixel.) We can thus use a technique proposed in [9] and test a point positioned behind the scan-converted surface by a small distance, *eps*. So, we subtract *eps* from the depth of the scan-converted point before comparing it to the tested point, whose depth is stored in Z2 (line 22).

The distance *eps* is chosen so as to exceed the combined effect of the depth-buffer limited resolution and of the round-off errors of the depth calculation during surface scan-conversion. When too large an *eps* value is used, details, such as shallow features, could disappear because their front-facing and back-facing faces would be considered coincident. To keep *eps* small and still correctly process the coincident face on/on cases, the staring depth along each scan-line must be accurate as elaborated in the next subsection.

### 3.3 Scan-conversion Consistent with the Supporting Surface

Scan-conversion procedures, which compute surface points for all the pixels covered by a face, produce approximate (truncated) depth values, because the z-buffer contains integer values. Consequently, the depth of a point that lies on the overlapping portion of two coplanar faces differs depending on which face is used (i.e., scan-converted) to produce the point. Therefore, to ensure that intended coincidences are correctly treated, we consider that two points that project onto the same pixel are identical if their depths differ by less than a small *eps* value computed from the size of the scene and the z-buffer resolution.

If a face is at a steep angle relative to the z axis, the sampled depth value may vary widely over the width of the pixel. To handle coincident faces correctly, it is important that every face be sampled at exactly the same point within the pixel (e.g., at the center of the pixel). If two faces are coincident, the sampling of depth values for the pixels covered by both faces must yield the same depth for both faces at any pixel.

We have obtained excellent results by computing the depth for the starting pixel of each horizontal span, not using a z-increment along the leading edge (as it is the case in most scanning algorithms), but precisely as the exact depth of the surface point that projects onto the center of the pixel. Consequently, within the numerical accuracy of the computation of the z-increment and its use along a scanline, the depth for all covered pixels will be correct with respect to the scanned surface, and will thus be the same for all faces lying in that surface.

### 3.4 Parity-based Point/Primitive Classification

In the original version of the Trickle algorithm [15], face trimming (i.e. testing face points) against a primitive Q in a product was done by checking whether the first face of Q encountered behind the tested point is front-facing or back-facing. Near the edges of Q, or if Q is flat within the depth buffer resolution, both front-facing and back-facing faces may have the same depth (due to truncated depth calculations). To solve the problem, we use the parity of the number of faces behind the tested point (line 25), as suggested in [14]. (An even number of faces of Q behind a point implies that the point is outside of Q.)

### 3.5 Scan-conversion Consistent with Primitive Boundary

The trickle algorithm requires that every pixel covered by the projection of a primitive be covered by a number of front faces that equals the number of back faces of that primitive. This requirement obviously indicates that primitives' boundaries should be valid two-cycles (no interior or dangling faces), which is the case theoretically in the definition of CSG. However, scan-conversion procedures dealing with two adjacent faces of the same primitive do not automatically ensure such parity. For example, the Bresenham or anti-aliasing algorithms do not.

A simple interpolation of the depth value over a span (horizontal row of pixels covered by the face projection) may lead to a wrong calculation of the depth at the end of the span if the end only partially covers the pixels. (The depth would be extrapolated using the slope of the plane containing the face, even though the actual pixel's center is not covered by the face.)

Consider a pixel whose rectangular region is traversed by the projection of an edge between a front and a back face, but whose center is not covered by these faces. If the scan-conversion algorithm visits that pixel for these two faces, a depth value will be computed for the center of the pixel. No matter how big the depth resolution or the *eps* tolerance value, one can choose the slope of the two faces such that the depth at the pixel's center computed for the front face exceeds the computed depth of the back face. This overshoot can lead to incorrect pictures near silhouette edges of primitives. The solution we have implemented simply processes, during scan-conversion, only those pixels whose centers are covered by the face.

Shadows are handled by using an auxiliary 'shadow' z-buffer that selects the surface portions visible from the light source. It is constructed by running the above trickle algorithm (without computing any intensity information) in the coordinate system that positions the eye at the light source. Then the standard trickle algorithm is run again from the eye orientation, except that, while computing the intensity reflected by visible points, their distance to the light is compared to the distance stored in the shadow buffer to establish if the surface point is visible from the light source, i.e., is lighted or is in the shadow of some other surface closer to the light source.

The above approach requires that during the final scan-conversion (after the shadow buffer has been computed) the coordinates of surface points be expressed in both coordinate systems (the coordinate system aligned with the viewer and the one aligned with the light source). To ensure that all pixels covered by the scan-converted surface are correctly processed, the scan-conversion uses increments in the viewer's coordinate system. These increments may be mapped into increments in the light coordinate system through a constant matrix so as to speed the scan-conversion process up.

The aliasing effect in the shadow buffer can be significantly accentuated if the surface upon which the shadow is projected is orthogonal to the viewing direction and nearly parallel to the light direction. Some techniques for dealing with such visual artifacts are discussed in [11].

An example, presented in the appendix, shows the result of this two pass algorithm.

## 4 Constructive Examples

Let us illustrate how the new trickle algorithm works by considering several examples. In these examples we will only concentrate on the computation of the visible front faces of simple products, because the sum (or union) of products is performed by the standard z-buffering hidden surface removal approach.

### 4.1 Intersection of Two Simple Primitives

Consider two convex primitives, A and B, of Figure 2. Our algorithm proceeds as follows. Before we start scan-converting primitives, we initialize the pixels' buffers memory. Z2 is initialized (line 6) to 0 (for simplicity, we assume that the world lies on the positive side of the Z=0 plane), and I2 to the background color (line 7), which we call 'black'. The count k of redundant passes is initialized to -1.

Primitive A appears first in the circular list of the primitives in our product, so we scan-convert it first. Since A is positive (and thus bounded), the parity bit flag 'ff' for each pixel is initialized to 1, so that points stored at pixels not covered by the projection of A will be properly treated as being exterior to A. Z3 is initialized to 'infinity' (a number representing the maximum depth of the z-buffer) and I3 is set to black (lines 15-17).

During the scanning of the faces of A, we find that, at least for the pixels we consider here, we have the following relation: $Z2 < F1 < F4 < Z3$. The test (line 22) succeeds, for small enough *eps*, and thus the depth of F1 is stored in Z3 and the color of F1 is stored in I3. In short: we are storing the front face of A in buffer 3. Both F1 and F4 are behind Z2, and thus the parity flag ff is toggled twice during the scan-conversion of A and remains 1 (the tested point in Z2 is outside of A and should be replaced by points further back).

During the update steps (lines 26-30), the contents of Z3 and I3 which corresponds to face F1 are copied into Z2 and I2. The count k of redundant passes is reset to 0, since we have updated some pixels. Note that pixels outside the projection of A now contain in buffer 2 the background depth and color.

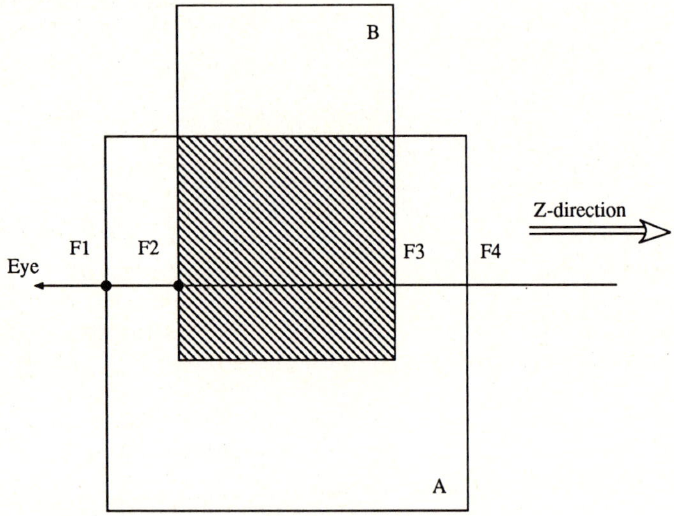


**Fig. 2.** Intersection of two convex primitives: The product is the intersection of two convex primitives, A and B. A has a front face F1 and a back face F4. B has a front face F2 and a back face F3. The other faces of A and B do not project onto the pixels of interest in this example and will thus not be considered. The eye is on the left and thus the z-axis direction is horizontal and left-to-right. We consider a particular pixel symbolized by a horizontal line through the eye. The face of the product that is visible through the pixel is the front face F2 of B.

Now we scan primitive B. We increase k to 1. The parity flag is also set to 1 and Z3 is initialized to 'infinity'. We find that: $Z2 < F2 < F3 < Z3$, so the depth and intensity of F2 are copied into Z3 and I3. Once more Z2 is less than F2 and F3, so, the parity flag is toggled twice. (The tested point is out of B.) The content of Z2 and I2 are overwritten with data from face F2 and the counter k is reset to 0 again. The algorithm has moved forward and F2 is stored in buffer 2.

The next primitive must be considered, but first we increase k to 1 and set the parity flag at each pixel to 1. Going through the circular list of the primitives in the product, we are back to primitive A. Scan-converting A again, we find that: $F1 < Z2 < F4 <$

$Z3$. Face F1 is not considered, because it does not lie behind Z2. The depth of F4 is stored in Z3, but, since F4 is back-facing, the color of F4 is not copied into I3! Only one face of A, F4, is behind Z2, so the parity flag is toggled only once and is set to 0. Consequently, Z2 is not changed and the counter k is not reset and is still 1.

The next primitive is B. K is incremented to 2. The parity flag is set to 1. Z2 contains the depth of F2 and scan-converting B we find that: $Z2 < F3 < Z3$. The depth of F3 is copied into Z3, but the color is not copied into I3 because F3 is back-facing. Only F3 is behind Z2 so the parity flag is toggled to 0 at each pixel covered by the projection of F3. Z2 is not changed and k remains at 2. Buffer 2 still contains the front face, F2, of B.

Since k equals the number of primitives in the product, we stop the loop (line 10). The product's visible front face is in buffer 2. The contents of Z2 and I2 are copied into the display buffers Z1 and I1, wherever Z2 is less than Z1, so as to merge this product with other products of the disjunctive form.

### 4.2 Coincident Face and One Non-convex Primitive

Now consider the intersection of a non-convex primitive A with a convex primitive B, as shown Figure 3. A has faces F1, F3, F4, and F5 and B has faces F2 and F6. The front face F1 and F2 are coincident.

As before, we first initialize buffer 2.

We start by scanning A. As in the previous example, the parity flag is set because A is positive. Because $Z2 < F1 < F3 < F4 < F5$, F1 is stored in buffer 3. Since there are 4 faces behind Z2, ff is set to 1 and F1 is copied into Z2 and I2 (lines 26-30).

Now, when we scan B, the face F2 is coincident with F1, and we have $F2 < Z2{+}eps < F6$. With only 1 face of B that is behind Z2, the parity flag is toggled to 0 and Z2 remains unchanged. The counter k is incremented to 1.

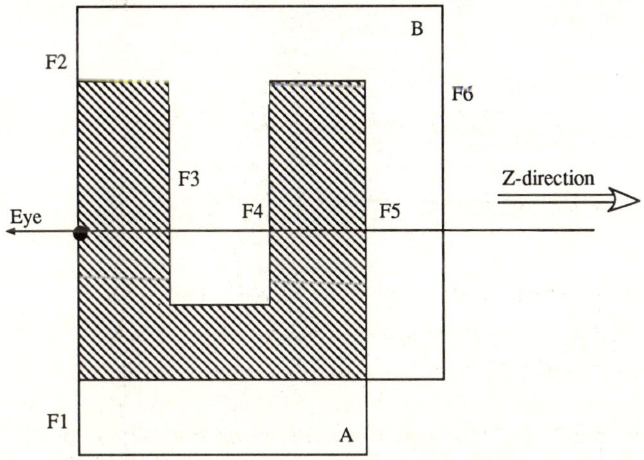


**Fig. 3**. A non-convex primitive: A has two front faces, F1 and F4, and two back faces, F3 and F5. B has a front face F2 and a back face of F6. The product is defined as the intersection of A and B.

When we scan A again, and find that $Z2 < F3 < F4 < F5$. The depth of F3 is stored in Z3, but I3 is not changed because F3 is back-facing. With an odd number of faces of A behind Z2, the parity flag is toggled to 0 and Z2 remains unchanged. The counter K is incremented to 2, which equal to the number of primitives in the product, and thus the loop stops. Buffer 2 contains F1, which is the front of the product, and can be merged into buffer 1.

### 4.3 Coincident Face and an Unbounded Primitive

Consider, the difference of one convex primitive, A, with another convex primitive, B, of Figure 4. The product is the intersection of A with the complement of B, which is a negative unbounded primitive. The front/back orientation of the faces of B are inverted because it is complemented.

Initialization takes place as usual.

We scan A, as in the previous examples, and F1 is stored in buffer 2.

Now, we scan B. Because B is negative, the parity flag ff is initialized to 0. We find that, $F2 < Z2 + eps < F3 < Z3$. Therefore, F3 is stored in buffer 3, including the intensity, because F3 is the front-facing (remember that B is negative). With 1 face of B behind Z2, the flag ff is toggled to 1 at the pixels visited by the scan-conversion: F2 is outside of B and we move forward. Buffer 3 is copied into buffer 2.

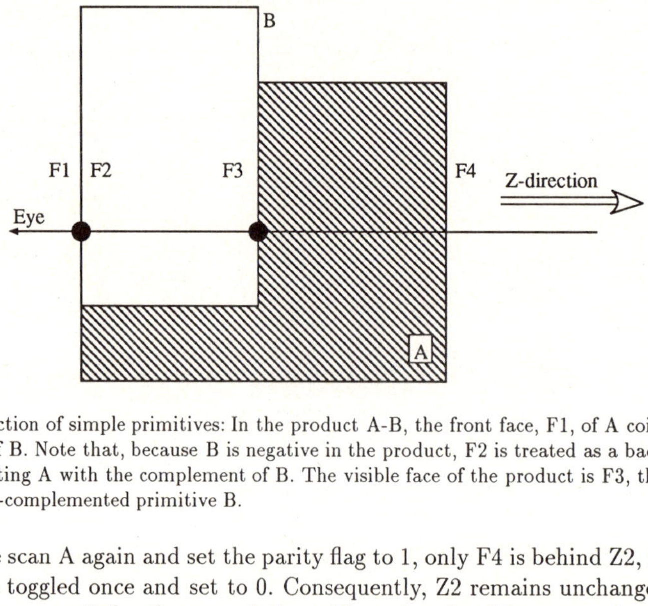


**Fig. 4.** Subtraction of simple primitives: In the product A-B, the front face, F1, of A coincides with the front face F2 of B. Note that, because B is negative in the product, F2 is treated as a back face, because we are intersecting A with the complement of B. The visible face of the product is F3, the original back face of the non-complemented primitive B.

When we scan A again and set the parity flag to 1, only F4 is behind Z2, therefore, the parity flag is toggled once and set to 0. Consequently, Z2 remains unchanged. The same happens as we scan B for the second time. Then the algorithm stops for this product, since k has reached 2. Buffer 2, containing F3, is merged into buffer 1.

### 4.4 Primitives with Internal Cracks

Finally, we look at the subtraction of one non-convex primitive, B, (which has an internal crack) from another non-convex primitive, A, (which also has an internal crack, which furthermore coincides with the crack in B) depicted in Figure 5. Such cracks are produced when, in the model—or because of the limited depth resolution—two faces of the same primitive are coincident. These situations also appear close to silhouette edges, as discussed earlier.

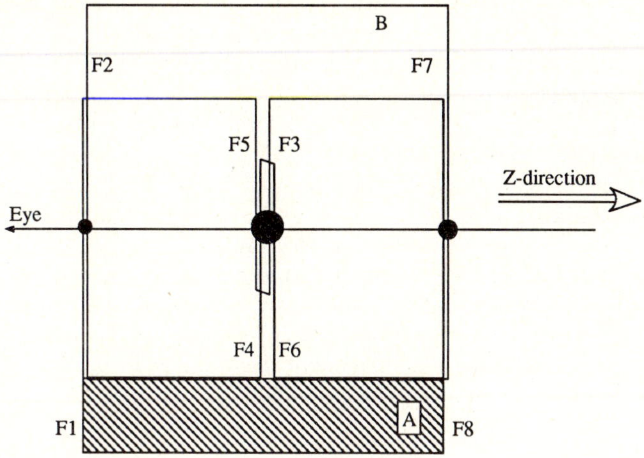


**Fig. 5.** Coincident cracks: A has faces F1, F4, F5, F7. B has faces F2, F3, F6, F8. The non-regularized difference A-B, that projects onto the pixels considered here is the empty set.

After scanning A, as in the previous examples, F1 is stored in buffer 2.

When we scan B, we set the parity flag to 0 since B is negative. F2 is coincident with F1, so $F2 < Z2 + eps < F3 = F6 < F8 < Z3$. The depth of either F3 or F6 is copied into Z3, depending on the order in which faces of B are scan-converted. However, the intensity of F3 is saved in I3, because F6 is backfacing.

Since there are 3 faces of B behind Z2, the parity flag is toggled to 1 and buffer 3 is copied into buffer 2.

We scan A again. The parity flag is set. F4 is coincident with F5 and with Z2. We have, $F1 < F4 = F5 < Z2 + eps < F7 < Z3$. F7 is written into Z3. Since only F7 is behind Z2, the parity bit is reset to 0 and Z2 remains unchanged. Buffer 2 still contains F3.

Now scanning B again, F6 and F3 are coincident with Z2. We have: $F2 < F3 = F6 < Z2 + eps < F8 < Z3$. F8 is written into buffer 3. Since only one face (F8) is behind Z2, the parity flag is toggled once to 1 and F8 is copied into buffer 2.

Scanning A again, the last face of A, F7 is coincident with F8. We have: $F1 < F4 = F5 < F7 < Z2 + eps < Z3$. There is no face of A behind Z2. Therefore, nothing is copied into Z3 and the parity flag remains set. Thus the background color (black) and maximum depth (infinity), with which buffer 3 was initialized are copied into buffer 2.

A further pass causes no change and the process stops when the count reaches 2.

## 5 Conclusion

To display regularized CSG solids using a multiple depth buffer algorithm, singular cases, where two faces have the same depth at some pixel, must be handled properly. These coincident-face situations do not only happen because the CSG primitives have been positioned with two-dimensional contacts along their boundaries. The situations also happen when surface points on constrictions or on sharp corners near silhouette edges project onto the same pixel and have depth-values that are sufficiently close to be rounded by the scan-conversion process to the same integer Z value.

First, the authors have decided to use a small *eps* tolerance value to remove the effects of round-off errors during scan-conversion. For example, faces that were designed to coincide, will, even if the actual depth may differ at some pixels. To keep *eps* small, relative to the size of the model, we have improved scan-conversion, so that it produces actual surface depths for all the visited pixels. This way, if two faces that overlap in space are scan-converted independently, the pairs of values generated for all the pixels covered by both faces will be equal, except for a very small round-off error that may occur during the depth increment cumulation.

To ensure that the scan-conversion may be used safely for point-in-primitive classification, we have modified the scan-conversion to guarantee that only pixels whose centers are covered by a face are visited during that face's scan-conversion.

To produce a picture that is correct with respect to the regularized interpretation of the CSG expression, toleranced depth tests are used within the trickle algorithm to remove dangling faces or edges that would otherwise appear.

Shadows, which may exhibit a fair amount of aliasing, may be produced using a simple two-pass algorithm with an auxiliary shadow-buffer.

## Acknowledgements

The original idea of combining a z-buffer depth-test with a CSG classification was described in [9]. The work at IBM on z-buffer techniques for shading from CSG was particularly inspired by the work of J. Goldfeather, S. Molnar, G. Turk, and H. Fuchs, at UNC reported in [14] and by some of Prof. F. Jansen's work [4]. It started as a collaboration between N. Gharacharoloo, C. Zoulas, and J. Rossignac at IBM Research, who were later joined by F. Jansen, visiting IBM from Delft Technical University in the Netherlands, and by D. Epstein. Our approach was originally focused on an improvement to the UNC algorithm, developed by Rossignac and based on the fact that the visible front-faces of products of convex (or z-connected) primitives or half-spaces can be computed in one pass by scan-converting only once each primitives' front faces into one depth and intensity buffer; by scan-converting only once each primitive's back faces into another depth-buffer; and by combining these two buffers. Several improvements were made to this approach in order to reduce the average complexity of the algorithm in terms of the number of primitives in the CSG tree. The work culminated in the trickle algorithm developed by D. Epstein, F. Jansen, and J. Rossignac and reported in [15]. The present paper relates recent progress made by its authors on simplifying the trickle algorithm and enabling it to correctly handle important singular situations and to deal with the round-off errors due to the z-buffer and scan-conversion limited resolutions.

## References

[1] Requicha, A. A. G. and Tilove, R. B.: Mathematical foundation of constructive solid geometry: General topology of closed regular sets, *Tech. Memo. No. 27a, Production Automation Project, Univ. of Rochester*, June 1978. (Available from CPA, 304 Kimball Hall, Cornell University, Ithaca, New York 14853.)

[2] Requicha, A. A. G. and Voelcker, H. B.: Boolean Operations in Solid Modelling: Boundary Evaluation and Merging Algorithms, *Proceedings of the IEEE*, Vol. 73, No. 1, January 1985.

[3] Roth, S. D.: Ray casting for modeling solids, *Computer Graphics and Image Processing*, vol. 18, no. 2, pp. 109-144, February 1982.

[4] Jansen, F. W.: Pixel-Parallel hidden-surface algorithm for Constructive Solid Geometry, *Proceedings Eurographics'86*, pp. 29-40, Elseviers Science Publishers, Amsterdam. 1986.

[5] Jansen, F. W.: CSG hidden-surface algorithms for VLSI hardware systems, in *Advances on Graphics Hardware I* W. Strasser (ed.), Springer Verlag, 1987.

[6] Jansen, F. W.: Solid modelling with faceted primitives, Delft University Press, *Doctoral Dissertation*, Technische Universiteit Delft, The Netherland, September 1987.

[7] Kedem, G. and Ellis, J. L.: The ray-casting machine, *Proc. ICCD'84*, pp. 533-538, October 1984.

[8] Kedem , G. and Ellis, J.: The Ray Casting Machine Prototype, *International Conference on Parallel Processing for Computer Vision and Display*, University of Leeds, UK, January 1988.

[9] Rossignac, J. R. and Requicha, A. A. G.: Depth buffering display techniques for constructive solid geometry, *IEEE, Computer Graphics and Applications*, vol. 6, no. 9, pp. 29-39, September 1986.

[10] Rossignac, J. R. and Voelcker, H. B.: Active Zones in CSG for Accelerating Boundary Evaluation, Redundancy Elimination, Interference Detection, and Shading Algorithms, *ACM Transactions on Graphics*, vol. 8, no. 1, pp. 51-87, January 1989.

[11] Woodward, C.: Methods for computer-aided design of free-form objects, *PhD dissertation, Mathematics and Computer Science Series number 56*, Helsinki University of Technology, Finland. 1990.

[12] Goldfeather, J., Hultquist, J. P. M. and Fuchs, H.: Fast Constructive Solid Geometry Display in the Pixel-Power Graphics System, *ACM SIGGRAPH'86 Proc.*, Computer Graphics, vol. 20, no. 4, August 1986.

[13] Tilove, R. B.: Set membership classification: A unified approach to geometric intersection problems, *IEEE Trans. on Computers*, vol. C-29, no. 10, pp. 874-883, October 1980.

[14] Goldfeather, J., Molnar, S., Turk, G. and Fuchs, H.: Near Real-Time CSG Rendering using Tree Normalization and Geometric Pruning, *IEEE Computer Graphics and Applications*, vol. 9, no. 3, pp. 20-28. May 1989.

[15] Epstein, D., Jansen, F. and Rossignac, J.: Z-buffer rendering from CSG: The Trickle Algorithm, *IBM Research Report RC15182*, IBM Thomas J. Watson Research Center, Yorktown Heights, New York, December 1989.

# Appendix A: A Case Study

The following sequence of pictures show how the regularized CSG expression $(A - (B \cup C)) \cup (B \cap D)$ is processed by the new trickle algorithm to generate a correct shaded image. Primitive A is the large green block; B is a non-convex primitive composed of two rectangular brown blocks. Primitive C is a purple block and D is a light blue block. A and B share coincident faces at the front and back sides. B and C share coincident faces at the back end, and B and D shard coincident faces at the right end. The expression is first converted into sum of products form. We obtain two products: $A \cap \bar{B} \cap \bar{C}$ and $B \cap D$. Each picture shows a series of time steps in the running of the algorithm. For each time step, the contents of the 3 buffers (Z3,I3 and Z2,I2 and Z1,I1) that are used are shown in three windows called 'buffer3', 'buffer2', and 'bufferl'. Buffer3 shows the result of the current primitive's scan-conversion. Buffer2, shows the current result of merging the scan conversion previously obtained in Buffer3 with the previous state of Buffer2. Bufferl stores the resulting products of the CSG sum of product forms.

We first scan A into buffer3. (Plate 6-a) Then buffer2 is updated with the contents of buffer3 and we see A's front faces in buffer2. Then we scan B into buffer3. Because the front flag is reversed and B's front face is coincident with A's front face, we see only the back faces of B in buffer3. (Plate 6-b).

In Plate 6-c, Buffer3 with B's back faces is merged into Buffer2. We see the back-faces merged into the image of A in Buffer2 creating the two shelves. The updating is not a simple merge, only those pixels for which the front flag ff is set are copied. Note that there is the dangling back faces of B which are coincident with the back face of A. It will disappear later to produce the correct image of a regularized solid. C, which is also negative, is scanned into Buffer3. Only the parts of the back faces of C that are behind Buffer2 appear in Buffer3.

In Plate 6-d, the faces of C are updated into Buffer2 creating the notch. Part of the back face of C is coincident with a back face of B; when this occurs the color of the visible face depends on the order in which the primitives are processed. The lightly colored area is from the coincident face of C that was behind Buffer2. Note the dangling backfaces of C are also present. We scan A again into Buffer3, and only the backfaces of A behind buffer2 are visible.

In Plate 6-e, the updating of Buffer2 by Buffer3 have trimmed away the dangling back faces of B from the image in Buffer2. We scan B into Buffer3 and we see only a small part of B's backfaces appearing in Buffer3.

In Plate 6-f, the updating of Buffer2 by Buffer3 has overwritten the dangling backface of C restoring the back faces of B. A dangling back face of B has been created. We scan C again.

In Plate 6-g, the updating of Buffer2 by Buffer3 has caused no change in the image. We scan A again and see the backfaces of A in Buffer3.

In Plate 6-h, the updating of Buffer2 by Buffer3 has trimmed the last dangling back face of B from the image in Buffer2. We scan B again.

In Plate 6-i, a repeated scanning of C has not changed the contents of Buffer2. So we know that we have computed the correct visible front faces of the product in Buffer2 and we copy it into Bufferl. (Plate 6-j,k)

In 6-k, we start processing the second product. B is scanned into Buffer3. Buffer3 is updated into Buffer2 in Plate 6-l. We scan D into Buffer3 and see the part of D that is behind the front faces of B.

In Plate 6-m, we see the result of the update of Buffer2. Note that one of the faces of the images belongs to B. Scanning B into Buffer3, we see the backface of B that is behind the image in Buffer2.

In Plate 6-n, the image in Buffer2 is trimmed by the contents of Buffer3 to produce a block. We scan D into Buffer3.

In Plate 6-o,p, because the passes over B and D have caused no change in Buffer2, we merge Buffer2 into buffer1 to get the final image.

In Plate 6-q, we apply the shadow algorithm to produce the shadows on the final image.

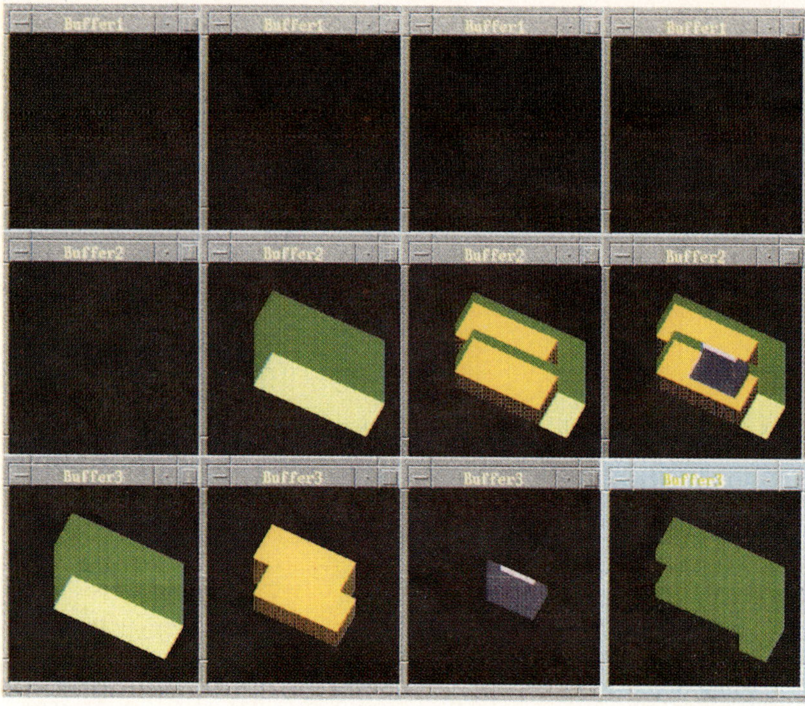


6 - a 6 - b 6 - c 6 - d

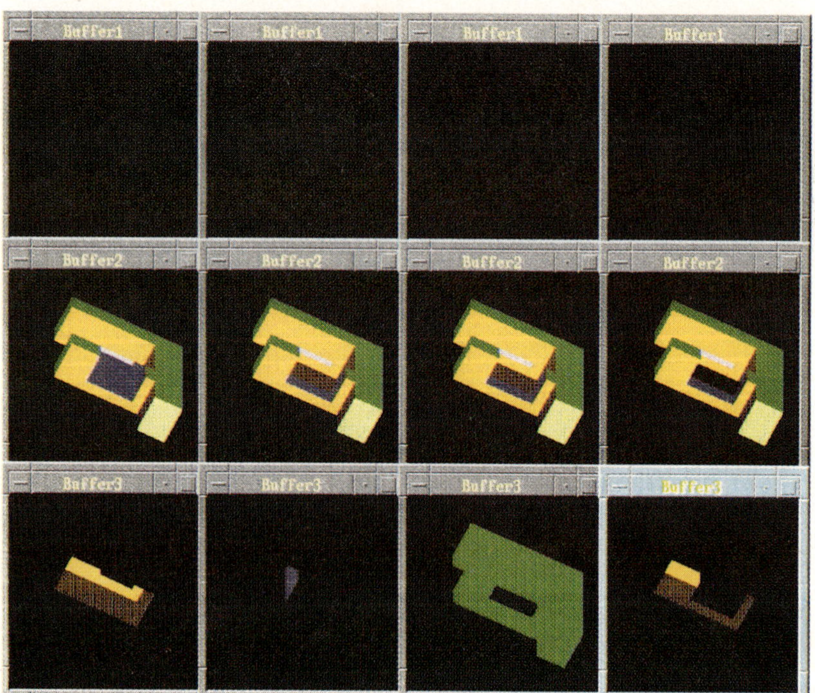


6 - e 6 - f 6 - g 6 - h

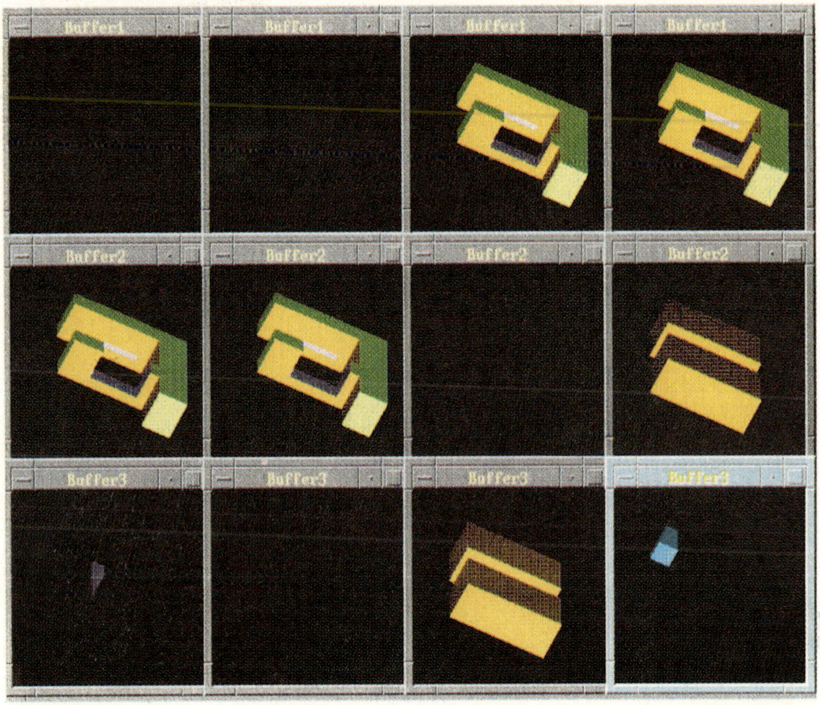


6 - i 6 - j 6 - k 6 - l

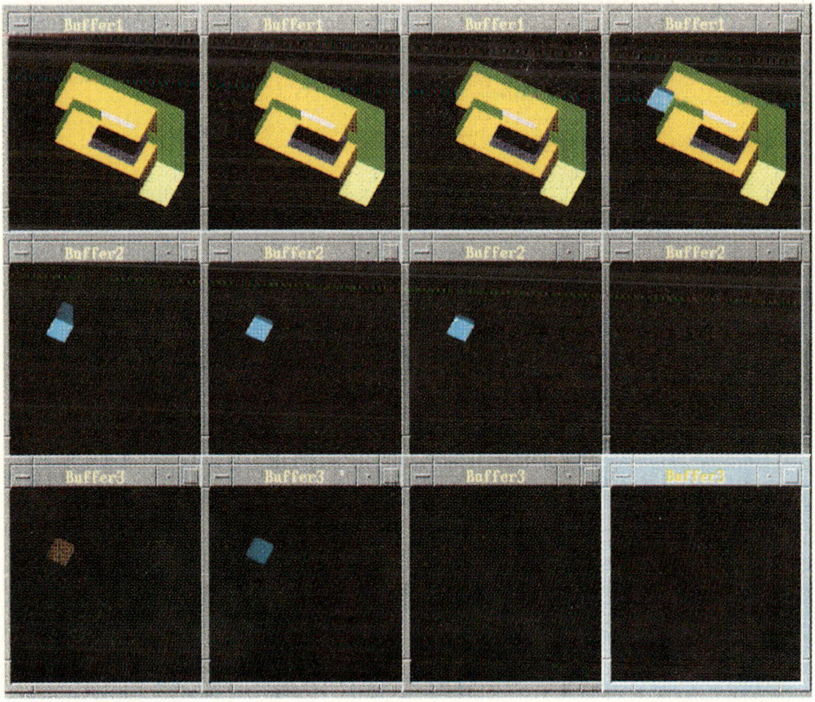


6 - m 6 - n 6 - o 6 - p

6 - q

# I.M.O.G.E.N.E.—A Solution to the Real Time Animation Problem

Christophe Chaillou, Michel Meriaux and Sylvain Karpf

ABSTRACT Current graphics processors are very slow for displaying shaded 3D objects. A lot of work is being done in order to define faster display processors by using massive parallelism and VLSI components. Our proposal goes along this line with the supplementary aim of displaying images in real time, i.e., 25 or 30 times per second. We choose to design a graphics module without any working memory and thus without frame buffer. A massive parallelism over objects, and thus a pixel pipe-line, are used. Each Object Processor handles one 3D object; all the processors work in a synchronous way, processing the same pixel simultaneously at pixel rate. These processors are built from very simple Elementary Processors (2 adders, 2 registers and 6 memory words) computing linear or quadratic expressions V(x,y), where (x,y) are the coordinates of a pixel. A pipelined tree made of basic operators (min, max, or, and, ...) gathers the results given by the Object Processors and makes inter-objects operations, i.e., at least hidden part elimination. Such a choice of course involves a high hardware complexity when displaying rather simple scenes. However, we feel that it is the price to pay for building graphics processors allowing real-time interactive animation (e.g., the graphics unit of a driving simulator).

## 1 Introduction

Our concern in this paper is to propose an original architecture for displaying images in real-time, thus obtaining a graphics processor for interactive animation. We use geometric rendering methods rather than ray-tracing or radiosity which are currently quite incompatible with the real-time constraint. Our choices are to associate graphics objects to processors and to use massive parallelism.

In a first part we shortly describe the display process of an image and the generally proposed architectural solutions. Then we present new solutions being studied and using a massive parallelism. At last we introduce a solution allowing for a real-time display processor.

The second part is a complete description of the I.M.O.G.E.N.E. machine. A special emphasis is put on the design and realization of Elementary Processors.

## 2 State of the Art

### 2.1 Rasterization [1]

The process generating pictures elements values from a geometric description of the image is called rasterization, and may be divided into four steps.

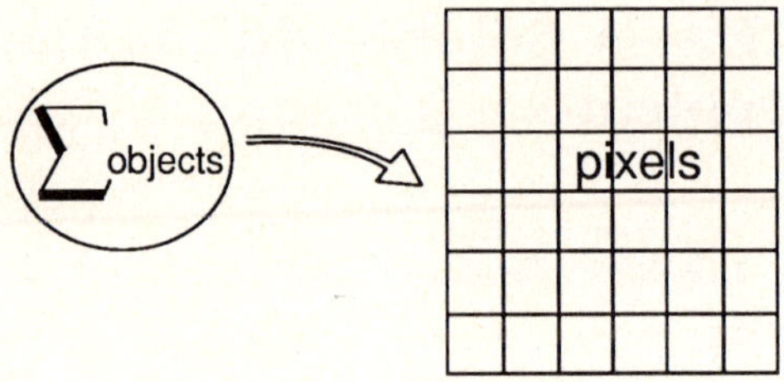


**Fig. 1.** Scan Conversion

- Traversal
  - Traverse the data structure, delivering graphics objects and light sources to the appropriate processor(s).
- Transformation
  - Objects and light sources positioning.
  - Coordinate system transformation.
  - Clipping.
- Scan Conversion
  - Transform each object into a set of pixels.
  - Hidden part elimination.
- Display

This description clearly shows that rasterization may be split into two main steps, one dealing with objects, and the other with pixels. As a matter of fact converting graphical objects into pixels requires many computations.

When real time animation is required, rasterization must be done for all the objects at image display rate. Moreover, rasterization may deal with more complex inter-objects computations (such as shadowing or transparency) that have not been presented here.

### 2.2 The Classical Architecture [2]

Figure 2 shows the architecture of currently available display machines.

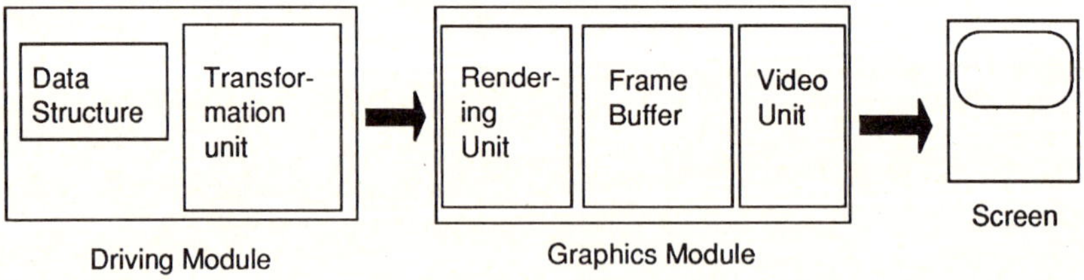


**Fig. 2.** Classical Rasterization Systems

All the current commercial graphics machines use this architecture. The most powerful ones are the Silicon Graphics 4D/240 GTX [3] and the STELLAR GS1000 [4]. They are able to display 100,000 small Gouraud-shaded three-dimensional triangles per second.

Such an architecture has the following limits:

- Limited real-time performances.
- Poor image quality due to Gouraud shading.
- Strong bottleneck between the rendering unit and the frame buffer.
- Triangle tesselation is not always an accurate solution.

## 2.3 New Architectures

In the recent years have been proposed many new architectures in order to build very powerful graphics modules. The most powerful ones use massive parallelism and VLSI components. When using such components, new constraints arise with regard to the machine design: the processors we intend to use must be simple enough to be realised in VLSI, and identical in order to limit costs. It is then interesting to choose a modular architecture in order to be able to increase machine capabilities only by adding new components.

With these assumptions, two approaches may be considered for the graphics module architecture:

- Image space partitioning, i.e., to associate processors to pixels. One processor per pixel is used, with massive pixel parallelism and thus object pipe-line. This solution can be viewed as an intelligent frame buffer.
- Object space partitioning, i.e., to associate processors to graphics objects. Thus object parallelism is used. Different objects are processed in parallel at pixel rate, pixels being processed in a pipe-lined way. With this solution the frame buffer appears to be unnecessary if inter-objects processings are done at pixel rate. Objects could be processed at a different rate, but this would involve the two following constraints:
  - There are access conflicts between the Objects Processors and the (necessary) frame buffer.
  - Inter-object operations can only be done in the frame buffer.

  Thus, object massive parallelism is interesting only when Object Processors do work at pixel rate.

## 2.4 Pixel-oriented Systems [5]

Such a machine has one processor per pixel. Two solutions with regular architecture can be considered for sending the objects to the processors:

- Broadcasting: all the objects are sent separately to all the pixels, all the processors being independent. The Pixel-Planes machine [6, 7] belongs to this class, if considering that all the objects are coded with linear expressions and that the adder trees are a broadcasting mechanism.
- Pipe-line network: the objects go from left to right through the network. The inputs are on the left edge; every processor receives the objects from its left neighbour and transmits them to its right one. The objects must have been split into horizontal spans. It is likely that such an intelligent frame buffer could be built by using one thousands of SAGE chips [8].

The main features of intelligent frame buffers are:

- Rigidness: as processors are designed for specific data types, any change would imply their full redesign.
- Uniformity, which allows an efficient VLSI implementation.

With regard to our aim (a graphics module for real-time animation), this solution appears to have some drawbacks:

- The execution time on different processors depends on the number of objects the processor has to deal with. So it is hard to guarantee that real-time will be obtained.
- There are access conflicts to the frame buffer between processors and video stream [9].
- It is not obvious that the whole scene could be loaded during the time of one image.

These are the reasons why we choose the other solution: associate the processors to the objects to be displayed.

### 2.5 Object-oriented Systems

Figure 3 shows the architecture of a general object-oriented machine. Every Object Processor (O.P.) outputs for every pixel at pixel rate the features of the corresponding object. The decision unit makes inter-objects operations, i.e., at least hidden part elimination.

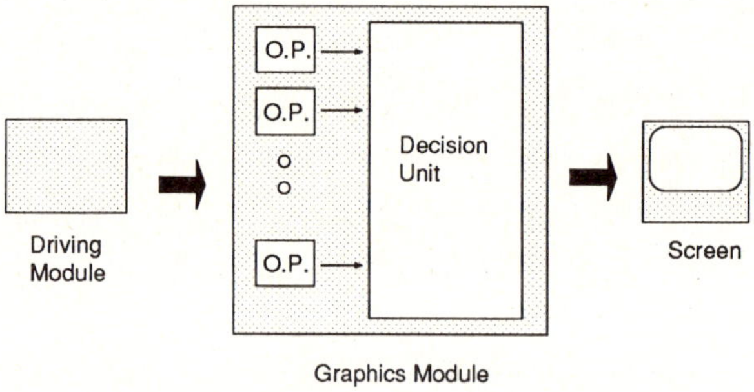


**Fig. 3.** Object-oriented rasterization system

Three open questions remain: i) how to make the decision unit, ii) with what strategy to allocate objects to the Object Processors, iii) what graphical primitives to choose?

The GSP-NVS machine [10] is a recently proposed massively parallel object-oriented machine. It uses the pipeline structure of the Weinberg machine [11], which was the first object machine proposed in 1981. GSP-NVS is made of a pipeline of VLSI processors. Every processor handles a 3D triangle. The hidden surface elimination is made by a pipelined Z-buffer algorithm. Every processor receives from the previous one in the pipeline the value to be displayed for every pixel. If, for a given pixel, the corresponding triangle has a smaller depth, the processor replaces the value by one of its triangles, else the 'old' value follows. Indeed the decision unit is distributed over every line. A pipelined post-processor computes the shading by a Phong's method for 5 light sources. PROOF [12] is another project using the same approach.

With regard to real-time display, such a machine reveals some drawbacks:

- It requires for every image a sort of the triangles depending on the vertex with the maximum ordinate, which is unthinkable in real-time.
- It may happen that on a given line there are more triangles than Object Processors. Thus all the triangles cannot be processed in one pass and real-time is lost.

The only solution to ensure real-time is to assign objects to processors before the display phase. Moreover, each Object Processor should handle only one object, because assigning several objects to the same processor would require preprocessing incompatible with the real-time display.

The idea of dealing with shading in a post-processor appears to be very fruitful, because the driving unit does not have to take care of these (heavy) computations. This post-processor must receive for every pixel the visible object with its depth and normal, and computes at pixel rate the RGB values. The driving unit must send at the beginning of every frame the positions and features of the various light sources. Another advantage of such a solution is that shading is computed for visible pixels only.

The previous analysis gives us the general architecture of a real-time object-oriented machine (see Figure 4).

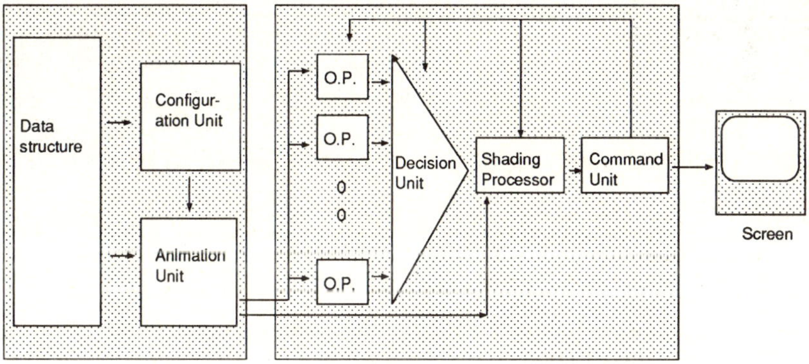


**Fig. 4.** Real-time object-oriented rasterization system

The configuration unit assigns the objects to the processors and defines the structure of the decision unit. The animation unit gives every processor at image rate the features of the corresponding object. The whole graphics module is synchronised by the command unit.

## 3 Description of I.M.O.G.E.N.E. [13]

I.M.O.G.E.N.E. (Image by Means of Objects GEnerated by Numerical Expressions) is a special implementation of the above architecture.

We choose to have synchronous Object Processors, i.e., they process the same pixel at the same time. Then the decision unit is a binary tree with $\log_2 N$ levels, $N$ being the number of objects. The decision unit makes the hidden part elimination by a distributed Z-buffer algorithm [13].

We will now describe in detail each unit of I.M.O.G.E.N.E.

## 3.1 Object Processors

*Introduction*

It is quite difficult to choose the object processors, since this choice on the one hand determines the kind of scenes that can be displayed, and on the other hand the VLSI feasibility. Indeed, if we choose a too simple basic object, the number of processors necessary for a good modelling will be very high; but if it is too complex, VLSI integration could be impossible.

Whatever the Object Processor may be, it has to indicate the decision unit whether the corresponding object is present or not at the current pixel. If it is the case, it outputs to the decision unit the depth of the object and the normal components at this point.

Moreover, it looks interesting to choose objects as close as possible to the forms they have in the data structure, in order to limit the host work. We have chosen rather complex basic objects, and thus rather complex Object Processors, but composed of several Elementary Processors working synchronously in parallel.

*The Elementary Processor*

**Definition** In the first part of this paper we have clearly shown that, with object partitioning, the Object Processors have to output values all over the scene. The Elementary Processors must have the same features. Moreover, these values must be produced with the correct sequence (i.e., after the value in (x,y), they have to produce the value in (x+1,y) then (x+2,y)...). A simple solution consists of defining the Elementary Processor as an entity computing an expression $V(x,y) = Ax^2 + By^2 + Cxy + Dx + Ey + F$ (or $F(x,y) = Ax + By + C$), with $A, B...F$ integer constants and $(x,y)$ the pixel coordinates; this value can be incrementally computed at pixel rate for every pixel at $(x,y)$.

Let us remark that this choice is not at all arbitrary, since Pixel-Planes 4 [6][7] and Pixel-Planes 5 [14] have clearly shown that such expressions could model rather realistic scenes.

**Realization** We will now detail the incremental method used for $V(x,y)$ evaluation. As the method for $F$ follows immediately, we will not present it.

N.B.: in the following, EP1 will be the Elementary Processor $F$ and EP2 the one for $V$.

Given $P(y) = Cy + D$ and $Q(y) = By^2 + Ey + F$, it follows that $V(x,y) = V1(x) = Ax^2 + Px + Q$.

The computation method consists of computing $P(y)$ and $Q(y)$ at the beginning of every line, and then for every pixel computing $V1(x)$.

Let us note that the opposite structure can be used to incrementally compute the first order expression Rx+S. Moreover, $V1(x+1) = V1(x) + (V1(x+1) - V1(x)), V1(x+1) - V1(x)$ being a first order expression, thus computable with this structure. $V1(x)$ can thus be incrementally computed by means of two serially connected structures. This new element may also be used for $P(y)$ and $Q(y)$ computations if backup registers are available. Figure 5 shows the Elementary Processor scheme and its working algorithm (assuming a non interlaced monitor).

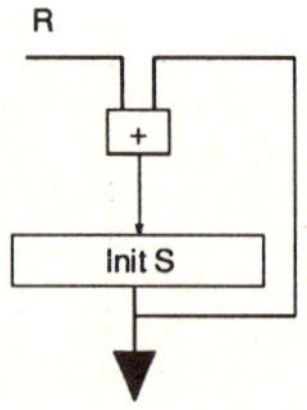

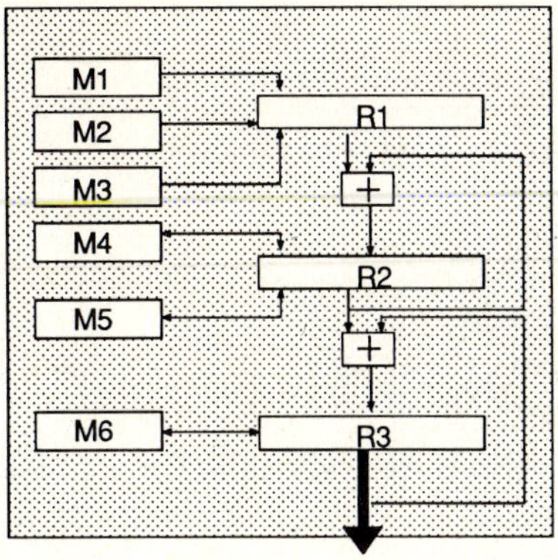


```
M1 ← 2A, M2 ← 2B, M3 ← C,
M4 ← E-B, M5 ← D-A, M6 ← F /initialization/
For every screen line Do
   R1 ← M2, R2 ← M4, R3 ← M6  /registers set up/
   first adder computation
   second adder computation
   M4 ← R2, M6 ← R3
   R1 ← M3, R2 ← M5   /registers backup/
   first adder computation
   M5 ← R2, R1 ← M1
   For every pixel Do
      first adder computation
      second adder computation
   Done
Done
```

Mi backup registers
Ri register

**Fig. 5.** Elementary Processor structure

Let us note that such a structure involves a high connection complexity and is not well suited for interlaced monitors. These are the reasons why we chose a less complex solution, using a unique backup RAM instead of backup registers (see Figure 6). The backup RAM must contain 6 memory words for a non interlaced monitor, and 12 for an interlaced one (since original coefficients must be available at the beginning of the second half frame).

A pipe-line effect appears in the Elementary Processor structure (the two additions may be computed simultaneously). Thus pixel generation time is set by the slowest element of the structure.

The working algorithm of the Elementary Processor is a bit different from that given in Figure 5: registers backups must be done through the whole structure, requiring at least three clock cycles (but during horizontal retrace). This algorithm is implemented on a microprogrammed controller.

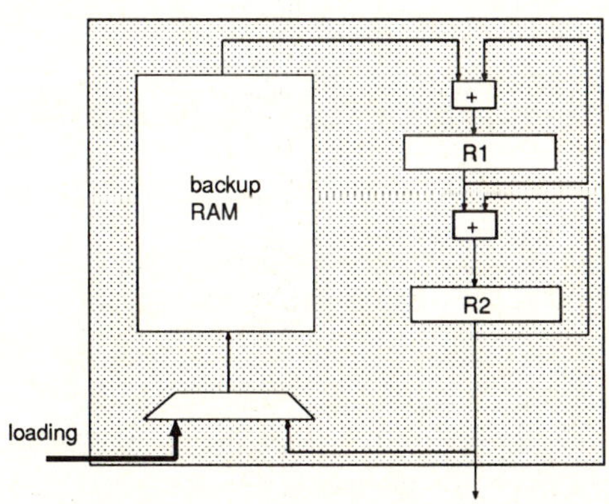


**Fig. 6.** Elementary Processor architecture

*Object Construction*

The outputs of the Elementary Processors may be interpreted as:

- A binary value (negative = absent; positive = present) indicating whether the object is present at the current pixel; combining such values allows to define the border of the object.
- The depth of the object in the viewer's reference.
- One of the components of the normal to the object at the current pixel.

These different values are combined in a pipelined tree called the Object Maker in order to define a given object. Thus an Object Processor has the following structure:

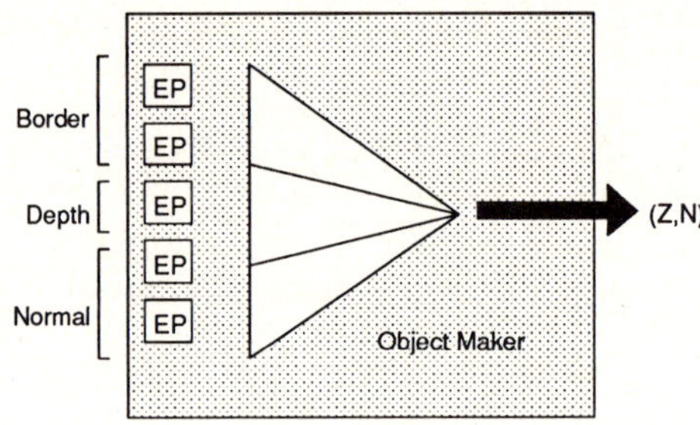


**Fig. 7.** An Object Processor Structure

Objects must be convex so that their screen border can be computed by combination of linear or quadratic expressions in a fixed structure whatever the perspective we use. Thus, the basic objects of I.M.O.G.E.N.E. are convex polyhedra, spheres, cylinders...

Let us remark that the explicit construction of convex polyhedra is unnecessary, since their faces can be considered as independent objects, the decision unit implicitly making the polyhedron construction by eliminating hidden parts with the Z-buffer algorithm.

We describe in the following Object Processors associated with a 3D triangle and a sphere.

*Triangular Face*

It may be defined by:

- Three Elementary Processors EP1 defining the border of the triangle by intersection of three half-planes.
- One Elementary Processor EP1 giving the depth for every pixel (i.e.,the equation of the 3D plane containing the triangle).
- Three Elementary Processors EP1 computing the three components (Nx, Ny, Nz) of the normal to the face by a bilinear Phong interpolation if the face approximates a surface, three constants if not.

Figure 8 shows a triangular face processor.

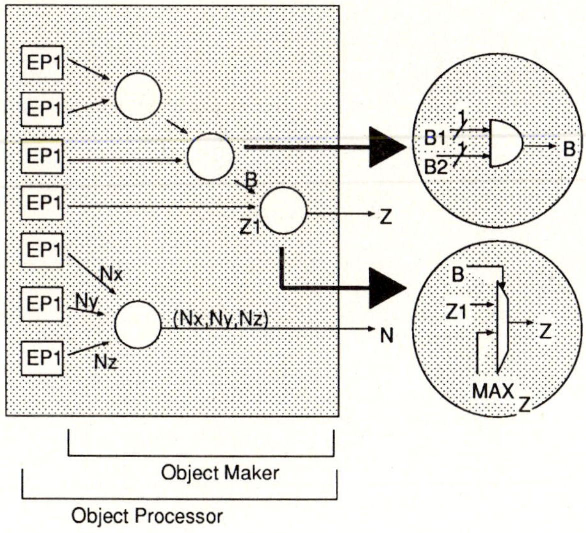


**Fig. 8.** A triangular face processor

*Sphere*

A sphere is defined by:

- One Elementary Processor EP2 to define the border of the sphere.
- One Elementary Processor EP2 to approximate the depth with a parabola.
- Three Elementary Processors (one EP2 and two Ep1s) to define the normal to the sphere.

The front half sphere is approximated with a parabola (the best parabola has been found using integral square error approximation). Simulations have shown that such an approximation is quite accurate. The Nz component is also an approximation of the same kind.

Figure 9 shows a sphere processor.

### 3.2 The Decision Unit

It is a pipelined binary tree implementing a distributed Z-buffer algorithm. All the nodes of the tree are identical; they keep the pair (Z,N) with the lower depth (see Figure 10). The decision unit may also deal with more complex inter-objects computations (e.g., shadowing and transparency), but this would involve a much higher hardware complexity.

### 3.3 The Shading Processor

It also works at pixel rate. It receives for every pixel the depth, the normal and the intrinsic features (basic colour, reflection coefficient) of the visible object, and computes the RGB values to be displayed according to light sources characteristics. In order to improve the quality of the images, the shading processor will handle diffuse and specular reflections.

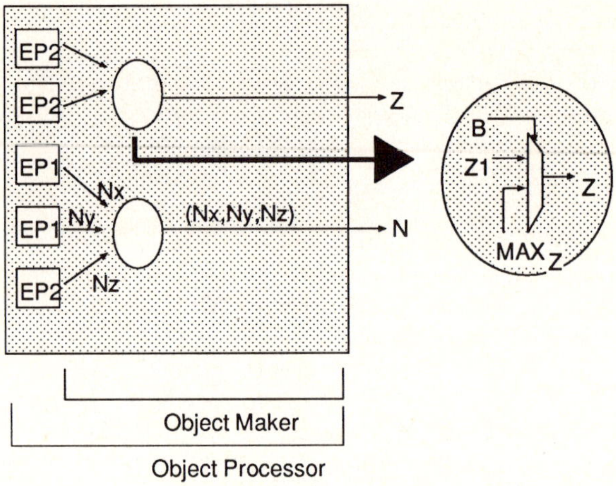


**Fig. 9.** A sphere processor

### 3.4 The Command Unit

It handles the system clock, micro-controllers and screen synchronization signals, and the Digital to Analogical conversions between the shading processor and the screen. It can be built with any standard graphics controller.

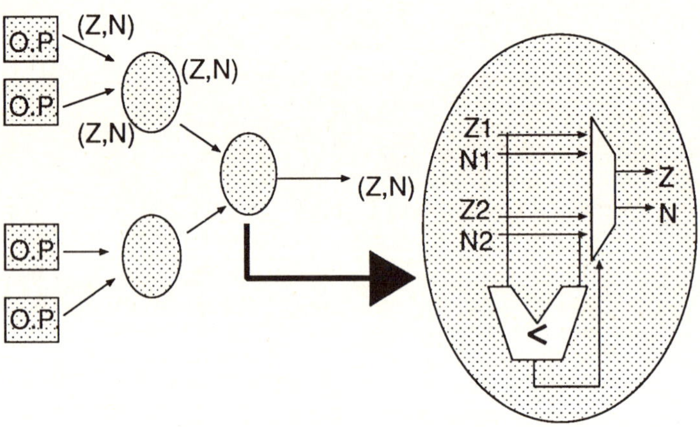


**Fig. 10.** The decision tree

### 3.5 The Driving Module

This unit is implemented on a general purpose computer, and is divided into two units.

*The Animation Unit*

The animation system computes the expressions coefficients according to objects and viewer positions. A real-time animation will be obtained only if the system is able to calculate them at screen rate; moreover, coefficients loading from the driving unit to the

Elementary Processors, and light sources information transfer to the shading unit must be achieved in the same time.

It is highly likely to use several processors for such computations in the (general) case when objects are independent. Thus coefficients loading is distributed over several links and the risk of bottleneck decreases.

*The Configuration Unit*

The Configuration Unit has to initiate the Display Unit, i.e., define the object processors structure and the way coefficients will be loaded into the Elementary Processors, before the real-time activity. The data structure must also describe for every object the elementary processor structure needed for its display.

*Link Between the Driving Module and the Graphics Module*

In order to guarantee real-time animation, the Elementary Processors backup RAMs must be refreshed at the beginning of every frame. In fact, time available for the host computer to compute and load all the Elementary Processors coefficients is $t1 + t2$, where $t1$ is display time and $t2$ vertical retrace period.

Our solution is to use a intermediate RAM where coefficients of the next frame to be displayed are stored. This RAM is controlled during period $t1$ by the host processor, and during period $t2$ by a wired automata that loads new coefficients into the Elementary Processors RAMs. Furthermore, this memory should be considered as an extension board of the host processor memory: this greatly reduces the host work, since coefficients allocation may be considered as a dynamic memory allocation.

Figure 11 illustrates the loading principle.

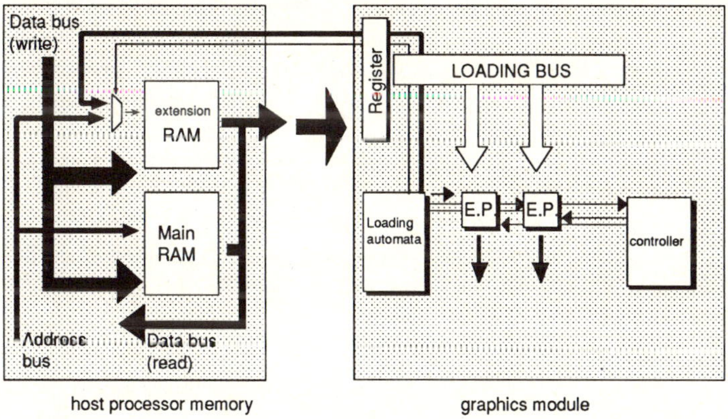


**Fig. 11.** Link between the driving module and the graphics module

# 4 Conclusion

## 4.1 Simulation

We are developing a simulation of the whole machine (Object Processors, Decision Tree and Shading Processor) on a Transputers-based workstation. This simulation has already given interesting results. Direct display of spheres or cylinders generated by means of few first and second order expressions looks better than the classical triangle tesselation. We are not studying how to build more complex objects with such expressions.

### 4.2 Realization

We have just finished the design of one second order Elementary Proccessor on a VLSI CAD software. We now intend to use these chips for designing an Object PCB, which would allow us to build a complete prototype (with of course only a small number of objects). The next step would be the design of a complete Object Processor, leading to a more powerful prototype. In the same time, we are developing the Shading processor.

### 4.3 Expected Performances

Performances directly depend on the number of Objects Processors. Moreover, classical performances tables (in number of small triangles per second) are inadequate for our machine. For example, 1000 spheres Processors would allow to display 50,000 spheres per second with a 50 Hz monitor (but only 1000 simultaneously on the screen), corresponding to at least 1,000,000 triangles per second for tesselation-based machines.

The main drawback of our machine is the limited number of simultaneously displayed objects according to the number of available object processors. This limitation can be easily overcome by connecting a classical frame buffer to the shading unit, using several frames to build a complete image (but of course losing true real-time display). With 1000 spheres processors, we could then display up to 50,000 spheres simultaneously, but at only one frame per second.

### 4.4 Future Work

As said in this paper, the objects our machine can handle are not true quadric volumes, since the second order Elementary Processor allows us to define only approximated objects (for the moment only spheres and cylinders). In order to overcome this limitation, and thus to build a dramatically more powerful machine, we are now working on a true Quadric Elementary Processor (called Q. E. P.), able to solve in real-time the general quadric equation $Ax^2 + By^2 + Cz^2 + Dxy + Exz + Fyz + Gx + Hy + Iz + K = 0$.

Such a processor will allow us to display in real-time any quadric (ellipsoid, cylinder, paraboloid, hyperboloid...). Moreover, these quadrics will be defined in the host computer directly by their equations in the screen reference.

## References

[1] Meriaux, M.: Contribution à l'imagerie informatique : aspects algorithmiques et architecturaux. *Thèse d'état* USTLFA Lille 1984.

[2] Gharachorloo, N. and Gupta, S.: A Characterization of Ten Rasterization Techniques. *ACM Computer Graphics* vol. 23 no. 3, 1989, pp. 355-368.

[3] Akeley, K.: The Silicon Graphics 4D/240GTX Superworkstation. *IEEE Computer Graphics and Applications*, vol. 9 no. 4, 1989, pp. 71-83.

[4] Apgar, B. and Bersack, B. and Mammen, A.: A Display System for the Stellar Graphics Supercomputer Model GS1000. *ACM Computer Graphics* vol. 22 no. 4, 1988 pp. 255-262.

[5] Lepretre E.: Algorithmique parallèle et architectures spécialisées pour la synthèse d'images. *Thèse de Doctorat* USTLFA Lille 1989.

[6] Fuchs, H. and Poulton, J.: Pixel-Planes:A VLSI oriented design for raster graphics engine. *VLSI Design* no.36, 1981, pp. 20-28.

[7] Eyles, J. Fuchs, H.: Pixel-Planes: a summary, in *Advances in Computer Graphics Hardware II*, Springer-Verlag, 1988, pp. 183-207.

[8] Gharachorloo, N.: Subnanosecond pixel rendering with million transistor chips. *ACM Computer Graphics* vol. 22, no. 4, 1988, pp.41-49.

[9] Cordonnier, V. and Meriaux, M.: Image display from multiprocessors. *SID International Symposium*, Digest of technical papers, vol. 21, 1990, pp. 49-52.

[10] Deering, M.: The triangle processor and normal vector shader: a VLSI system for high performance graphics. *ACM Computer Graphics* vol. 22, no. 4, 1988, pp. 21-30.

[11] Weinberg R.: Parallel Processing Image Synthesis and Antialiasing. *ACM Computer Graphics* vol. 15, no. 3, 1981, pp. 55-62.

[12] Schneider, B. and Claussen, U.: PROOF: An Architecture for Rendering in Object Space. *Advances in Computer Graphics Hardware III*, Springer-Verlag, 1989.

[13] Chaillou, C. et al.: A real-time Image Generator. *Proc. of the Eighth IASTED International Symposium Applied Informatics*, ACTA PRESS, 1990, pp. 140-143.

[14] Goldfeather, J.: Fast constructive solid geometry display in the Pixel-Powers graphics system. *ACM Computer Graphics* vol. 20, no. 4, 1986, pp. 107-116.

# A New Space Partitioning for Mapping Computations of the Radiosity Method onto a Highly Pipelined Parallel Architecture

Li-Sheng Shen, E. Deprettere and P. Dewilde

ABSTRACT Despite the fact that realistic images can be generated by ray-tracing and radiosity shading, these techniques are impractical for scenes of high complexity because of the extremely high time cost. Several attempts have been made to reduce image synthesis time by using parallel architectures, but they still suffer from communication problems. In this paper, we present a new space partitioning which is adaptive to the local environment seen by a bundle of rays. Two tracking mechanisms are embedded to guarantee adaptation. When using a shared memory parallel architecture, the communication load between the host and the PEs can be alleviated with this approach. Furthermore, the partitioning provides a better balancing between processing throughput and I/O bandwidth which will enhance the pipelinability of computations, especially when a high speed cache memory is allowed for each PE. Combining those factors, a highly pipelined parallel architecture can be used to accelerate computations in ray-tracing and radiosity methods. The technique has been tested on different scenes with randomly generated patches in a 2D setting. When compared with the conventional technique, promising results have been observed. This technique can be easily extended to 3D.

## 1 Introduction

In the fields of solid modeling and computer graphics, the most promising method to render realistic images is based on ray-tracing and radiosity shading, because it can account for all important physical effects occurring in the scene. Ray tracing, first described by Appel [1], cannot alone account for global illumination, since that is dependent on all objects in the environment. Although some fairly realistic images have been obtained using solely ray-tracing, this technique ignores the interreflection of light between diffusely reflecting surfaces. In 1984, Goral [2] introduced a radiosity method borrowed from radiative heat transfer to model the interreflection between diffusely reflecting surfaces. After that, substantial efforts have exerted on it: Cohen [3,4] presented the hemi-cube algorithm to calculate form-factors by projecting patches onto a hemi-cube and presented the substructuring technique to render areas possessing high intensity gradients by adaptive patch subdivision. Immel [5] extended the radiosity method to treat an environment consisting of non-diffuse surfaces. Wallace [6] proposed a combined radiosity and ray-tracing method to render a complex environment; they called it the two-pass approach.

Despite the fact that the two-pass approach can generate realistic images, it is impractical for scenes of high complexity because of extremely high time and storage costs. In ray-tracing, a large amount of intersection computations is needed. In fact, it is proportional to the number of screen pixels (even more when supersampling is used to accommodate for anti-aliasing, or when secondary rays are taken into account) and the number of surfaces in the environment. This situation becomes even worse if form-factor computations are also based on ray- tracing, because the number of intersections computed for calculating form-factors is at the order of $(N^2 \times R)$, where $N$ is the number of patches in the environment and $R$ is the number of rays on a hemisphere. Apart from this computation cost, the storage capacity needed to store the form-factor matrix is extremely high. Indeed, assuming the form-factor matrix is 90% sparse, it still requires 400 gigabytes of storage for an environment consisting of 1M patches.

To overcome the storage problem in the radiosity method, Cohen [7] proposed a progressive refinement approach to reduce the storage capacity to $O(N)$. To overcome the computation problem in ray-tracing, two main strategies have been devised. The first strategy is to exploit coherence. One kind of coherence is called ray coherence: Heckbert [8] proposed a beam-tracing algorithm in which a beam of rays, instead of a single ray, traces an environment consisting of polygons. Speer [9] also exploit this coherence in their coherent ray-tracing algorithm. Another kind of coherence is called spatial coherence. This sort of coherence is exploited in space partitioning techniques to reduce the number of patches to be considered. Many different encoding schemes for space partitioning have been proposed: octree [10], binary tree [11] and voxel [12]. Basically, the 3D object-space is subdivided into cells based on a specific encoding scheme. One ray is shot and tested against each patch in the first cell. If the ray hits some patches in this cell, a nearest distance test must be invoked to determine the intersection point. Otherwise, the next cell (or cells) will be traversed and tested again until there is a hit or the boundary of the data structure is reached. After that, the procedure proceeds to the next ray and iterates again. One very promising result of the space partitioning technique is that the performance is nearly independent of the scene complexity.

The second strategy relies on parallel processing. Parallel architectures can be classified into three classes: processing without dataflow [13,14], processing with ray dataflow [15,16], and processing with object dataflow [17,18]. The drawback of the first class is that it cannot render complex scenes due to the limited size of local memories. As for the second class, a ray might pass through a number of processors such that the efficiency of the system will be degraded due to this communication overhead. This can be resolved by assigning rays to processors as the third class does, but it requires an efficient way to access the whole database. For comparison purpose, we refer to the third class as the conventional technique throughout this paper.

Ray tracing has already been used as a method for determining the form-factors in the radiosity method. We have capitalized on a hardware oriented two-pass approach [19] in which both the preprocess and the postprocess are ray tracing based. Unfortunately, the two strategies stated above can not be applied successfully in this case. This is due to the following:

- In the radiosity method, each patch in the environment will be chosen as a source to start a ray-tracing algorithm to compute form-factors. For each source patch, a costly depth-sorted list of polygons must be constructed. The time spent on constructing such a list will be at the order of $O(N^2)$ at worst, where $N$ is the number of polygons after splitting which is larger than the original number [20].

- Since any patch in the environment will become the source patch, the architecture with ray dataflow is certainly undesirable. As for the architecture with object dataflow, many regions can be processed in parallel, but each processor still works on a serial ray base within its own region. Consequently, a patch might be loaded many times from the global or local memory because the neighboring rays are most likely to traverse similar cells and even hit the same patch. This accounts for a lot of waste in the sense of communication.

In this paper we present a new space partitioning technique to alleviate the communication problem stated above. Moreover, two tracking mechanisms are considered to exploit the ray coherence with low cost.

The outline of the paper is as follows. After defining some basic terms in Section 2, we present the main technique in a two-dimensional setting and suggest two possibilities to extend it to 3D in Section 3. We formalize the intersection computation time and the speedup factor of this technique in Section 4. In Section 5, the results from a number of scenes with randomly generated patches are shown and compared with the conventional technique.

## 2 Basic Terms

In this section we define some basic terms to facilitate the discussion in subsequent sections.

**Definition 2.1 (Polygonal Patch)** A polygonal patch $P$ with $v$ vertices ($v \geq 3$) is defined by the inner area of a convex planar polygon with simple or non-self-intersecting boundary. It will be represented by the coordinates of its vertices $V_i = (x_i, y_i, z_i)$, $i = 1, 2, \ldots, v$, the coordinates of its center point $O = (x_c, y_c, z_c)$, and the unit normal vector $\vec{n}$ of the plane enclosing P, i.e.,

$$P = \{V_i, O, \vec{n} \mid i = 1, 2, \ldots, v\}.$$

Usually, a polygonal patch can only emit light energy into its front side, i.e., the half-space containing $\vec{n}$. Similarly, a polygonal patch can only receive light energy from its front side.

**Definition 2.2 (Backward Polygonal Patch)** Given polygonal patches $P$ and $P'$, $P'$ is said to be a backward polygonal patch for $P$ when it is not located at the front side of $P$.

**Definition 2.3 (Spherical Bounding Box of a Polygonal Patch)** Let

$$P = \{V_i, O, \vec{n} \mid i = 1, 2, \ldots, v\}$$

be a polygonal patch with $v$ vertices, and let the polar coordinates of vertex $V_i$ be $r_i$, $\Theta_i$, and $\Phi_i$. The spherical bounding box $B$ of $P$ is defined as the region bounded by six surfaces represented in the polar coordinates: $r = r_{min}, r = r_{max}, \Theta = \Theta_{min}, \Theta = \Theta_{max}, \Phi = \Phi_{min}, and\ \Phi = \Phi_{max}$, where the min and max denote the minimum and maximum value of the corresponding polar coordinates.

**Definition 2.4 (Spanning Angle and Flatness of a Polygonal Patch)** Let $B$, which is the region bounded by six surfaces represented in the polar coordinates: $r = r_{min}, r = r_{max}, \Theta = \Theta_{min}, \Theta = \Theta_{max}, \Phi = \Phi_{min}$, and $\Phi = \Phi_{max}$, be the spherical bounding box of a polygonal patch $P$. The spanning angles $\omega_\theta$, and $\omega_\phi$ of $P$ are defined as $\omega_\theta = \Theta_{max} - \Theta_{min}$, and $\omega_\phi = \Phi_{max} - \Phi_{min}$. The flatness $\eta$ of $P$ is defined as $\eta = r_{max} - r_{min}$.

**Definition 2.5 (Sector)** Let a hemisphere ray $\vec{r_i}$ be represented by its origin that is the centroid of the hemisphere, and the unit direction vector

$$\vec{a_i} = (\sin\Phi_i \cos\Theta_i, \sin\Phi_i \sin\Theta_i, \cos\Phi_i).$$

A sector bounded by the boundary rays $\vec{rb_1}, \vec{rb_2}, \vec{rb_3}$, and $\vec{rb_4}$, i.e., the hemisphere rays with the following unit direction vectors:

$$(\sin\Phi_1 \cos\Theta_1, \sin\Phi_1 \sin\Theta_1, \cos\Phi_1),$$
$$(\sin\Phi_2 \cos\Theta_2, \sin\Phi_2 \sin\Theta_2, \cos\Phi_2),$$
$$(\sin\Phi_2 \cos\Theta_1, \sin\Phi_2 \sin\Theta_1, \cos\Phi_2),$$
$$(\sin\Phi_1 \cos\Theta_2, \sin\Phi_1 \sin\Theta_2, \cos\Phi_1),$$

is defined as the set of hemisphere rays $\vec{r_i}, i = 1, \ldots, r.$, with the following properties:

- The angular component $\Theta_i$ of the unit direction vector $\vec{a_i}$ is bounded by the real numbers $\Theta_1$ and $\Theta_2$, i.e., $\Theta_1 \leq \Theta_i < \Theta_2$.
- The angular component $\Phi_i$ of the unit direction vector $\vec{a_i}$ is bounded by the real numbers $\Phi_1$ and $\Phi_2$, i.e., $\Phi_1 \leq \Phi_i < \Phi_2$.

**Definition 2.6 (Shell)** Let $V$ be a sector bounded by $\vec{rb_1}, \vec{rb_2}, \vec{rb_3}$, and $\vec{rb_4}$ as defined in the definition. A shell $\nabla$ in $V$ is defined as the region bounded by six surfaces represented in the polar coordinates: $r = r_1, r = r_2, \Theta = \Theta_1, \Theta = \Theta_2, \Phi = \Phi_1$, and $\Phi = \Phi_2$. It can be represented as,

$$\nabla = \{\vec{rb_1}, \vec{rb_2}, \vec{rb_3}, \vec{rb_4}, \zeta_1, \zeta_2\}$$

where $\zeta_1$ and $\zeta_2$ denote the surfaces represented in the polar coordinates: $r = r_1$ and $r = r_2$, respectively.

**Definition 2.7 (Spanning Angle and Depth of a Shell)** Let

$$\nabla = \{\vec{rb_1}, \vec{rb_2}, \vec{rb_3}, \vec{rb_4}, \zeta_1, \zeta_2\}$$

be a shell as defined in the definition. The spanning angles $\Omega_\theta$, and $\Omega_\phi$ of $\nabla$ are defined as $\Omega_\theta = \mid \theta_1 - \theta_2 \mid$, and $\Omega_\phi = \mid \Phi_1 - \Phi_2 \mid$. The depth $\Gamma$ of $\nabla$ is defined as $\Gamma = \mid r_1 - r_2 \mid$.

**Definition 2.8 (Degree of Local Coherence)** For a prescribed discretization (and hence a prescribed number of rays confined to a hemisphere) of the surface of a hemisphere, the degree of local coherence of a patch $P$ with respect to a point $O$ is defined as the number of rays shot from $O$ through the hemisphere placed over $O$, that hit $P$.

**Definition 2.9 (Active Patch)** Let $O$ be a point over which a hemisphere is placed to start a ray-tracing algorithm. An active patch with respect to the point $O$ is a patch whose degree of local coherence with respect to the point $O$ is nonzero.

**Definition 2.10 (Average Degree of Local Coherence)** Consider an environment which consists of a number of patches. Let the degree of local coherence of active patches with respect to a point $O$ over which a hemisphere is placed to start a ray-tracing algorithm, be $D_1, D_2, \ldots, D_N$. The average degree of local coherence of the environment with respect to the point $O$, which we denote $ADLC$, is defined as,

$$ADLC = \frac{\sum_{i=1}^{N} D_i}{N}$$

## 3 The Main Technique

In this section, a technique relying on an adaptive tracking mechanism to construct a shell structure which can support a highly pipelined parallel architecture for the radiosity method is described. For simplicity, we first explain it in a two-dimensional setting. Then we propose two possibilities to extend it to 3D. We already mentioned the communication problems which may arise from parallel architectures. This motivates us to think out a new space partitioning technique featuring the following properties:

- The partitioning of space should be consistent with the direction of rays such that a ray does not travel through many partitions.
- The partitioning of space should be adaptive to the local environment seen by rays such that each active patch needs to be loaded only once from the memory that stores it.

This is just what we have called the shelling technique. Conceptually, it can be viewed as a method that strives to construct an ideal structure as shown in Figure 1. The half-space seen by the source patch is first subdivided into sectors. Then, a sector is subdivided into a number of shells. Ideally, a shell can be matched with the the active patch which actually defines the shell[1]. When this structure has been constructed, the bundle of rays in a sector is shot and tested against the active patch within the shell currently considered. With the ideal structure considered here, each active patch needs to be loaded only once as desired. Furthermore, when assigning sectors to processors, it is clear that a ray is always processed by one processor.

Besides the saving in communication cost, the shelling technique has a further advantage is that the resulting shell structure is amenable to a highly pipelined parallel architecture. To see this, recall first that for achieving high throughput, the conventional technique can exploit concurrency at the patch side, i.e., each ray traced can be tested against all the patches within a cell in a pipelined fashion. However, the following two factors will jeopardize the pipeline efficiency[2]:

- When using a shared memory parallel architecture, it is very time-consuming to load a patch from the memory. This will preclude the applicability of pipelined computations.
- In general, a ray can only hit one patch at most. This implies that the conventional technique can only fill up pipeline stages with irrelevant hidden patches, which would be meaningless.

On the contrary, the shelling technique exploits concurrency at the ray side, i.e., a bundle of rays can be tested against each relevant patch within a shell in a pipelined fashion. With this approach, the two detrimental factors mentioned above do not exist. This is because:

- When using a shared memory parallel architecture, the shelling technique provides a better balancing between processing time and I/O time such that the pipeline

[1]A shell is said to be matched with a patch when the shell is aligned perfectly with the visible part of the patch. Hence one necessary condition for this definition is that the spanning angle of the shell must be equal to the degree of local coherence of the patch.

[2]The pipeline efficiency is used to measure the performance of a pipeline and is defined as the ratio of busy time-space span over the total time-space span.

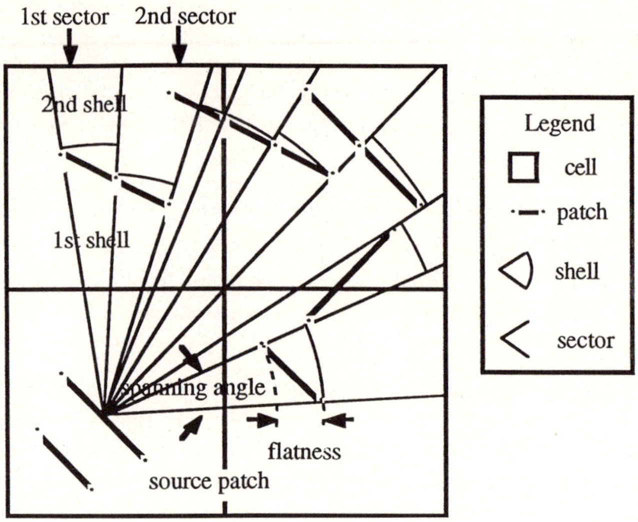


**Fig. 1.** The ideal shell and sector structures in the shelling technique.

efficiency will be higher than the conventional technique. This property will be very promising when a high speed cache memory is allowed for each PE. This is because the intersection computation time between a bundle of rays and a patch can readily balance with the loading time of the next patch for an environment with reasonable degree of local coherence.

- In general, a patch can be hit by many rays, it is desirable to fill up pipeline stages with those rays.

However, there are two major problems in constructing the shell structure. First, this specific structure cannot be chosen as an original data structure because it varies with the source patches. Second, it is costly to match a shell with the active patch which defines the shell. A simple solution to the first problem is to superimpose this structure on an uniform grid data structure as shown in Figure 1 such that relevant patches can be found by working on this well-developed data structure. As for the second problem, the actual degree of local coherence of an active patch can be estimated from its neighborhood with low cost. This is due to the fact that in realistic situations, neighboring patches appear to possess similar shapes. This can be understood from the following:

- Neighboring patches most likely belong to the surface of the same object. For an object with smooth surface, neighboring patches are often similar in some sense.

- When using the substructuring technique as proposed in [4] to account for the effect of high intensity gradients, it is necessary to provide a reasonable initial subdivision for the surfaces of a scene such that neighboring patches will become similar indeed.

Exploiting these facts, an adaptive tracking mechanism which employs the neighborhood information to estimate the degree of local coherence is devised. In the next section, we shall discuss the shelling technique with this tracking mechanism. We shall call it the stochastic shelling technique hereafter.

## 3.1 Main Procedures

From the above discussions, the stochastic shelling technique can be broken into four main procedures: preprocessing, screening, tracking, and intersection computation.

- Preprocessing

  The main purpose of this step is to build a data structure on which the shell structure can be superimposed such that relevant patches can be searched efficiently. We have chosen the uniform grid cells with macro-regions proposed in [21] as our underlying data structure.

- Screening

  Because the intersection computation for each patch will proceed with a bundle of rays in the shelling technique, it is necessary to screen out irrelevant patches before computing intersection points. This step is similar to that of searching small sets of surfaces by cell traversal in the conventional space partitioning technique, but additional angle comparisons are necessary to cull patches which reside within (at least partly) the shell currently considered. Meanwhile, backward patches which are located at the back side of a source patch will be screened out.

- Tracking

  After the screening step, the spanning angle and flatness of relevant patches in the shell are computed and they will contribute to the *ADLC* and the average flatness of the shell. We use the *ADLC* of the first shell in a sector to set up the next sector. All the shells in the next sector can be constructed by subdividing the sector along the radial direction. In order to pass neighborhood information smoothly, we choose a constant shell depth, but shells can be further subdivided based on the *ADLC* and the average flatness coming from one of their neighboring shells to reduce the number of intersection computations. In the case when there is no such neighborhood information, the algorithm will choose default values. Conceptually, the way of tracking is to traverse a region, which is most probably empty as match as possible in the radial direction but as narrow as possible in the angular direction. On the contrary, it will traverse a region which is most probably nonempty as narrow as possible in the radial direction but as match as possible in the angular direction.

- Intersection Computation

  When the local shell structure has been constructed, the bundle of rays in a sector proceeds to compute the intersection points with each relevant patch within the shell currently considered. Only remaining rays leaving one shell will enter the next shell and need to be processed again until there is no ray left or the boundary of the data structure is reached. Intersection computation is the most time-consuming step because a huge number of intersection points need to be computed, but the regular and repeatedly executed nature of this operation makes it very appealing for a pipelined circuit. For polygonal patches, we can adopt the circuit as proposed in [22] which is built from commercial chips or the circuit as proposed in [23] which is built from pipelined Cordic processors.

### 3.2 Extension to 3D

It is easier to explain the concept and the nature of the shelling technique in 2D. Nonetheless, it is only the 3D version that is of major interest to us. In the following, we suggest two possibilities to extend it to 3D.

- Intuitively, we can extend the 2D version directly to 3D. In 3D, a shell is defined by three polar coordinates instead of two. In order to pass neighborhood information smoothly, we must fix the shell depth and one of the two angles. Just like in 2D, a shell can be subdivided further in radial and two angular directions based on neighborhood information. However, we have found two difficulties for this approach. First, it is difficult to compute the spanning angle wj because max and min do not necessarily occur at vertices of a patch. Second, the spherical bounding box of a patch might be a loose convex hull of this patch.

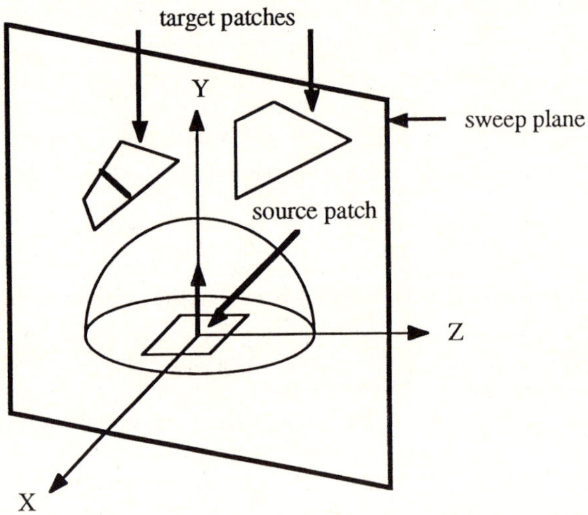


**Fig. 2.** The geometry of a sweep plane and patches in 3D.

- We can also transform our 3D problem into a 2D problem. A simple way is to use a sweep plane to slice 3D hemisphere rays and polygonal patches (see Figure 2) into 2D rays on the hemicircle and line segments, and then rotate the sweep plane to coincide with the YZ-plane as shown in Figure 3. Now we can use the technique described above to treat it. With this approach, a modification must be made in the tracking step. Instead of using *ADLC* coming from neighboring shells, the actual degree of local coherence of a patch must be derived. This is because the orientation of line segments originating from slicing a patch will not in general parallel with the orientation of one of the subdivision axes of the patch such that neighboring line segments do not possess similar shapes at all. In order to derive actual degree of local coherence, a sorting procedure is necessary to sort patches by increasing angle. In addition to the overhead introduced by the sorting procedure, another drawback of this approach is that the degree of local coherence captured in 2D is far less than

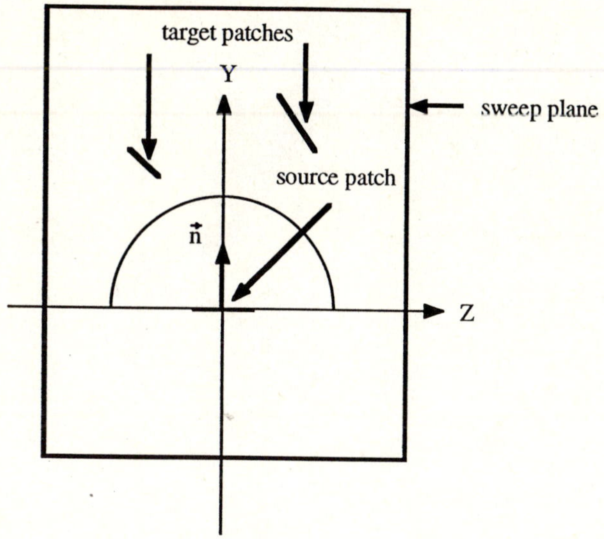


**Fig. 3.** A coordinate system to represent rays and patches in 2D.

the actual degree of local coherence. For clarity, we refer to the shelling technique with this tracking mechanism as the deterministic shelling technique.

Finally, we want to show the resulting shell structures of the stochastic and deterministic shelling techniques in Figure 4, and 5. In Figure 4, we can see sectors, shells, and subshells which are constructed by using neighborhood information. Some degree of mismatch between a subshell and a patch can be observed from the figure. This is because the stochastic shelling technique can only estimate the degree of local coherence of a patch but not its position. In Figure 5, each shell is exactly matched with the active patch which actually defines the shell. Notice that only a small portion of patches in an environment are necessary to be considered in both cases. This is due to cell traversal procedure.

## 4 Formal Comparisons

In this section, we derive an estimate of the intersection computation time for the shelling technique and the conventional technique. In order to simplify the derivation, we make the following assumptions:

- The patches are uniformly distributed in the space, and
- For a given number of rays, the percentage of rays leaving a shell will be constant if the product of the number of patches in the shell and the density of the rays in the shell is constant.

Based on those assumptions, we can derive a shell structure as shown in Figure 6 (represented conceptually in 2D) such that the percentage of rays leaving all the shells can be kept the same. Let $R$ be the number of rays in the starting shell, $P$ the number of patches in this shell, and let $S$ be the percentage of rays leaving any shell. Moreover,

**Fig. 4**. The actual shell structure of the stochastic shelling technique.

**Fig. 5**. The actual shell structure of the deterministic shelling technique.

let $T_\lambda$ be the pipeline period of the intersection computation circuit as proposed in [22] or [23]. The intersection computation time for the shelling technique, $T_1$, can be estimated to be

$$T_1(R\,P + S\,R\,2^2\,S\,P + S^2\,R\,3^2\,S^2\,P + \ldots)T_\lambda \tag{1}$$

Here we assume that the intersection computation time of one patch with respect to a bundle of rays can balance the arrival time of the next patch. Notice that the remaining rays need to visit only a fraction of patches because of cell traversal procedure. Evaluating the series in Equation 1, we obtain

$$\begin{aligned} T_1 &= \frac{(1+S^2)\,R\,P\,T_\lambda}{(1-S^2)^3} && (2)\\ &= K_1\,R\,P\,T_\lambda && (3) \end{aligned}$$

where

$$K_1 = \frac{(1+S^2)}{(1-S^2)^3} \tag{4}$$

The effect of $S$ on $K_1$ is depicted in Figure 7. From this, we observe that $K_1$ increases slowly when $S$ is small, but it rises up very quickly when $S$ approaches to 1. This explains the purpose and the necessity of introducing a tracking mechanism in the shelling technique.

From the definition of $ADLC$, we can derive the $ADLC$ of shell $i$ as follows:

$$ADLC_i = \frac{K\,R}{i^2\,P} \tag{5}$$

We compute the intersection computation time of the conventional technique in shell $i$, $T2_i$, as follows:

$$T2_i = \begin{cases} (S^i\,i^2\,P + S^{i-1}\,K\,R)\,T_c & \text{if } ADLC_i > 1, \\ (S^{i-1}\,i^2\,P)\,T_c & \text{if } ADLC_i \le 1 \end{cases} \tag{6}$$

where $K = (1 - S)$ denotes the percentage of rays screened out in a shell, and $T_c$ is the data arrival time of the intersection computation circuit which will be dominated by the loading time of one patch from the host when using a shared memory parallel architecture.

From Equation 1, we can express the portion of time of $T_1$ spent on shell $i$, $T_{1_i}$, as follows:

$$T_{1_i} = \begin{cases} S^{2(i-1)}\,R\,i^2\,P\,T_\lambda & \text{if } S^{i-1}\,RT_\lambda > T_c \\ S^{i-1}\,i^2\,P\,T_c & \text{if } S^{i-1}\,RT_\lambda \le T_c \end{cases} \tag{7}$$

Here we have allowed the intersection computation time of one patch not to balance the arrival time of the next patch. If balancing is achieved, then only the first part of Equation 7 will apply as was in Equation 1.

Comparing Equation 6 and Equation 7, we see that:

- When $ADLC_i$ is not larger than 1, there is no advantage at all to use the shelling technique. This is because

$$\begin{cases} T_{1_i} > T_{2_i} & \text{if } S^{i-1}\,RT_\lambda > T_c \\ T_{1_i} = T_{2_i} & \text{if } S^{i-1}\,RT_\lambda \le T_c \end{cases} \tag{8}$$

- From the above, only in case that $ADLC_i$ is larger than 1 is of major interest to us. If we can subdivide a shell into subshells such that the number of rays within a subshell $i$ is equal to $ADLC_i$, then we have

$$T_{1_i} = \begin{cases} K\,S^{i-1}\,RT_\lambda & \text{if } \left(\frac{K\,R}{i^2\,P}\right) T_\lambda > T_c \\ S^{i-1}\,i^2\,P\,T_c & \text{if } \left(\frac{K\,R}{i^2\,P}\right) T_\lambda \le T_c \end{cases} \tag{9}$$

From Equation 6 and Equation 9, we obtain

$$SF_i = \begin{cases} (1+ \frac{S}{ADLC_i})\left(\frac{T_c}{T_\lambda}\right) & if \left(\frac{KR}{i^2P}\right) T_\lambda > T_c, \\ S + ADLC_i & if \left(\frac{KR}{i^2P}\right) T_\lambda \le T_c \end{cases} \tag{10}$$

where $SF_i = T_{2_i}/T_{1_i}$ is called the speedup factor in shell $i$ that denotes the ratio of the intersection computation time that spent on shell $i$ in both techniques. The optimum point lies at $S = 0$,i.e., $K = 0$, in which case $SF_i$ is given by

$$SF_i = \begin{cases} \frac{T_c}{T_\lambda} & if \left(\frac{KR}{i^2P}\right) T_\lambda > T_c \\ ADLC_i & if \left(\frac{KR}{i^2P}\right) T_\lambda \le T_c \end{cases} \tag{11}$$

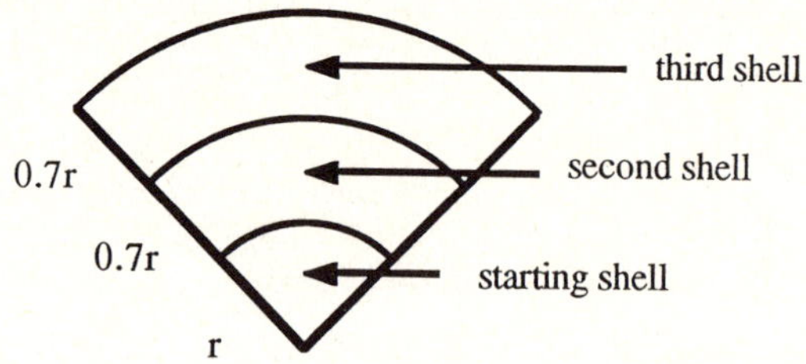


**Fig. 6.** A shell structure to keep the percentage of rays leaving all the shells the same.

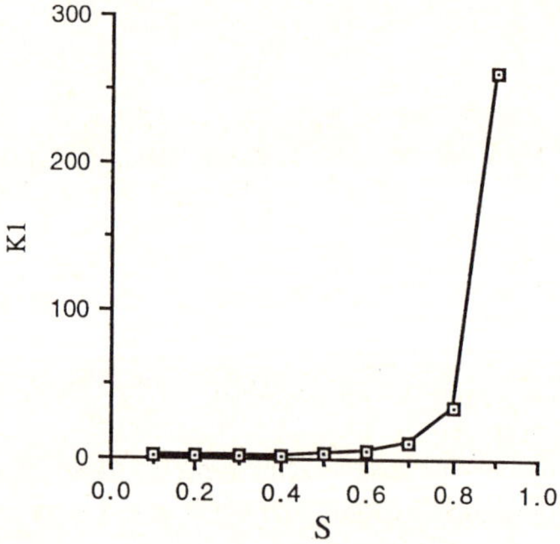


**Fig. 7.** The effect of S on K1.

We can make some remarks as follows:

- The shelling technique provides a more balanced structure for processing time and I/O time.

- A considerable speedup can be obtained when the environment consists of large patches (actually large $ADLC$). If a shared memory parallel architecture is adopted, the speedup factor will be $ADLC$ because the data arrival time $Tc$ is dominated by the loading time of one patch from the host. However, when a high speed cache memory is allowed for each PE and the next patch can be loaded immediately from that memory, the speedup factor will be the ratio of $Tc$ over $T_\lambda$. In general, the speedup factor lies in-between which can be determined only when the detailed statistics about the environment and the underlying architecture are known.

## 5 The Results

The two shelling techniques as described in Section 3 have been implemented in the C language. Different scenes with randomly generated patches (actually 1000 line segments in 2D) have been tested. The length of the segments is within the following: 4, 8, 16, 32, 64, and 128. In this section, we compare the results of three techniques: the stochastic shelling technique, the deterministic shelling technique, and the conventional technique. For convenience, the stochastic and deterministic shelling techniques are referred to shelling technique S and shelling technique D, respectively.

In the following, three factors will be taken into account for comparison purpose:

- The number of patches read in (refer to Figure 8 and 9)

  When using a shared memory parallel architecture, this is the most important factor in determining the performance. The saving from the two shelling techniques strongly depends on the actual $ADLC$ of an environment. A considerable saving can be observed when the actual $ADLC$ is high. Notice from the figure that the number of patches read in after screening in shelling technique D will approach that of shelling technique S. This motivates us to screen irrelevant patches out before loading them.

- The Number of Cells Traversed (refer to Figure 10)

  The results of three techniques are much the same. This is because we did not use radius comparison to cull relevant patches. As said before, one drawback of shelling technique S is that the prescribed shell depth will limit the span of passing empty regions.

- The Number of Intersection Computations (refer to Figure 11)

  In order to see the overhead of introducing wasteful intersection computations, here we compare results with actual value. It is interesting that the result of shelling technique S is always about twice that of the actual value. This is reasonable because shelling technique S can only estimate the degree of local coherence of a patch in a shell but not its position. So one additional bundle of rays must be introduced to compute intersection points. This bears a similarity with the Nyquist theory in communication. As for the result of shelling technique D, it is close to the actual value when the $ADLC$ is low, but it will approach that of shelling technique S when the $ADLC$ is high. This is due to the fact that it is difficult to isolate large patches by decreasing cell size.

So far we have compared the three factors separately. From a hardware perspective, they are related to each other as will be discussed in the following. In fact, two-level

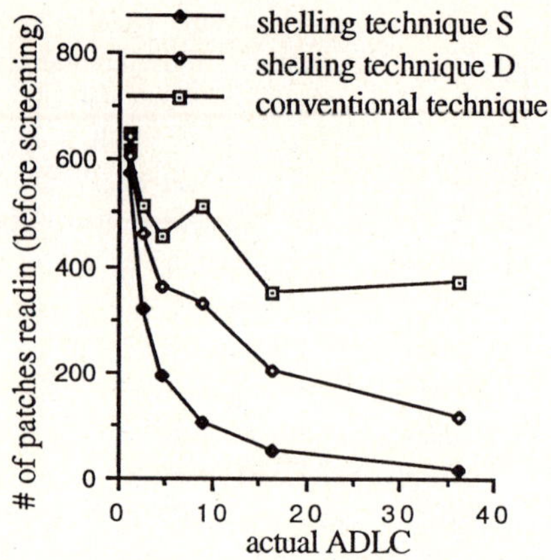


**Fig. 8**. The number of patches read in before screening.

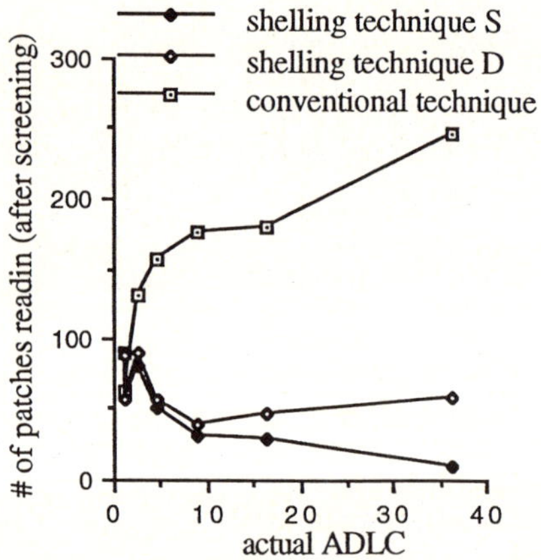


**Fig. 9**. The number of patches read in after screening.

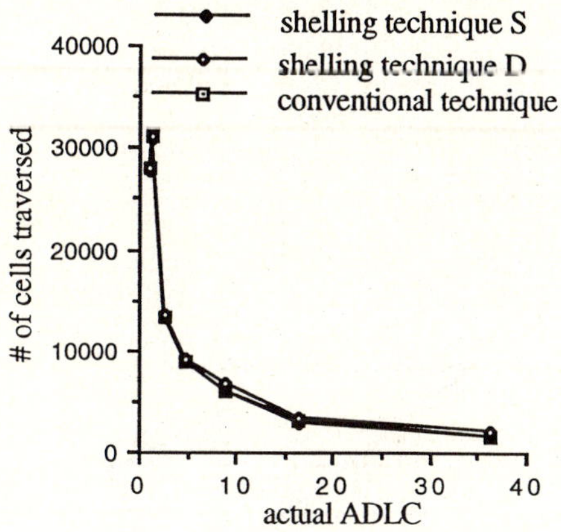


**Fig. 10**. The number of cells traversed.

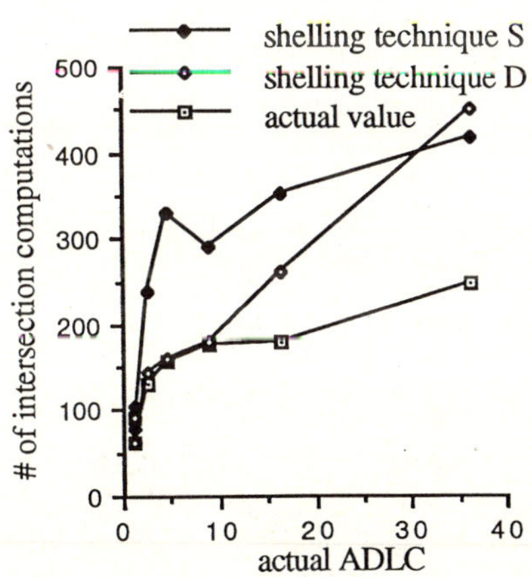


**Fig. 11**. The number of intersection computations.

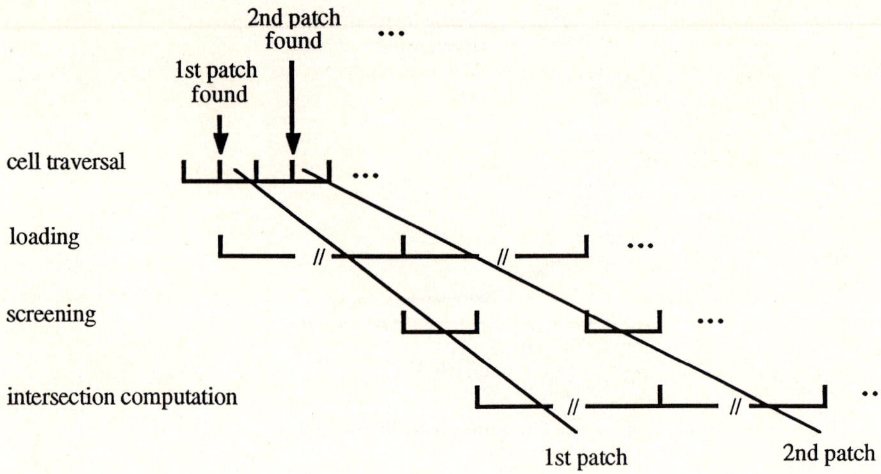


**Fig. 12.** The four steps in the shelling technique are processed in an overlapped fashion.

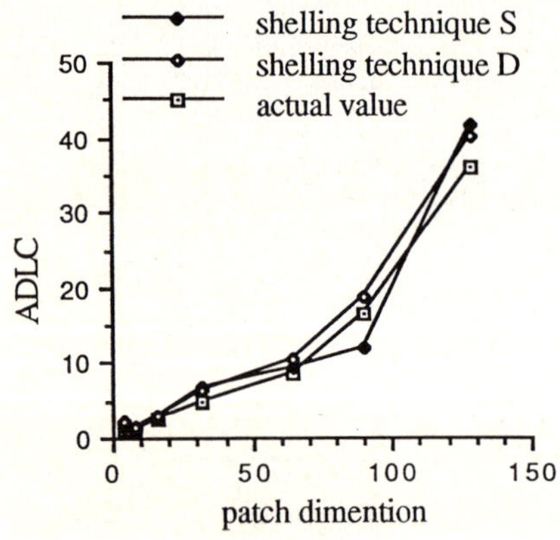


**Fig. 13.** The average degree of local coherence.

pipelining can be exploited in the shelling technique, in which the first level refers to pipelining at the four steps as shown in Figure 12 and the second refers to pipelining within each step. The second level pipelining can be understood when realizing them with pipelined circuits. As to the first level pipelining, it can be understood as follows:

- When the neighborhood information is known, we can start the cell traversal of the next shell.
- After traversing some empty cells (or macro-regions), a patch is found and then loaded from the host. During this time, the cell traversal still keeps on searching patches.
- After loading a patch from the host, we can start the preprocessing to check whether it is a backward patch or not. During this time, the cell traversal and loading still keep on searching and supplying patches for the preprocessing.
- If it is not a backward patch, then a bundle of rays proceeds to compute the intersection points with this patch. During this time, the cell traversal, loading, and preprocessing still keep on traversing, supplying, and screening out patches.

In the conventional technique, there is only one intersection computation for one patch. Without solving the bottleneck, i.e., the loading, it cannot benefit from the pipelining at all. By contrast, a bundle of rays will proceed to compute the intersection points with one patch in the shelling technique. This provides a more balanced structure for the abovementioned four steps. From this point of view, we can assert that the shelling technique can outperform the conventional technique. Nonetheless, the comparison can be made only when the detailed statistics about the environment and the underlying architecture are known.

It is known that pipeline efficiency is a measure of the performance of a pipeline. In the shelling technique, the *ADLC* plays an important role in determining the pipeline efficiency. If the *ADLC* of a shell is too small to fill up the pipeline, then the pipeline efficiency will be degraded. This can happen in an environment consisting of small patches or in an environment consisting of large patches when the tracking mechanism cannot capture the actual degree of local coherence. For this purpose, we use the *ADLC* as an index to show how close the coherence of an environment can be captured. In Figure 13, we see that the results of both techniques are desirable.

## 6 Conclusion

In this paper we have proposed a new space partitioning technique such that the requirement of loading patches can be reduced considerably. It can be used as a replacement of accommodating a large local memory for each PE. Of course, it is favourable to use a reasonable size of cache memory in each PE. This leads to a more balanced structure to fill up the pipeline such that a highly pipelined parallel architecture is applicable to speedup the form-factor computations in the radiosity method.

## Acknowledgements

This research has been supported in part by the commission of the EEC under the NANA project (BRA 3280) and by ITRI.

## References

[1] Appel, A.: Some techniques for shading machine renderings of solids. *Proc. AFIPS JSCC*, Vol. 23, No. 6, 1968, pp. 37-45.

[2] Goral, C., Torrance, K., Greenberg, D. and Battaile, B.: Modeling the interaction of light between diffuse surfaces. *Computer Graphics (SIGGRAPH '84 Proceedings)*, Vol. 18, No. 3, July 1984, pp. 213-222.

[3] Cohen, M. and Greenberg, D.: The Hemi-Cube: A radiosity solution for complex environments. *Computer Graphics (SIGGRAPH '85 Proceedings)*, Vol. 19, No. 3, July 1985, pp. 31-40.

[4] Cohen, M., Greenberg, D., Immel, D. and Brock, P.: An efficient radiosity approach for realistic image synthesis. *IEEE Computer Graphics and Applications*, Vol. 6, No. 2, March 1986, pp. 26-35.

[5] Immel, D., Cohen, M. and Greenberg, D.: A radiosity method for non-diffuse environments. *Computer Graphics (SIGGRAPH '86 Proceedings)*, Vol. 20, No. 4, August 1986, pp. 133- 142.

[6] Wallace, J. Cohen, M. and Greenberg, D.: A two pass solution to the rendering equation: A Synthesis of Ray-Tracing and Radiosity Methods. *Computer Graphics (SIGGRAPH '87 Proceedings)*, Vol. 21, No. 4, July 1987, pp. 311-320.

[7] Cohen, M., Chen, S., Wallace, R. and Greenberg, D.: A progressive refinement approach to fast radiosity image generation. *Computer Graphics (SIGGRAPH '88 Proceedings)*, Vol. 22, No. 4, August 1988, pp. 75-84.

[8] Heckbert, S. and Hanrahan, P.: Beam tracing polygonal objects. *Computer Graphics*, Vol. 18, No. 3, July 1984, pp. 119-127.

[9] Speer, L., Tony, D. and Barsky, B.: A theoretical and empirical analysis of coherence ray-tracing. *Computer-Generated Images (Proceedings of Graphics Interface '85)*, May 1985, pp. 11-25.

[10] Glassner, A.: Space subdivision for fast ray tracing. *IEEE Computer Graphics and Applications*, Vol. 4, No. 10, October 1984, pp. 15-22.

[11] Tamminnen, M., Karonen, O. and Mantyla, M.: Ray-casting and block model conversion using spatial index. *Computer-Aided Design*, Vol. 16, No. 4, July 1984, pp. 203-208.

[12] Fujimoto, A., Tanaka, T. and Iwata, K.: ARTS: Accelerated ray-tracing system. *IEEE Computer Graphics and Applications*, Vol. 6, No. 4, April 1986, pp. 16-26.

[13] Murakami, K., Hirota, K. and Ishii, M.: Fast ray tracing. *FUJITSU Sci. Technical Journal*, Vol. 24, No. 2, June 1988, pp. 150-159.

[14] Naruse, T., Yoshida, M., Takahashi, T. and Naito, S.: Sight : A dedicated computer graphics machine. *Computer Graphics Forum*, Vol. 6, No. 4, 1987, pp. 327-334.

[15] Cleary, J., Wyvill, B., Birtwistle, G. and Vatti, R.: Multiprocessor ray tracing. *Computer Graphics Forum*, Vol. 5, No. 1, January 1986, pp. 3-12.

[16] Dippé, M. and Swensen, J.: An adaptive subdivision algorithm and parallel architecture for realistic image synthesis. *SIGGRAPH'84*, 1984, pp. 149-157.

[17] Green, S., Paddon, D. and Lewis, E.: A parallel algorithm and tree-based computer architecture for ray traced computer graphics. *Parallel Processing for Computer Vision and Display*, University of Leeds, January 1988.

[18] Priol, T. and Bouatouch, K.: Static load balancing for a parallel ray tracing on a MIMD hypercube. *The Visual Computer*, Vol. 5, 1989, pp. 109-119.

[19] Yilmaz, A., Hagestein, S., Deprettere, E. and Dewilde, P.: A hardware algorithm for fast realistic image synthesis. *Eurographics '89.*

[20] Fuchs, H., Kedem, Z. and Naylor, B.: On visible surface generation by a priori tree structures. *Computer Graphics (SIGGRAPH '80 Proceedings)*, Vol. 14, No. 3, July 1980, pp. 124-133.

[21] Devillers, O.: The macro-regions: an efficient space subdivision structure for ray tracing. *Eurographics '89*, pp. 27-38.

[22] Ullner, M.: Parallel machines for computer graphics. *Doctor Thesis*, California Institute of Technology, January 1983.

[23] Bu, J. and Deprettere, E.: A VLSI system architecture for high-speed radiative transfer 3D image synthesis. *The Visual Computer*, Vol. 5, No. 3, June 1989.

# List of Contributors

**Hans-Josef Ackermann**
Fraunhofer-Arbeitsgruppe für Graphische Datenverarbeitung, Wilhelminenstrasse 7, D-6100 Darmstadt. Germany.
Phone: +49-6151-155-183

**Abdelghani Atamenia**
Laboratoire d'Informatique Fondamentale de Lille, URA 369 CNRS, Bat M3, Université de Lille Flandres-Artois, 59655 Villeneuve d'ascq Cedex, France.
Phone: +33-204-342-58

**Didier Badouel**
CSRI University of Toronto, 10 King's College Road, Toronto, Ontario M5S 1A1, Canada.
Phone: +0101-416-978-6320
email: badouel@dgp.toronto.edu

**Reuven Bakalash**
Department of Computer Science, State University of New York at Stony Brook, Stony Brook, NY 11794-4400, U. S. A.

**Christophe Chaillou**
Laboratoire d'Informatique Fondamentale de Lille, URA 369 CNRS, Bat M3, Université de Lille Flandres-Artois, 59655 Villeneuve d'ascq Cedex, France.
Phone: +33-204-342-58
email: chaillou@lifl.lifl.fr

**Ute Claussen**
Aitec GmbH & Co., Informationstechnologie, Am Hartweg 106, D-4600 Dortmund. Germany.
Phone: +49-231-179911

**Samuel Degrande**
Laboratoire d'Informatique Fondamentale de Lille, URA 369 CNRS, Bat M3, Université de Lille Flandres-Artois, 59655 Villeneuve d'ascq Cedex, France.
Phone: +33-204-342-58

**E. Deprettere**
Delft University of Technology, Faculty of Electrical Engineering, 2628 CD Delft, The Netherlands.

**P. Dewilde**
Delft University of Technology, Faculty of Electrical Engineering, 2628 CD Delft, The Netherlands.

**Steven Evans**
VLSI and Computer Graphics Research Group, School of Engineering, University of Sussex, Falmer, Brighton, U.K.

**Richard. L. Grimsdale**
VLSI and Computer Graphics Research Group, School of Engineering, University of Sussex, Falmer, Brighton, U. K.
Phone: +44-273-606755 ext 8047
email: dickg@central.sussex.ac.uk

**Marie-Pierre Hébert**
VLSI and Computer Graphics Research Group, School of Engineering, University of Sussex, Falmer, Brighton. U. K.

**Christoph Hornung**
Fraunhofer-Arbeitsgruppe für Graphische Datenverarbeitung, Wilhelminenstrasse 7, D-6100 Darmstadt. Germany.
Phone: +49-6151-155-234

**Sylvian Karpf**
Laboratoire d'Informatique Fondamentale de Lille, URA 369 CNRS, Bat M3, Université de Lille Flandres-Artois, 59655 Villeneuve d'ascq Cedex, France.
Phone: +33-204-342-58

**Arie Kaufman**
Department of Computer Science, State University of New York at Stony Brook, Stony Brook, NY 11794-4400, U. S. A.

**Eric Lepetre**
Laboratoire d'Informatique Fondamentale de Lille, URA 369 CNRS, Bat M3, Université de Lille Flandres-Artois, 59655 Villeneuve d'ascq Cedex, France.
Phone: +33-204-342-58

**Paul Lister**
VLSI and Computer Graphics Research Group, School of Engineering, University of Sussex, Falmer, Brighton, U. K.
Phone: +44-273-606755 ext 8060
email: paull@central.sussex.ac.uk